CONTESTED BRITAIN

Brexit, Austerity and Agency

Edited by Marius Guderjan,
Hugh Mackay and Gesa Stedman

First published in Great Britain in 2020 by

Bristol University Press
1-9 Old Park Hill
Bristol
BS2 8BB
UK
t: +44 (0)117 954 5940
www.bristoluniversitypress.co.uk

North America office:
c/o The University of Chicago Press
1427 East 60th Street
Chicago, IL 60637, USA
t: +1 773 702 7700
f: +1 773-702-9756
sales@press.uchicago.edu
www.press.uchicago.edu

© Bristol University Press 2020

British Library Cataloguing in Publication Data
A catalogue record for this book is available from the British Library

Library of Congress Cataloging-in-Publication Data
A catalog record for this book has been requested

ISBN 978-1-5292-0500-8 (hardback)
ISBN 978-1-5292-0502-2 (paperback)
ISBN 978-1-5292-0503-9 (ePub)
ISBN 978-1-5292-0501-5 (ePdf)

The right of Marius Guderjan, Gesa Stedman and Hugh Mackay to be identified as editors of this work has been asserted by them in accordance with the Copyright, Designs and Patents Act 1988.

All rights reserved: no part of this publication may be reproduced, stored in a retrieval system, or transmitted in any form or by any means, electronic, mechanical, photocopying, recording, or otherwise without the prior permission of Bristol University Press.

Every reasonable effort has been made to obtain permission to reproduce copyrighted material. If, however, anyone knows of an oversight, please contact the publisher.

The statements and opinions contained within this publication are solely those of the editor and contributors and not of The University of Bristol or Bristol University Press. The University of Bristol and Bristol University Press disclaim responsibility for any injury to persons or property resulting from any material published in this publication.

Bristol University Press works to counter discrimination on grounds of gender, race, disability, age and sexuality.

Cover design by blu inc
Front cover: image iStock/robertiez

Contents

List of Tables		v
Notes on Contributors		vi
Acknowledgements		ix
Introduction		1
Marius Guderjan, Hugh Mackay and Gesa Stedman		

Part I The Politics and Culture of Austerity: Impacts and Resistance

1	The Contracting State: Austerity and Public Services *Simon Griffiths*	19
2	Breaking Britain's Working Class: the Left Out *Lisa Mckenzie*	33
3	Political Activism and Agency under Austerity and Brexit *Tom Montgomery and Maria Grasso*	45
4	Culture Matters: Cuts and Resistance *Ingrid von Rosenberg*	59
5	Agents and Agency in the Face of Austerity and Brexit Uncertainty: the Case of Legal Aid *Steven Truxal*	73

Part II The Politics and Discourse of Brexit

6	The Economy of Brexit: Performance, Interests and Agency *Carlo Morelli*	89
7	Brexit Populism: Disenfranchisement and Agency *Marius Guderjan and Adrian Wilding*	103
8	A Sovereign People? Political Fantasy and Governmental Time in the Pursuit of Brexit *John Clarke*	117

| 9 | 'Not an International Health Service': Xenophobia, Brexit and the Restoration of National Sovereignty
Kirsten Forkert | 131 |
| 10 | 'Uni-Culti' Myths and Liberal Dreams: Brexit and Austerity from the Perspective of Migrants
Magdalena Nowicka | 145 |

Part III Austerity and Brexit in a Divided Union

11	From Brexit to the Break-Up of ... England? Thinking in and Beyond the Nation *Allan Cochrane*	161
12	Understanding Brexit in Wales: Austerity, Elites and National Identity *Hugh Mackay*	175
13	Scotland, Brexit and the Broken Promise of Democracy *Klaus Stolz*	189
14	Brexit, Devolution and Northern Ireland's Political Parties: Differential Solutions, Special Status or Special Arrangements? *Derek Birrell and Paul Carmichael*	203
15	More Than the Border? Looking at Brexit through Irish eyes *Kevin Bean*	219

Conclusion 233
Marius Guderjan, Hugh Mackay and Gesa Stedman

Index 247

List of Tables

11.1	Votes in the 2016 referendum	163
12.1	Outcome of the 2016 referendum in the nations of the UK	177
12.2	Percentage of Leave voters (by age) in the 2016 referendum	178
12.3	Welsh and British identification as reflected in the 2016 referendum	184
14.1	UK 2016 referendum result on the question of remaining in or leaving the European Union	205

Notes on Contributors

Kevin Bean
Institute of Irish Studies, University of Liverpool
Lecturer in Irish Politics

Derek Birrell
School of Applied Social and Policy Science, Ulster University
Professor

Paul Carmichael
Faculty of Arts, Humanities and Social Sciences, Ulster University
Professor / Associate Dean (Global Engagement)

John Clarke
Faculty of Arts and Social Sciences, The Open University
Professor Emeritus

Allan Cochrane
Faculty of Arts and Social Sciences, The Open University
Emeritus Professor of Urban Studies

Kirsten Forkert
School of Media, Birmingham City University
Reader

Maria Grasso
Department of Politics, University of Sheffield
Professor

NOTES ON CONTRIBUTORS

Simon Griffiths
Department of Politics and International Relations, Goldsmiths, University of London
Reader

Marius Guderjan
Centre for British Studies, Humboldt-Universität zu Berlin
Lecturer and Researcher

Hugh Mackay
Faculty of Arts and Social Sciences, The Open University
Honorary Visiting Fellow

Lisa Mckenzie
Department of Sociology, London School of Economics
Fellow

Tom Montgomery
Glasgow School for Business and Society, Glasgow Caledonian University
Researcher

Carlo Morelli
School of Business, University of Dundee
Senior Lecturer in Economics

Magdalena Nowicka
Deutsches Zentrum für Integrations- und Migrationsforschung (DeZIM e.V.)
Professor for Migration and Transnationalism, Humboldt-Universität zu Berlin

Gesa Stedman
Centre for British Studies, Humboldt-Universität zu Berlin
Professor for British Culture and Literature

Klaus Stolz
Institute for English and American Studies, Technische Universität Chemnitz
Professor for British and American Social and Cultural Studies

Steven Truxal
The City Law School, City University of London
Reader in Law

Ingrid von Rosenberg
Institute for English and American Studies, Technische Universität Dresden
Professor Emeritus for British Cultural Studies

Adrian Wilding
Centre for British Studies, Humboldt-Universität zu Berlin
Fellow

Acknowledgements

The editors would like to thank contributors to the meetings of the Berlin-Britain Research Network at the Centre for British Studies at Humboldt-Universität zu Berlin. Several of the contributors to this collection were involved in those meetings, where the idea for this book originated. We would like to thank especially Allan Cochrane, who helped to get the project off the ground. Catherine Smith and the student assistants, David Bell, Lorenz Böttcher, Esmé Ellis, Michael Griff, Sarah Meyer and Adina Reza, of the Centre for British Studies were meticulous in their proof-reading. Corinna Radke's outstanding reliability, technical know-how, and commitment were instrumental in turning the manuscripts into a printable typescript. Lastly, the editors are grateful to Stephen Wenham at Bristol University Press for working with us on this publication.

Marius Guderjan, Hugh Mackay
and Gesa Stedman
September 2019

Introduction

Marius Guderjan, Hugh Mackay and Gesa Stedman

Governing the UK has always been complex and fluid, but recent years have been particularly turbulent. Political parties were forced into coalition at Westminster in 2010, Scotland came close to leaving the union in 2014, the UK voted to leave the EU in 2016 and the Conservatives were forced into a minority government in 2017 under the leadership of Theresa May, who was forced to resign by her own party and was replaced as Prime Minister by Boris Johnson in July 2019. While by the time this book is published a new Prime Minister or a new party may be in power, this book offers a powerful and distinctive analysis of how the politics of the UK and the lived experience of its citizens have been contested in the first decades of the 21st century. It sets out to explore and understand the Brexit vote, not only in its own right but also as an expression of wider shifts in the UK's social and political structures and discourses, in particular regarding the experience of and responses to austerity. In order to comprehend the complexity of what Britain is or will be, the book links Brexit and austerity to a crisis of agency and who is or is not able to exercise agency in the UK, and to what degree. Notions of agency are mobilized because they help to understand the role of austerity (as politics and lived experience) as a fundamental cause of Brexit.

The book brings together authors from the constituent parts of the UK with others from Germany. It is the product of an ongoing set of debates fostered by an interdisciplinary research network. Incorporating sensibility and thinking from beyond the UK, the voices from the outside add a mainland European perspective on what is developing in the UK. In doing so, it goes beyond traditional disciplinary approaches by drawing on insights from cultural studies, political science, sociology, geography and law. It uses comparative material from the regions of England and from the other nations of the UK, and explores the profound differences – of geography (the social zoning of cities and the disparities between regions), generation, gender, 'race' and class – in how austerity is experienced.

This introduction outlines first the origins and nature of Brexit before it focuses on the politics, discourse and ideology of the recent austerity policies. Agency is then introduced as a way of understanding a range of phenomena related to the politics and discourses of austerity and Brexit. An agencyfocused perspective helps to subsequently demonstrate the links between voting Leave and austerity, and to assess the prospects of Brexit during times of fast-changing developments and great uncertainty. The introduction ends with an outline of the book's chapters and their multidisciplinary approaches.

The origins of Euroscepticism and Brexit

The underlying reason for this book is the result of the referendum on 23 June 2016, in which a slight majority of 51.9 per cent voted to leave the EU. The Prime Minister David Cameron resigned shortly afterwards and his successor Theresa May reiterated *ad nauseam* that 'Brexit means Brexit' – an assertion that we shall here unpack and problematize, because its banality obscures a remarkable range of political, economic, social and cultural concerns. Each of these had its own significance prior to the Brexit referendum, though the EU was rarely the focus of how they were articulated. Though Europe has long been a major issue for the Conservative Party, it has not been for the British public, at least not until Cameron came to power and decided in 2013 to hold the Brexit referendum.

There has, however, been a long history in the UK of scepticism towards the EU. The British, it is often said, are 'reluctant Europeans' living in 'splendid isolation'. Dissatisfaction over the loss of sovereignty, EU budgets and regulation are longstanding, with the UK public and politicians being the least committed of the member states to the EU. British ambivalence to the EU can be traced back to at least the founding of the European Coal and Steel Community and the European Economic Community, which the UK joined only in 1973. The Thatcher administration added to this negativity, demanding 'our' money back; and this grew under John Major – as was evident in Britain's resistance to further economic and political integration in the Maastricht Treaty of 1992, and to the direction of European federalism. In general, the UK was enthusiastic about the single market (for example in its promotion of the Single Europe Act, 1987), but not about the political or other dimensions of integration. Opposition to Europe has never been confined to the Conservative Party; conversely, the European project has always depended on cross-party support. For a long time, polls have shown strong opposition to the EU, and much lower identification as 'European' on the part of UK citizens compared with those of other EU member states. UK voting in the Euro elections is among the lowest in the EU (24 per cent–36 per cent depending on which election), and lower than all countries bar some of the eastern accession states.

Britain's imperial legacy and its national identity has until today served the narrative of exceptionalism and independence, which competed with ambitions to integrate politically with Europe. At the turn of the 20th century, the British Empire comprised 20 per cent of the world's landmass, 400 million subjects, and the UK was the industrial and financial centre of the world. With the financial pre-eminence of the City of London and its often referenced special relationships with the US and links to the Commonwealth, Britain continues to command a role as a global force. While its history and culture make it problematic to scale back its ambitions, despite considerable economic, military and diplomatic capacities, its international standing and prospects are uncertain (McTavish, 2019, pp 14–22).

Brexiteers hope and have promised to restore imperial greatness and national sovereignty (see Chapter Clarke). They have been able to draw on nearly a decade of retro-conservative cultural and media hegemony, as evinced by TV show design styles and panegyrics to Winston Churchill. Everyday culture – in Raymond Williams' sense (1976) – as well as parts of culture in the narrow sense – the arts – have thus helped to entrench in mainstream representation a self-centred normalcy. This is of course fiercely opposed by the 98 per cent of those working in the creative industries who intended to vote Remain and who find it increasingly difficult to be taken into account by political decision makers (Dawood, 2016). Beyond a rethinking of Britain's role in the context of post-colonialism, a major recent catalyst for Brexit is the austerity measures introduced by the Coalition and following Conservative governments, the short- and long-term consequences of which are introduced in the next section.

Austerity politics, discourse and ideology

Since 2008, following the banking crisis, the dominant policy framing has been austerity. David Cameron apportioned the blame for this to the Labour government, whose alleged overspending was identified as the reason for economic retrenchment. That it was the consequence of the insufficiently regulated banking sector and its centrality to the

British (and global) economy was sidelined in the debate. What was presented as necessity-driven economic measures are really a politics of social engineering. Quite apart from the fact that, in purely economic terms, austerity measures have not only failed but slowed down economic growth and financial investments (Blyth, 2013), their social impact suggests a different agenda altogether. This has been so successfully normalized that it is no longer necessary to use the term 'austerity' to mask the fact that an 'illusion' of a change in fiscal policy has led to increased social inequality (Berry, 2015). At the core of austerity measures are cuts in state expenditure, with austerity involving the massive rolling back of the boundaries of the state, as state services have been reduced, marketized and privatized to an extent that even Margaret Thatcher would or could not have dreamed of (see Chapters Montgomery and Grasso, and Griffiths).

In dismantling substantial parts of the welfare state, Cameron referenced postwar austerity politics. Austerity in and after the Second World War was a collective matter, fairly evenly spread, and generally understood as necessary and in the national interest. As Kynaston (2008) points out, austerity then was involved in building a more egalitarian society: it coincided with the building of the welfare state. Today, the politics and policies of austerity are very different. Rather than collective, it is a cost-cutting exercise designed to implement a policy agenda informed by a powerful political ideology. This involves a moral discourse about living beyond one's means.

Everyday cultural practice (Williams, 1976) has a direct impact on all areas of society. The postwar imagery which is invoked whenever the term 'austerity' is deployed reinforces notions of solidarity, thrift and nostalgia for a fictitiously homogenous colonial and largely English national identity (Bramall, 2013; Bauman, 2017). At the same time, stigmatization and objectification of those in need of support and a return to a Victorian-style discourse of the 'deserving' and, more commonly, the 'undeserving' poor have led to increasing social inequalities and divisions (see for instance Tyler, 2013; Mckenzie, 2015; Forkert, 2017). These play out in different ways, including reduced access to public services, such as welfare and education (see Chapters Montgomery and Grasso, Griffiths, Mckenzie, and Morelli), healthcare (see Chapter Forkert), justice (see Chapter Truxal) and cultural opportunities (see Chapter von Rosenberg).

Despite Cameron's rhetoric that 'we are all in this together', between 2008 and 2014 wages in the UK in real terms declined by over 10 per cent, whereas they have increased by 23 per cent in Germany and an average of 7 per cent in OECD countries (OECD, 2019). Cuts in public expenditure halved local government expenditure in England in the period 2010–17, meaning the closure of libraries, swimming pools and parks, and the cutting of all but the most essential of services. Support for people in need, disability and housing benefits and working tax credits have all suffered cuts, and child poverty and homelessness have increased dramatically. In this context, significant numbers were 'left behind' and 'left out', surviving on reduced benefits, part-time work, zero-hours contracts, involuntary self-employment, increasing job insecurity and low wages. Meanwhile, although income inequality remained broadly static over the decade to 2018, the gulf between the richest 1 per cent and the rest of the population has grown. Voting for leaving the EU can be seen as opposition to injustice and inequality, albeit with anger directed at immigrants rather than the elite (see Chapters Forkert, Guderjan and Wilding, and Mckenzie).

With the Brexit referendum, the rise of Jeremy Corbyn as Labour leader and Theresa May's losses in the 2017 general election, the austerity discourse has come under serious challenge. Although in October 2018, the Conservative government, if only rhetorically, abandoned austerity and announced an increase in public spending, the impact of austerity has been too deep to be reversed overnight and will shape British society for a long time.

'Acting otherwise'? Agency and agents

The notion of voters expressing their beliefs or needs connects with the other theme of this book: agency, a concept used widely today across various theoretical schools and disciplines, including law, economics, sociology and cultural studies. While this book is not intended as a contribution to theoretical debates about agency, it is nevertheless necessary to explain the editors' take on the concept and how it allows one to understand the specific and at times contradictory strands of Brexit and what led to the decision to leave the EU.

It is particularly productive to think of agency as the capability to make a difference and to act otherwise. As Anthony Giddens expressed it:

> Agency refers not to the intentions people have in doing things but to their capability of doing those things in the first place. Agency concerns events of which an individual is the perpetrator, in the sense that the individual could, at any phase in a given sequence of conduct, have acted differently.

> To be able to 'act otherwise' means being able to intervene in the world, or to restrain from such intervention, with the effect of influencing a specific process or state of affairs. This presumes that to be an agent is to be able to deploy (chronically, in the daily life) a range of causal powers, including that of influencing those deployed by others. Action depends on the capability of the individual to 'make a difference' to a pre-existing state of affairs or course of events. An agent ceases to be such if he or she loses the capability to 'make a difference', that is, to exercise some sort of power. (1984, p. 14)

Agency is exercised by agents who are defined by their capacity to formulate and act upon situations (Sibeon, 1999, p. 141). Agents are not individuals but collectivities with shared characteristics. For instance, people who are born into a pre-existing environment or a socio-cultural system and share the same properties, privileges and life chances are a collective of agents (Archer, 1995, p. 257). A set of agents has been important in linking austerity and Brexit, for example those who are living precariously, those who feel excluded and stigmatized, working class people, cosmopolitan graduates or urban elites. Actors, by contrast, occupy a specific role and function, such as governments, politicians, lawyers, institutional decision-makers. 'Unlike agency, which is universal to members of society, not everyone can succeed in becoming an actor – that is in finding a role(s) in which they feel they can invest themselves' (Archer, 2004, pp 261–2).

This approach invokes the old debate on the relationship between structure and agency, as Hay suggests:

> Every time we construct, however tentatively, a notion of social, political or economic causality we appeal, whether explicitly or (more likely) implicitly, to ideas about structure and agency. The way our explanations are formulated reflects a deeper set of understandings about the (relative) autonomy of actors or agents in the settings in which they find themselves. (1995, p. 189)

This book is not concerned with providing any resolution to this debate, or to add to the perspectives of Michel Foucault on agency and discourse, Pierre Bourdieu on habitus, field and capital, Anthony Giddens' theory of structuration or others. In general, it seeks to bridge structuralist with intentionalist accounts: 'agency is understood as a kind of mediating relationality. [...] we make ourselves, but not under conditions of our own choosing' (Kockelman, 2007, p. 376). Within this relationality, power is always an essential determinant (Hay, 1995), with hegemonic discourses – probably more unconsciously than consciously – influencing the strategies of actors (McAnulla, 2002, p. 284). Although structures or contexts endure and predate agents, they are still the outcome of human interaction (though not always intended or acknowledged). Hence, this socio-cultural shaping is exercised by people and simultaneously affects them (Archer, 1995, p. 196).

Most importantly, agency is not a universal phenomenon but constituted by multi-causal contexts that produce particular types of agents, actors and agency (Clarke, 2013, p. 31). Agency is context-dependent; it is not desirable or even possible to generate a timeless or context-transcending definition (Ahearn, 2001, pp 112–13). Such structural and contextual properties can be enabling or constraining, preventing or facilitating the actions of different types of agents (Archer, 2003, p. 7). In other words, agency 'can be constrained by unequal power relations and/or the absence of enabling affordances and thus is not regarded as dependent on an individual's will or capacity alone but as a contextually enabled and constrained capacity' (Miller, 2016, p. 350).

As agency depends on the availability of means to achieve specific ends, it is commonly connected to notions of choice, freedom, selfhood, motivation, desire or resistance to unjust conditions, such as patriarchy, oligarchy, capitalism, colonialism or globalization (Kockelman, 2007, pp 375–6). The ability of agents to actively (re-)shape society's distribution of resources 'depends upon their capacity to realise collective action' (Archer, 2004, p. 11) (see Chapter Montgomery and Grasso).

The EU referendum, austerity and agency

This book explores the connections between the EU referendum, austerity politics and discourses, and agency. In the UK, a key issue of the past decade has been the rise in social inequality as a consequence of austerity measures, deepening the rifts in an already very unequal society. Those who have been affected most by austerity measures have experienced 'devaluation', stigmatization and a loss of social and political rights (Mckenzie, 2015; Cummins, 2018). This has undermined their confidence and ability to take collective action which would improve their conditions (Atkinson, 2017, pp 12–13; Edmiston, 2018, p. 143). Hence voting Leave may well represent an act of collective contestation, with agents deciding that the benefits of leaving the EU outweigh the expected costs and penalties. Austerity may have constrained the living conditions of some agents to such an extent that their hopes for 'taking back control', shaking up the establishment or achieving any kind of change resonated more strongly than the predicted economic risks.

It is important to acknowledge that Brexit was supported not only by the victims of austerity. Certainly, 63 per cent of the working classes voted Leave, and only 44 per cent of the middle classes. But Leave was supported too by those who belong to the middle classes and have benefited from a globalized economy rather than suffered from poverty and precariousness (Williams, 2016). It was supported by people from the libertarian left, Trotskyists, trade unionists and members of the Labour Party, as well as the free-market right and those concerned about the loss of empire and sovereignty – so it is a more complex and nuanced movement than suggested by the simple binaries (of north–south, young–old, rich–poor, urban–rural, cities–towns, provincial–metropolitan, etc.). The typical Leave voter was older, less-educated, Conservative-supporting, middle class, a reader of the *Daily Mail* or the *Daily Express* and tending towards 'authoritarian, nativist and xenophobic values and attitudes' (Taylor, 2017, p. 98).

Correspondingly, there has been a rise of right-wing populist actors who put the liberal consensus to the test (see Chapters Clarke, and Guderjan and Wilding). UKIP set the agenda, representing itself as the voice of the people and portraying society as run by a corrupt elite. Nigel Farage, despite attending a public school and working in the City, presents himself as the plain-speaking representative of the ordinary person. Brexit gave a huge boost to the radical right, which has increased its scale and prominence, in the process increasing racial tension in the UK. In the 2013 local elections, across 35 local authorities in England and Wales, UKIP won about 25 per cent of the vote. Buoyed by this, at the UKIP conference in February 2014, Farage said that mass migration was making parts of the country 'unrecognisable' and 'like a foreign land'. The appeal of the Leave campaign was emotional (regarding control, sovereignty and nationalism), dramatized and in places deceitful.

In stirring up racial tensions and denigrating Brussels, the Leave campaign deployed wilful misinformation, such as the £350m weekly saving which could fund the NHS or that the UK would not be able to block Turkish admission to the EU. Of major concern was immigration. Refugees were conflated with economic migrants in the toxic propaganda war – notably on UKIP's poster image of a massive queue of refugees that was headed 'breaking point'. Only through leaving the EU, argued Nigel Farage, could Britain regain control of its borders. The rise of UKIP and the outcome of the referendum meant that more people felt that it was legitimate to express racist and intolerant views (see Chapters Nowicka, and Forkert).

Xenophobic and nationalist voices gained prominence during and after the EU referendum, and public discourse since then has focused very much on who belongs and has (or should have) rights and who does not. In this racialized debate, which was able to draw on a centuries-long tradition of othering (Winder, 2005), the metropolitan elite was seen as being more concerned with immigrants than 'their own people' – a notion which became blurred when the Windrush scandal revealed how long-standing UK citizens were treated, highlighting that othering processes in public discourse are highly contradictory.

This connects with notions of English identity (see Chapters Cochrane, and Mackay), as devolution has enhanced the distinctiveness of each of the nations of the UK – in terms of policies and politics, but also national identification. Strong opposition to Brexit in the referendum in Northern Ireland and Scotland highlights the question of agency in the devolved territories (see Chapters Bean, Birrell and Carmichael, and Stolz). Moves towards a hard and especially a no-deal Brexit make Scottish independence and a united Ireland look more likely than they have hitherto. This in turn would raise questions about the future status of Wales and, of course, the Union and Britain. It reinforces concerns regarding the democratic deficit in England, of its lack of a separate parliament, government or even a clear identity that is distinct from those of Britain or the UK.

Overall, the referendum allowed people to express their will in an unusually significant way. As the individual chapters of this book demonstrate, there are evident links between voting Leave and austerity. Brexit can therefore be understood as a drastic example of agency, either 'to make a difference' or to resist and 'act otherwise' regardless of the costs. This has challenged much of the consensus in British society that had been taken for granted for a long time. These concern the political system, social coherence, pluralist and (neo)liberal values, and territorial integrity. The transformation of the hegemonic discourse in the UK has turned the Leave campaign's standpoint on immigration, national identity, sovereignty and the role of the EU into mainstream discourse. Nostalgic imperial notions of the UK's place in the world feed into this discourse, while protest against Brexit, and proponents of a different UK identity, as more open, diverse and part of a multilateral network, are marginalized.

The prospects of Brexit

So where does this leave us, and what might happen as Brexit develops? Clearly there had been little planning for Brexit when the referendum was initiated by Cameron. Leave campaigners presented no detail of the future they envisaged. It was a vote against something but without any detail of an alternative. From the January 2017 Lancaster House speech through to the Chequers Brexit deal of July 2018 and later, Theresa May defined Brexit in terms of a hard Brexit, involving withdrawal from the single market (at least for services) and the customs union, meaning controlling immigration, striking trade deals with non-EU countries and being outside the remit of the European Court of Justice. This was picked up and hardened by Boris Johnson in his failed efforts to 'get Brexit done' by the end of October 2019. Apart from being unacceptable to the EU negotiators, in large part because it does not fit with the Good Friday Agreement (see Chapters Bean, and Birrell and Carmichael), few economists saw what May or Johnson has put on the table as other than disastrous for the economy (see Chapter Morelli).

The UK parliament and government are part of and are constrained by broader social and cultural dynamics. With the rise of a professional class of politicians, less representatives of the working class and with neoliberalism being the orthodoxy across most of the political spectrum, there has been a long-term trend of growing mistrust in politicians, and generally low turnouts in elections (Flinders, 2018). The Labour and Conservative parties have become unstable alliances, struggling to hold together members with widely divergent views, on Brexit especially. The formation of the Independent Group in February 2019, joined by a small number of Labour and Conservative MPs is one example of this.

As the hard Brexiteers in the Conservative Party and the DUP subjected the Prime Minister Theresa May to repeated defeats over the EU withdrawal bill, the House of Commons was incapable of making a decision, as there was never a majority of MPs who could agree on what they wanted (as distinct from what they opposed). Subsequently, a 'hard Brexit' has become mainstream in a way that was unthinkable only a few months ago. When 92,153 Conservative party members voted for Boris Johnson to be Prime Minister in July 2019, the rhetoric of a hard Brexit was replaced by the rise to the status of 'normal' of a 'no-deal Brexit'. Yet, in early September 2019 Johnson's hardliner cabinet suffered heavy defeats when former Conservative minister Phillip Lee defected to the Liberal Democrats and 21 MPs voted with the opposition to stop a no-deal Brexit, for which they were subsequently suspended from the Conservative Party.

Throughout the Brexit process, the virtues of the EU have been presented in only the most pragmatic, largely economistic way. At best, the EU has been defended in terms of a market. Other merits of European integration – for example, sustaining peace in Europe – have been almost absent from the debate. European integration has made member states less independent but allowed them to pool their sovereignty and to deal more effectively with transnational problems than they could on their own. Brexit is a setback for that project. However, because of the protracted Brexit process, debates in mainland Europe have increased in volume and intensity regarding European integration, the value of the EU, and the need to reform it and maintain and build on its successes.

Meanwhile, the costs have added up. While the economy did not plunge into crisis in response to the Brexit vote as had been predicted, in autumn 2018 it was estimated that the cost to the UK economy was about £500m per week, the economy had reduced by about 2.5 per cent (Springford, 2018) and the value of the pound to the dollar and euro had dropped by 15 per cent–20 per cent. Several major multinational investors have cancelled investments or moved jobs from the UK, and more have said that they will reduce their activity in Britain if Brexit occurs. The anticipated job losses and economic damage would increase inequality and have disastrous consequences for people's agency. Time will show whether the acerbic debate, the widening polarization and the absence of compromise or unity which it has fostered can be overcome, or whether the downward spiral of a heated debate, misinformation, hatred, extremism and parochialism will lead to further political divisions, more social inequality, and loss of individual and collective agency.

Structure of the book

The book has three parts and starts with contributions that examine the impact of austerity politics and culture on the UK's economy, public services, social classes, cultural sector and legal assistance, as well as how this has triggered acts of resistance. Simon Griffiths demonstrates that under austerity the transformation of public service delivery has promoted a retrenchment of state tasks which have been underfinanced or contracted to private service providers.

Lisa Mckenzie's chapter follows on the socio-economic impact of austerity. It uses ethnographic research to examine the transformation of representations of the working class under austerity, suggesting that the exclusion and 'breaking' of the working class made people vote Leave to resist their precarious conditions. Tom Montgomery and Maria Grasso's chapter also builds on the uneven effects of austerity across social groups and geographies, suggesting that for people in the most exposed communities, the EU referendum was an opportunity to exercise agency. Their chapter uses survey data to analyse collective actions against austerity, capitalism and gender inequality within activist groups. Ingrid von Rosenberg explores the impact of local and national funding cuts on the UK's cultural sector, its venues and activities, and how the sector is reconstituting itself to survive with reduced funding. Finally, Steven Truxal explains how the justice system and the rule of law have been affected by cuts in legal aid funding.

The second part links the impact of austerity to the politics and discourse of Brexit. It opens with a chapter by Carlo Morelli who outlines the scale of austerity policies and the consequences for both capital and labour from the UK's withdrawal from the EU. Marius Guderjan and Adrian Wilding analyse how economic, political and cultural disenfranchisement and questions of agency connect with populist politics in the EU referendum. This is followed by John Clarke's examination of the construction of 'a sovereign people' in populist Leave discourses. Kirsten Forkert then focuses on the politics and discourses around immigration and shows how xenophobia and nationalism shaped the Leave campaign, in particular regarding immigrants' access to the NHS. Magdalena Nowicka's chapter elaborates on debates about immigration by looking at the perspectives of Polish immigrants in the UK. She explains how these differ from the dominant discourses of migrants as rational economic agents or passive victims of anti-immigrant policies.

The third part of the book turns to the different nations and territories of the UK and beyond. First, Allan Cochrane investigates the diversity and uneven socio-economic developments in England, characterized by a domination by London and the South East, and how this connects with English national identity. Hugh Mackay then studies what is and is not different about the Brexit vote in Wales, compared with England, and examines some implications of the historical relationship between the nations, their elites and national identifications. Klaus Stolz examines the distinctiveness of Scottish attitudes to the EU, and to fiscal austerity. His chapter argues that compared to England and Wales, the referendum result in Scotland was pro-European because of Scotland's more social-democratic nature and because, unlike the British government, the Scottish government is seen as a facilitator of 'Scottish agency'. Derek Birrell and Paul Carmichael outline the exceptionalism of Northern Ireland, and how the strong social and political divisions have enabled Unionist and constrained Republican preferences in the Brexit negotiations. Kevin Bean completes this third part of the book with an examination of the relationship between the Irish Republic and both the UK and the EU, and suggests that Ireland's EU membership has enabled 'Irish agency' vis-à-vis the UK.

Finally, the conclusion draws together the main strands of the book and focuses on the nexus between Brexit, austerity and agency. In a review of the phases of Brexit so far it takes a cautious look at the prospects for the UK and its relations to the EU before outlining future research possibilities.

References

Ahearn, L. M. (2001) 'Language and Agency', *Annual Review of Anthropology*, 30: 109–37.

Archer, M. (1995) *Realist Social Theory: The Morphogenetic Approach*, Cambridge: Cambridge University Press.

Archer, M. (2003) *Structure, Agency and the Internal Conversation*, Cambridge: Cambridge University Press.

Archer, M. (2004) *Being Human: the Problem of Agency*, Cambridge: Cambridge University Press.

Atkinson, H. (2017) *Local democracy, civic engagement and community: From New Labour to the Big Society*, Manchester: Manchester University Press.

Bauman, Z. (2017) *Retrotopia*, Cambridge: Polity Press.

Berry, C. (2015) *Austerity Politics and UK Economic Policy*, London: Palgrave Macmillan.

Bienkov, A. (2016) 'Half of Leave Voters Believe EU Referendum Will Be Rigged', *politics.co.uk*, 21 June.

Blyth, M. (2013) *Austerity. The History of a Dangerous Idea*, Oxford: Oxford University Press.

Bramall, R. (2013) *The Cultural Politics of Austerity. Past and Present in Austere Times*, London: Palgrave Macmillan.

Clarke, J. (2013) 'Contexts: Forms of Agency and Action', in Ch. Pollitt (ed.) *Context in Public Policy and Management: The Missing Link?*, Cheltenham: Edward Elgar, pp 22–34.

Cummins, I. (ed.) (2018) *Poverty, inequality and social work: The impact of neoliberalism and austerity politics on welfare provision*, Bristol: Policy Press.

Dawood, S. (2016) 'Creative Industries Federation members survey shows 98% want to stay in EU', *Design Week*, 27 May.

Edmiston, D. (ed.) (2018) *Welfare, inequality and social citizenship: Deprivation and affluence in Austerity Britain*, Bristol: Policy Press.

Evans, G. and A. Menon (2017) *Brexit and British Politics*, Cambridge: Polity Press.

Flinders, M. (2018) 'The (Anti-)Politics of the General Election: Funnelling Frustration in a Divided Democracy', *Parliamentary Affairs,* 71(1): 222–36.

Forkert, K. (2017) *Austerity as Public Mood. Social Anxieties and Social Struggles,* London: Rowman & Littlefield International.

Giddens, A. (1984) *The Constitution of Society. Outline of the Theory of Structuration*, Cambridge: Polity Press, 1997 reprint.

Goodwin, M. and O. Heath (2016) 'The 2016 Referendum, Brexit and the Left Behind: An Aggregate-level Analysis of the Result', *The Political Quarterly,* 87(3): 323–32.

Guderjan, M. (2016) *The Future of the UK: Between Internal and External Divisions*, Berlin: Centre for British Studies.

Hay, C. (1995) 'Structure and Agency', in D. Marsh and G. Stoker (eds) *Theory and Methods in Political Science*, Basingstoke: Palgrave Macmillan, pp 189–206.

Kockelman, P. (2007) 'Agency: The relation between meaning, power, and knowledge', *Current Anthropology*, 48(3): 375–401.

Kynaston, D. (2008) *Austerity Britain 1945–51*, London: Bloomsbury.

McAnulla, S. (2002) 'Structure and Agency', in D. Marsh and G. Stoker (eds.) *Theory and Methods in Political Science*, Basingstoke: Palgrave Macmillan, pp 271–91.

Mckenzie, L. (2015) *Getting By. Estates, Class and Culture in Austerity Britain,* Bristol: Policy Press.

McTavish, D. (2019) *Themes and Flux in British Politics. Evolution, Change and Turbulence*, London: Routledge.

Miller, E. (2016) 'The ideology of learner agency and the neoliberal self', *International Journal of Applied Linguistics*, 26(3): 348–65.

OECD (2019) 'Average annual wages', *OECD.stat.*

Sibeon, R. (1999) 'Agency, Structure and Social Chance as Cross-Disciplinary Concepts', *Politics*, 19(3): 139–44.

Springford, J. (2018) *The Cost of Brexit to June 2018*, London: Centre for European Reform.

Taylor, G. (2017) *Understanding Brexit. Why Britain Voted to Leave the European Union*, Emerald: Bingley.

Tyler, I. (2013) *Revolting Subjects. Social Abjections and Resistance in Neoliberal Britain*, London: Zed Books.

Williams, R. (1976) *Keywords. A Vocabulary of Culture and Society*, London: Croom Helm.

Williams, Z. (2016) 'Think the North and the Poor Caused Brexit? Think Again', *The Guardian*, 7 August.

Winder, R. (2005) *Bloody Foreigners. The Story of Immigration to Britain*, London: Abacus.

PART I

The Politics and Culture of Austerity: Impacts and Resistance

1

The Contracting State: Austerity and Public Services

Simon Griffiths

Introduction

At the Conservative Party conference in October 2018, Theresa May bounced on to the stage to the sound of Abba's *Dancing Queen* to declare that austerity was 'over' (CCHQ, 2018). Putting aside the scepticism of opposition parties over this claim (BBC, 2018), the speech did mark a significant shift, rhetorically at least, for the Conservatives. Speaking in 2009, May's Conservative predecessor, David Cameron, had argued that 'the age of austerity demands […] some incredibly tough decisions on taxation, spending, borrowing' (Cameron, 2009). In practice, 'tough decisions' meant deep cuts to public services.

Underlying the rhetoric about 'austerity' was an ideological debate around the role and scope of the state. By 2010, the routes that the Conservatives and the Labour Party offered to economic recovery had diverged along increasingly explicit ideological lines. The election of Cameron's Conservative-led coalition ended New Labour's 'reform-and-invest' approach to public services. Cameron had long been sceptical about the size of the state, and its ability to achieve desirable social ends. Throughout his speeches, the state was portrayed as inefficient, bureaucratic and outdated – although this scepticism was often downplayed through a rhetoric of 'modernization' and political centrism while in opposition (Griffiths, 2014). However, it was the economic crisis of 2008 that offered Cameron the opportunity to explicitly challenge the state that had emerged during the New Labour years. While the Labour leadership had accepted the need for some spending cuts during the party's final years in power, Cameron blamed Labour's overspending for the scale of the crisis, arguing that the party had 'maxed out on our nation's credit card' (Lee, 2009, p. 69). He claimed that the high-cost public services of the New Labour years were untenable. On entering office in 2010 his government set out to radically transform the state.

This chapter focuses on the 'contracting state' under Cameron, and reviews developments in three major public services since 2010: health, education and welfare, paying attention to the way in which these reforms affect the agency of the people who rely on these services.

Austerity in the contracting state

Public services, such as education or healthcare, are those services generally considered to be so essential to well-being that they are available to all citizens of a state, regardless of their income. They enable or enhance agency, as they allow citizens to realize their potential. In the UK, during the postwar period, public services were generally provided directly by the state and paid for from general taxation. Over the last 40 years, public services have increasingly been contracted out to private sector organizations, which deliver services funded (or co-funded) by the state. This trend has been particularly pronounced during the last decade. Using the rhetoric of austerity, Cameron, and his chancellor George Osborne, created a 'contracting' state: one that both contracted in terms of relative size and contracted out many of its activities to third parties. Although many of these changes had begun a generation before, Cameron's premiership was marked by the *extent* of the expansion of the market into areas previously occupied by the state.

The first aspect of the contracting state concerns the reduction of the size of state spending as a proportion of the total economy. This had a direct impact on the capital and revenue available for public services after 2010. Cameron and his government consistently put forward an economic position that criticized the 'overspending' of New Labour and focused on the perceived need for austerity. Even before the economic crisis, Cameron characterized the state as corpulent, outdated and inefficient (Griffiths, 2014). However, it was only after the economic crash that the implications Cameron drew from this became clear. In office, Cameron and Osborne set out a hawkish response to the deficit, involving deep cuts to public spending, and consequently public services. According to the Institute for Fiscal Studies (IFS), the Emergency Budget introduced by Osborne in 2010 would have resulted in 'the longest, deepest and most sustained period of cuts in public services spending at least since the Second World War' (Chote, 2010). Two years into office, Osborne would claim: 'I'm the Chancellor who is cutting the size of Government faster than anyone in modern times. We're reducing the size of government, from almost 50% of our national income to 40%, in just five years' (Osborne, 2012).

Writing in 2011, Peter Taylor-Gooby and Gerry Stoker pointed out that, '[o]n current projections, public expenditure in the UK appears likely to fall below that in the US by 2014 or 2015. This is simply unprecedented and, if fully implemented, indicates a radical new departure in British policy directions' (2011, p. 6). In practice, sluggish economic growth over the next few years meant that the state spending was reduced less than originally planned as a proportion of the overall economy. This reduction was further complicated because some public services – notably, schools, the National Health Service (NHS) and pensions – were protected by the government, fearful of the political backlash that cutting popular public services might cause. This meant that the brunt of the cuts fell on particular areas. Nevertheless, under Cameron state spending as a proportion of the overall economy was still to shrink considerably. In this sense, public services in the UK after 2010 were being reformed against a backdrop of a contracting state.

The second aspect of Cameron's contracting state came from the form that public services took after 2010: the role of the state was increasingly limited to 'contracting out' services to third parties, largely in the private sector, rather than providing them directly. This shift predated Cameron's leadership of the party. Since the 1980s governments of all colours had begun to move away from the idea that the state should provide services directly. This was accompanied by the practice of 'contracting' public services to external organizations wherever feasible – and where it was not, reconstituting existing state institutions to operate within market or quasi-market structures. Third party providers of public services overwhelmingly came from the private sector. The intellectual underpinnings of this idea can be traced back through the Thatcher governments to various neoliberal thinkers. With Cameron, however, it was not just the extent of the cuts to public services, but the radicalism of the pro-market reforms that was unexpected. To Taylor-Gooby and Stoker the 'reforms also include a far-reaching restructuring of state services involving significant transfers of responsibility from the state to the private sector and to the citizen' (2011, p. 4). The clearest statement of this trend came with the Coalition's white paper, *Open Public Services* (2011), which took plans to contract out public services further than ever before. Trailing the paper, Cameron argued that public services needed a complete transformation: 'the grip of state control will be released and power will be placed in people's hands'. To achieve this

> public services should be open to a range of providers competing to offer a better service [...] [I]nstead of having to justify why it makes sense to introduce competition in some public services – as we are now doing with schools and in the NHS – the state will have to justify why it should ever operate a monopoly. (Cameron, 2011)

The state's role was increasingly limited to be a contractor of services provided by third parties.

Before reviewing developments in specific public services, it is worth noting that multilayer governance complicates the analysis of changes in the UK. Since 1999, responsibility for many public services, including health, education, housing, local government, transport and other areas, has been devolved to Scotland, Wales and Northern Ireland. Local authorities are also significant providers of public services, and have been hit particularly hard by austerity. In the UK, they remain hugely dependent on Westminster and the devolved governments for their revenue and spending decisions. This comes in the form of central grants, as well as stipulations on the amount of local tax they can raise and the services they must provide. Indeed, for every pound raised in taxation in England 91 pence is controlled and allocated by central government (Crewe, 2016). As chancellor, Osborne passed down significant responsibilities for deficit reduction to local government. This meant most local authorities have made huge cuts to local public services, including transport, parks, libraries, public amenities, adult social care, housing services for the vulnerable, and services for young children over the last decade. Some local councils will have lost more than 60 per cent of their revenues between 2010 and 2020. Simon Parker, former Director of the New Local Government Network – a think tank specializing in local government – describes the consequences as 'perhaps the biggest shift in the role of the British state since 1945' (quoted in Crewe, 2016). However, while there is much that could be discussed in more detail on the constraining effects of budget cuts on local governments and other public services, this chapter focuses on austerity and the contracting state in three of the largest public services: education, health and welfare.

Education and austerity

In December 2010, Michael Gove, the Conservative Secretary of State for Education, wrote that it has become fashionable 'to refer to the Coalition as a Maoist enterprise. Not so much because the government is inhabiting the wilder shores of the Left, but because of the relentless pace of modernization being pursued across government' (Gove, 2010). Over the next five years, the Coalition government undertook one of the most radical periods of structural reform to the education system in recent history, driving through a marketizing agenda from the top across significant areas of education policy in England. (Education is a devolved responsibility in the UK, with Scotland, Wales and Northern Ireland operating different systems.) It is the pro-market radicalism of the reforms to the system of schools and higher education in England that is likely to be one of the most significant legacies of the period after 2010.

It was in higher education in England that marketization went furthest. (Scotland also faced austerity cuts, but the devolved Scottish government implemented them within a different ideological framework, which meant that higher education institutions avoided high tuition fees.) While earlier reforms under New Labour ended 'free' university education, coalition policy had radical implications for the way in which higher education is provided in England. The Browne Review – *Securing a sustainable future for higher education: an independent review of higher education funding and student finance* – published its findings in October 2010. Among other things, the review argued that there should be no limit on university fees, with universities subject to a levy on all fees charged above £6.000. The review also argued that a new body, the Higher Education Council, should be responsible for investing in priority courses; enforcing quality standards and improving access; having the power to bail out struggling institutions; and exploring options such as mergers and takeovers if institutions faced financial failure. There was also scope for new providers to enter the system. Browne proposed that students should not have to pay any tuition fees up front, but would begin to pay their loans back (with interest) once their earnings reached £21,000.

By the time the Browne proposals reached parliament in November 2010, certain concessions had been made. In particular, the government put forward an absolute cap on fees of £9,000 per year. In an effort to mitigate criticism that the review would discourage poorer students from applying, the government also proposed that universities charging fees of over £6,000 per year would have to contribute to a National Scholarships programme and introduced a stricter regime of financial sanctions, encouraging high-charging universities to increase participation. However, despite government assurances that this would lead to price variation in the market, the overwhelming majority of universities chose to charge fees at the top rate. Other proposals, such as the creation of a Higher Education Council to invest in those areas of study deemed to be in the national interest, were sidelined.

This adoption of a 'Revised Browne Review' provides an example of a contracting state. It promoted a very different view of students as agents. In theory at least, they were significantly empowered as consumers of a service. Gone was the idea that higher education was a public good, determined by academics, and paid for by the state. In its place was the view that consumer choice, determined by student numbers, would decide which institutions, subjects and modules would survive in a market context (Collini, 2010, p. 23). Universities must now compete for students and, like any other business, can fail if they do not attract these consumers.

Schools were protected from the worst of the cuts, with government pledging to 'ringfence' their budgets from the austerity agenda. Yet, as in higher education, the marketizing push has been radical. Schools policy has been dominated by the hollowing out of local authority power, which was passed upwards to the Secretary of State and downwards to academies operating in a quasi-market system. The Academies Act (2010) allowed all state schools in England to gain 'academy status'. Academies are publicly funded schools that have significant autonomy from the state. Most academies are at secondary level, although there are some at primary level too. In May 2010, Gove wrote to every head teacher in England to encourage them to apply for academy status; either as academies on their own or as part of a 'chain', run by private or charitable organizations. The result was a dramatic rise in the number of academies: by 2018 there were around 7,000 of them, teaching almost half of the pupils in England (NAO, 2018).

These reforms were controversial. Critics of the academy models have, among other things, attacked the freedoms these new schools have from state control and the influence that private and third-sector sponsors exert – described by one teachers' leader as the ability to teach 'creationism instead of literacy' (Sellgren, 2010). For some analysts, the academy programme, with its extensive use of non-state providers to run schools, meant 'the beginning of the end of state education' (Ball, 2012, p. 89).

Academies mark a long-term move from a (theoretically) universal service to one in which the school system is shaped by parental choice. To some degree, 'academization' is an extension of policies put forward by New Labour or the Conservative's Grant Maintained Schools of the 1980s, but the scope and radicalism of the Coalition reforms – rolling out a market-based system to all schools – constitutes a step-change from anything that went before. This marketizing approach, with the contraction of state oversight and responsibility, is consistent with the radical reform of higher education undertaken during the same period.

Market-based reforms under the Cameron administration have fundamentally changed education in England. They assume a very different view of pupils (and their parents) and students, who are now seen to act as 'consumers' of education. According to this understanding of agency, students are expected to make choices about education, with reduced state oversight supposedly allowing for greater diversity and experimentation between academy chains or universities. These increasingly 'privatized' bodies providing education must, in turn, compete for the custom of those who use them.

Health and austerity

The Coalition agreement between the Conservatives and Liberal Democrats in May 2010 pledged to 'stop the top–down reorganizations of the NHS'. Yet, within just a few months, Andrew Lansley, then Secretary of State for Health, began a process of radical reform to the health system. These reforms were set out in the *Equity and Excellence* white paper (DH, 2010), subtitled 'Liberating the NHS'. There is no further mention of this latter phrase, but the implication was that the NHS had to be liberated from state control to reach its full potential. The white paper applied only to the NHS in England, as the devolved administrations in Scotland, Wales and Northern Ireland are responsible for developing their own health policies. Curiously, given the centrality of austerity to the 2010–16 government's political programme, there is no mention of the term in the white paper. This is perhaps due to the commitment to ring-fence NHS funding and the risks of justifying such fundamental reforms to a popular institution as part of a 'cutting' agenda. However, after 2010, the Conservative-led government set about radically transforming the NHS on the basis of 'cutting-costs' of bureaucracy and the inefficiencies of monopolistic state provision.

Equity and Excellence set out radical plans to give patients in England 'choice of any provider, choice of consultant-led team, choice of GP practice and choice of treatment' (DH, 2010, p. 3).

The governance structure of the NHS after these reforms, set out in the resulting Health and Social Care Bill, was hugely complex. Key elements saw groups of General Practitioners – organized into Clinical Commissioning Groups – acting as commissioners of health services. The 150 or so Primary Care Trusts and ten Strategic Health Authorities which previously had commissioning roles were abolished. At the same time – in a move that mimicked the academy school programme to some degree – all hospitals in England were compelled to become foundation trusts. These institutions were largely autonomous from central government and gained new freedoms, including the freedom to generate up to 49 per cent of their income from private patients (a huge increase on the average incomes generated from private practice before 2012). They also operated under a new regulatory structure, with foundation hospitals operating like businesses competing for patients.

The reforms were described in the medical journal, *The Lancet*, as 'the biggest changes in the National Health Service (NHS) in England since the service began in 1948' (Whitehead et al, 2010, p. 1373), and led to a range of criticisms. Concerns included the ability of new Clinical Commissioning Groups to determine whether particular procedures should be funded. They also included provision for new charging powers for services previously provided free through the NHS. The reforms also abolished the duty of Primary Care Trusts to secure health services for everyone living in a defined geographical area. This led to fears that vulnerable citizens could be excluded. Finally, reforms gave hospitals the right to carry out extensive private care. In short, although the reforms theoretically provided greater flexibility in patients' choice of providers and greater agency over their treatments, there were concerns that wealthier, better informed patients would gain greater agency over more vulnerable patients.

To Lansley and his colleagues, the financial pressures on the NHS justified this wholesale reform. However, writing in *The Lancet* on the blueprint that led to the changes, Margaret Whitehead and her colleagues argued that

> [t]he white paper's proposals are ideological with little evidential foundation. They represent a decisive step towards privatization that risks undermining the fundamental equity and efficiency objectives of the NHS. Rather than 'liberating the NHS', these proposals seem to be an exercise in liberating the NHS' £100 billion budget to commercial enterprises. (2010, p. 1373)

As with the education reforms in England discussed in the previous section, these changes demonstrated the lack of faith in the central state to directly plan for the public good – a contraction of the scope of its previous responsibilities.

Welfare under austerity

While health and schools' policy were sheltered, to some degree, from the full effects of austerity, public services related to welfare were not. Welfare reform since 2010 involved radical structural changes combined with deep, UK-wide spending cuts. There are areas of welfare policy that are not discussed here – notably the reform of pensions under the Liberal Democrat minister, Steve Webb – which proceeded relatively smoothly. However, the most controversial shifts came under four headings: deep cuts to the working-age welfare budget; the amalgamation of all of Labour's welfare-to-work schemes for the unemployed into one 'Work Programme'; the use of Work Capability Tests and increased benefit sanctions for claimants; and the introduction of Universal Credit to replace six of the largest working-age benefits. Because devolution of welfare began later with the Scotland Act of 2016, these reforms took place across the UK. The reforms largely fit the notion of a contracting state, particularly when they contained the fingerprints of the Chancellor, George Osborne, whose focus was on radically reducing welfare expenditure. This set up frequent clashes with the Secretary of State for Work and Pensions, Iain Duncan Smith, whose focus was increasingly on radical reforms as a solution to entrenched deprivation.

The Coalition introduced various welfare cuts in the name of austerity. These included the withdrawal of the spare room subsidy for working-age Housing Benefit claimants deemed to be underusing their home (a policy dubbed the 'Bedroom Tax' by critics); a £500 a week benefit cap for couples; a seven-day waiting period for new benefit claims; the restriction of (non-pensioner) benefits to increases of 1 per cent per year from 2013 to 2016 and an absolute freeze from 2016. Changes to the inflation measure used to upgrade benefits also saved money in the long run. In an effort to demonstrate the 'fairness' of their reforms, the Coalition also pointed to the withdrawal of Child Benefit for households containing a higher tax payer. However, it is clear that the bulk of these changes hit the poorest hardest (see Chapters Grasso and Montgomery, Guderjan and Wilding, Mckenzie, and Morelli). Spending on welfare benefits for the UK's poorest families had shrunk by nearly a quarter after nearly a decade of austerity. It is estimated that £37bn less will be spent on working-age social security by 2021, compared with 2010, despite rising prices and living costs (Butler, 2018). In all, the cuts to welfare spending as a proportion of the size of the economy represent a significant contraction of the state's role in this area.

The amalgamation of all Labour's welfare-to-work schemes for the unemployed into one Work Programme, was meant to provide a more efficient way of supporting those in long-term unemployment back into work. This support was contracted out to mostly large, private sector organizations, known as 'prime contractors', on a 'payment-by-results' basis. Higher payments were made for successes in getting individuals who needed more support, such as those claiming health-related out-of-work benefits, into the workplace. However, the scheme was criticized for getting far fewer people back into the workplace than the Department for Work and Pensions (DWP) and the contractors had estimated (Page, 2015). As private providers missed their contractual targets, the payment by results model meant that they then received less money to provide the service, creating a vicious cycle of underperformance and taking even more money out of frontline services.

The use of Work Capability Tests for those receiving health-related out-of-work benefits and 'sanctions' for benefit claimants also significantly increased under the Coalition. This reflected a dispute about the agency and motives of claimants. Underlying the government's reforms was an assumption that many claimants had the capacity to work but not the willingness. There was therefore a rise in the use of financial sanctions for welfare claimants deemed to have failed to meet certain conditions – such as arriving late for a meeting with a Jobcentre adviser. Adults claiming out-of-work benefits due to disability or a long-term health condition were also required to undergo a Work Capability Test to determine whether they were able to work, and what support would be required. The test itself dated from New Labour's Welfare Reform Act (2007), but its conditions became harsher with the austerity cuts. The administration of the Work Capability Test was also contracted to private companies. Critics noted the impersonal and mechanistic approach of assessors, the lack of transparency over the decision-making process and its complexity (Page, 2015). There were a large number of appeals related to the Test, with around three fifths of formal appeals against the assessment decision being successful (DWP, 2016, p. 9). Atos Healthcare, one of the largest private companies carrying out the assessments eventually withdrew from the role following negative publicity and criticism by DWP officials.

One of the Coalition's most controversial policies was the introduction of Universal Credit. The project was the brainchild of the former leader of the Conservative Party, Iain Duncan Smith, who was given the role of Secretary of State for Work and Pensions. After undergoing something of an 'epiphany' on poverty, he championed the idea of Universal Credit with almost evangelical zeal. The new benefit was designed to bring together a variety of existing benefits for working-age people – such as working tax credit, child tax credit, income support and housing benefit – under one programme. Before 2010, it had a degree of cross-party support as a way of simplifying a complex system of different welfare benefits, supposedly offering claimants greater control and agency in bringing all support into a single monthly payment. However, the implementation of the reforms was deeply problematic. Concerns were raised about the online application process, with many claimants lacking the technological skills or internet access to apply. The switch to paying benefit monthly and in arrears (following the standard practice for professional salaried positions) also caused budgetary problems for many claimants used to weekly wages or fortnightly benefit payments. The removal of the option for rent to be paid directly to landlords led to an increased risk of eviction. The programme also became bogged down by wider welfare cuts introduced by the Coalition, with Duncan Smith forced by the Chancellor to agree to cuts to Universal Credit in order to cover the costs of its implementation. This meant that a major purported benefit of the new programme was lost, as the level at which Universal Credit was set failed to lift many claimants out of poverty (Hirsch and Hartfree, 2013).

Social security, as a share of national income, is projected to fall from 12.5 per cent in 2009–10 to 9.8 per cent by 2020–21 (IFS, 2015). The state's involvement has literally contracted in size relative to the overall economy and has retreated in terms of contracting services out, largely to private providers. For many welfare claimants, or former welfare claimants now struggling without state support, the promises made of a more efficient, effective benefit system, offering them greater agency and control, have failed to materialize.

Conclusion

If the construction of a contracting state was the aim, then Cameron was certainly successful: austerity provided the opportunity for a radical reconstruction of the state and public services in the UK after 2010. In November 2018, a politically controversial report on the effects of austerity in the UK was produced by Philip Alston, the United Nations' *rapporteur* on extreme poverty and human rights. Alston argued that austerity and its consequences were a 'political choice', rather than a fiscal necessity (Alston, 2018, p. 22). It was austerity that provided the opportunity for a transformation of the state and public services in the UK, particularly in England. It allowed key players, particularly Cameron and Osborne, to create a contracting state, which would both contract out services and which literally contracted in relative size.

The decision to contract state spending as a proportion of the economy draws on a very different conception of agency to that which characterized the New Labour years. Under the Coalition, in those areas where the state withdrew through the abolition of certain types of welfare payments, for example, citizens were increasingly expected to support themselves. To many Conservatives, over-reliance on the state caused dependency, rather than increasing agency. To Cameron's critics, the withdrawal of the state limited agency through forcing citizens into poverty.

Contracting out public services to other providers also had implications for the agency of citizens. Where public services had been contracted out under monopoly conditions, such as the provision of Work Capability Tests, incentives were often set for private providers to focus on reducing benefit spending, rather than claimant needs. This resulted in many vulnerable claimants being deemed 'fit for work', denying them additional support for living costs and reducing their agency rather than increasing it.

Where citizens faced a choice of third-party providers of public services, or public providers competing under quasi-market conditions, they were increasingly treated as consumers of services, and granted choices over provider – deciding which foundation hospital or school is best for them or their families, for example. In this sense, the agents needed to choose between public services increasingly aped other market choices. Critics noted that some citizens – who had more social or financial capital, for example – were better able to meet the expectations implicit in this conception of agency than others.

Comparing Cameron's radicalism with that of his Conservative predecessor, Margaret Thatcher, Eric Pickles, the former Conservative Party Chairman, is said to have claimed that, 'I think we have probably achieved more in the first term, [than] the blessed Margaret did in hers ...' (Guido Fawkes, 2014). Thatcher had set about to 'roll back the frontiers of the state' in the 1980s through a programme of privatization and free market economics. Cameron went further than Thatcher ever could. Austerity provided the opportunity for further contracting the state.

References

Alston, P. (2018) *Statement on Visit to the United Kingdom*, Office of the High Commissioner for Human Rights, 16 November: https://www.ohchr.org/Documents/Issues/Poverty/EOM_GB_16Nov2018.pdf.

Ball, S. J. (2012) 'The reluctant state and the beginning of the end of state education' *Journal of Educational Administration and History*, 44(2): 89–103.

BBC (2018) 'May's end of austerity claim 'not credible'', *BBC News*, 4 October.

Booth, R. and P. Butler (2018) 'UK austerity has inflicted 'great misery' on citizens, UN says', *The Guardian*, 16 November.

Butler, P. (2018) 'Welfare spending for UK's poorest shrinks by £37bn', *The Guardian*, 23 September.

Cameron, D. (2009) 'The Age of Austerity', *Conservative Party Speeches*, 26 April: https://conservative-speeches.sayit.mysociety.org/speech/601367.

Cameron, D. (2011) 'How We Will Release the Grip of State Control', *The Telegraph*, 20 February.

CCHQ [Conservative Campaign Headquarters] (2018) *Prime Minister: Our future is in our hands*: http://press.conservatives.com/post/178695544270/prime-minister-our-future-is-in-our-hands.

Chote, R. (2010) 'Post Budget Presentations: Opening Remarks', *Institute for Fiscal Studies*: http://www.ifs.org.uk/budgets/budgetjune2010/chote.pdf.

Collini, S. (2010) 'Browne's Gamble', *London Review of Books*, 32(21): 23–5.

Crewe, T. (2016) 'The Strange Death of Municipal England', *London Review of Books*, 38(24): 6–10.

DH [Department of Health] (2010) *Equity and Excellence: Liberating the NHS*, London: The Stationary Office (Cm 7881).

DWP [Department of Work and Pensions] (2016) *Employment and Support Allowance: Work Capability Assessments, Mandatory Reconsiderations and Appeals*, https://assets.publishing.service.gov.uk/government/uploads/system/uploads/attachment_data/file/558953/esa-wca-summary-september-2016.pdf.

Gove, M. (2010) 'Michael Gove: my revolution for culture in classroom', *The Telegraph*, 28 December.

Griffiths, S. (2014) 'What was Progressive in 'Progressive Conservatism'?', *Political Studies Review*, 12(1): 29–40.

Guido Fawkes (2014) 'Tory Cabinet Minister: We've Done More Than Maggie', *Guido Fawkes*, 2 July: https://order-order.com/2014/06/02/tory-cabinet-minister-weve-done-more-than-maggie/.

Hirsch, D and Y. Hartfree (2013) *Does universal credit enable households to reach a minimum income standard?*, Joseph Rowntree Foundation: https://www.jrf.org.uk/sites/default/files/jrf/migrated/files/universal-credit-income-standards-full.pdf.

Institute for Fiscal Studies [IFS] (2015) *Social security spending*, https://www.ifs.org.uk/tools_and_resources/fiscal_facts/social_security.

Lee, S. (2009) 'Convergence, Critique and Divergence: the development of economic policy under David Cameron', in S. Lee and M. Beech (eds) *The Conservatives under David Cameron: Built to Last?*, Basingstoke: Palgrave.

NAO [National Audit Office] (2018) *Converting maintained schools to academies*, https://www.nao.org.uk/wp-content/uploads/2018/02/Converting-maintained-schools-to-academies-Summary.pdf.

Osborne, G. (2012) 'Speech to the Conservative conference: full text', *New Statesman*, 8 October.

Page, R. (2015) 'The Coalition, Poverty and Social Security', in M. Beech and S. Lee (eds) *The Conservative-Liberal Coalition*, Basingstoke: Palgrave.

Sellgren, K. (2010) 'Tory free schools 'barking mad'; says teachers' leader', *BBC News*, 31 March.

Taylor-Gooby, P. and G. Stoker (2011) 'The Coalition Programme: A New Vision for Britain or Politics as Usual?', *Political Quarterly*, 82(1): 4–15.

Whitehead, M., Hanratty, B. and Popay, J. (2010) 'NHS reform: untried remedies for misdiagnosed problems?', *The Lancet*, 376(9750): pp 1373–5.

2

Breaking Britain's Working Class: the Left Out

Lisa Mckenzie

Introduction

The foundation of this chapter is inspired by the work of Pierre Bourdieu, who spent his life exposing the unfairness and the damage that is done to society through a structured and structuring classified system. In *The Weight of the World: Social Suffering in Contemporary Society*, an in-depth collection of case studies, Bourdieu (1999) pulls together the lived experience of working-class people from around the globe at the end of the last century. They also connect the logic and practice of people, groups and institutions purposefully depriving the working class of the subjective social, cultural, symbolic and economic capital that is passed on and inherited, thus reproducing an unjust and highly structured society. For that reason, throughout this chapter the term 'breaking' is describing a purposeful process, or as Bourdieu would argue 'a logic of practice', a structured and structuring system unfairly advantaging some simultaneously and unfairly disadvantaging others.

As the neoliberal economy has matured and globalized there is undoubtedly a growing and distinct group of people (or agents in the context of this book) throughout Europe (and globally) that are faring badly. The first two decades of this century have been dominated by the term and the experience of wealth inequality – in Britain wealth inequality is ever widening the gap between people at the top and those at the bottom of society. It has expanded and for the working class, life has become far more precarious (Savage, 2015). This globalized neoliberal economic system has been disastrous for

European working-class people but unlike previous generations they have little in the way of self or state organized stability, from trade unions, political parties or from culture, networks and identities once connected to their employment.

Social goods have always been important to agents of the working class. However, over the last 30 years there has been a marked retreat from the postwar consensus and a definite policy of 'rolling back' public-owned and public-run social services. These policies have been purposeful, and have been guided through a de-valuing process of Britain's working class. The de-industrialization and loss of manufacturing industries, and the privatization of those industries that were once publicly owned have devastated working-class communities, economically but also culturally, socially and symbolically. Housing policy has shifted over the last 30 years towards the home-owning democracy and away from a large social renting culture. Consequently, changing the way that the population view housing from 'home' to 'asset' has serious implications upon how communities organize and operate (Hodkinson, Watt, Mooney, 2013). Simultaneously removing state support for further education for all adults over the age of 25 and introducing and raising fees within higher education have ensured that even the myth of social mobility is now unbelievable (Bathmaker, Ingram, Waller, 2013).

There has been a severe lack of political will or until recently debate in Britain in challenging social and political systems to tackle poverty and inequality. Rather the focus has shifted onto the usefulness of an individual, their productivity, and how their behaviour, their culture and their values are problematic (Skeggs, 2004, 2014). Although this is not an entirely new phenomenon, there have been institutional and moral judgements regarding the poorest for as long as there has been a 'poor law' naming them (Welshman, 2006). Consequently, naming and identifying the poor has been used to divide them into two distinct groups: the deserving poor, those deemed 'the respectable' doing their best and perhaps becoming 'unlucky' in opposition to those who are undeserving, the deviant, dangerous, and criminal.

Breaking Britain's working class into two separate groups of the underserving and the deserving has been well practiced; John Welshman (2006) maps this process of classification through identifying and naming the poor as far back to the 17th century. However, this chapter argues that poverty, class and inequality is distinct as working-class people's lives are becoming increasingly precarious. Working-class people who have historically used many forms of collectivism within their class identities, employment, and social lives, are now struggling in an ever-competitive low-skilled race to the bottom jobs market, while more skilled and stable jobs are out of reach as technology is changing faster than they can accumulate the skills they require. Added to this is the rolling back of many state social programmes as governments follow the ideology of a neoliberal market-driven economy for both its public and private services. Public services have been hollowed out yet there has been little in the way of empathy towards those working-class communities and the struggles they face, instead they have been demonized, stigmatized and ridiculed for their apparent failure. Subsequent government policy for almost 40 years has compounded this with rhetoric that has shifted the focus from the market to the individual by looking specifically at the culture and the practices of the poorest. Policy and rhetoric from the full spectrum of British politics have followed the undeserving/deserving mantra from the Conservative government's theories of the underclass during the 1980s (Levitas, 2005) to New Labour's social exclusion agenda and back to the Conservative government's concept of 'Broken Britain' (Mckenzie, 2015, p. 7).

Breaking Britain's working class

As large organized industries disappear, the debate around how working-class people are valued and devalued during this period of advanced capitalist ideology is central for understanding the purposeful act of breaking Britain's working class. Sociologists who study class, for example Savage (2015), Sayer (2015) and Skeggs (2014), have all placed the financialization of society through an advanced capitalist economy at the centre of their analysis of contemporary class relationships. Frank (2001, p. 19) succinctly pointed out that the 'market has become God' and is dominated by the logic that capital is to make capital. The concept of value becomes central, who we value, and why we value them has replaced the debate around class struggle. Rather than understanding inequality as structural with collective beneficiaries at the expense of collective losers we attribute value to an individual (Sayer, 2015).

The debate is often subtle, and can be addressed in many ways, for example in 'the hardworking families' rhetoric that is used in Westminster political language. This is slight but effective in removing the concept of class but also removing the critique of social structure, making distinctions between 'hardworking' people and others that we must assume are not hard working. Bev Skeggs' (2014) recent research on 'value' argues that this forceful logic opens out and 'commodifies' every aspect of our lives, making everything – every person and every interaction – subject to a value that can be bought, sold or exchanged.

This logic and practice has had severe consequences for working-class people through stigmatization, and re-branding them as of a lesser value, and in some cases valueless. This connection between an individual's market value and their moral value has been central in producing new ways of exploitation through the fields of culture and media, strengthening established forms of class differentiation but also inventing new forms of class prejudice. A process of differentiation that can be subtle, and can move amongst society unseen but has terrible consequences for those whose social value is being undermined, a process that Bourdieu (1986) would term 'symbolic violence'. An act of violence that is symbolic and often difficult to detect through the normalization process of everyday practice that is inflicted upon a less powerful group by a more powerful group.

Drawing upon the author's own ethnographic research in St Ann's Nottingham and in Bethnal Green in London's East End, this chapter argues that despite 'value' being linked to an exchange value within the market, working-class people in both locations resist this neoliberal model of society through placing their own understanding of value firmly located within and amongst their families, friends and local communities. Despite growing and deeply ingrained class inequality in the UK, the working-class people that were part of the author's research both acknowledged the de-valuing process and narrative of their communities but simultaneously demonstrated agency by resisting that narrative, by telling their own stories of class, local and cultural pride.

Ethnographic tales of value and resistance

Bethnal Green

It is July 2014, in the backyard of a local pub in Bethnal Green sits a group of people who have lived within staggering distance to this establishment for either all or most of their lives, as have their families and friends. Most of the people who drink in this pub in the East End did not vote in the 2015 general election and would be known as the 'politically disinterested'. Although conversations change daily, the constant is the talk about how difficult it is to make ends meet in London, this conversation never changes and never ends. The men are on very precarious contracts within the building trade, sometimes a day at a time, and the women mostly work cleaning the offices and homes of the more affluent and they are unlikely to earn the London living wage. The talk in this pub is what will happen to them, will they be allowed to stay in this neighbourhood, and if not what will happen to their relatives, particularly the elderly who have more secure social housing and are more difficult to move. Constantly changing cuts in welfare keep them precarious. They never know what new cuts will be implemented and how it will affect them. This is particularly salient relating to housing benefit capping and the cost of renting privately, the benefit just does not fit the rent. This means that whole communities that have been stable for generations are forced to move further out of London.

The value of 'the social' and of family and of community is becoming increasingly diminished and over-ridden by the needs of a capitalist system extracting as much market value as possible out of each and every relationship, interaction and person. This method of de-valuing low-income working-class people is not subtle, it is extremely blunt. If you live in Bethnal Green and within walking distance to the City of London and the financial district, and you are not worth the £80,700 that the estate agent Savills has calculated as the cost of the space you are taking up, you need to leave, no value can be extracted from you. This type of blunt and simplistic logic is having a severe effect on working-class families within London and wider within the South East as rents rise and house prices skyrocket. The bottom line to whether you are allowed to stay in a neighbourhood where you have perhaps lived most or all of your life, where you have a job, a family and a connection is based upon 'are you worth it'?

St Ann's in Nottingham

The East Midlands have been hit over 30 years with total de-industrialization by the closure of the mining industry, the large engineering industries, and the textile industry. The de-valuing process here has been more culturally pitched because of the levels of unemployment and the extremely low paid work it has fixed upon a moral worth. Out of the eight years of ethnographic research in this neighbourhood the author spent almost every day for two years in a community centre that was in the centre of the St Ann's council estate in Nottingham. This community had suffered high unemployment, low wages, and increasing amounts of class prejudice for generations (Mckenzie, 2015). It was home to almost 15,000 people, and social housing was still predominantly controlled by the local council. The estate itself had no real aesthetic value for gentrifiers or property developers; being built in the 1970s using grey concrete pre-moulded or pre-casted sections of square and uniformed small terraced houses. The estate throughout Nottingham was known as a pretty lawless place, but also ugly with nothing worth going to within the neighbourhood. Both place and people have been devalued and stigmatized as valueless over several generations.

The community centre was busy and vibrant, often very noisy, and was well used. There was one woman, Sharon, who volunteered in the kitchen every day. She would arrive at 9.15am after dropping her own children off at school. She made all the drinks, cleaned up the tables and did some washing up. Her constant presence at the community centre was comforting; she knew everyone by name and made everyone feel welcome. Her contribution to the community was enormous, although her contribution to wider society was de-valued. Sharon claimed full state benefits to live, she received income support for her two children and herself that amounted to £110 per week, she lived in a three-bedroom council house on the estate and received the full rental amount in housing benefit of £52.50 a week. She was costing the taxpayer approximately £8,500 a year in living and subsistence costs. Sharon worked in the community centre approximately 16 hours a week but received no pay.

In 2010, things had really changed for her personally, the global financial and political events had affected her life and sledgehammered into this small community centre on a council estate in Nottingham. In 2008, the then Chancellor of the Exchequer for the Labour Government, Alistair Darling, agreed a bank rescue package totalling £500bn in response to the instability of the British banking sector. This measure according to all politicians within the British parliament was crucial in safeguarding the stability of the UK's economic future following a global banking crisis that was born out of a reckless banking industry borrowing and trading on the debts of others. Subsequently, similar measures were introduced by the US and the EU in response to the financial crisis. The developed world went into recession and most governments in Europe and the US applied austerity measures to their finances, warning their citizens that there would be significant cuts in public spending.

About this time, Sharon had received a letter telling her to go to an appointment at the local benefits agency. During the interview she had been questioned about her availability to work and she told them she was working albeit without pay in the community centre. The advisor asked her whether she thought it was about time she stopped taking from society and gave something back, in the form of paid work. Sharon wanted to work in the local community but Nottingham City council had just sent out thousands of 'under threat' redundancy letters to current public sector workers, put a freeze on recruitment and announced that there needed to be £28m in public sector cuts. The benefit agency pushed on with Sharon's case that she needed to get a paid job and contribute to society. Sharon was eventually sanctioned, her benefits were cut from £110 per week to £30. She did not manage well, and admitted defeat taking the offer of 'help' that the job centre extended to her in putting her forward for a job in a cheese packing factory six miles away. This meant that Sharon no longer could volunteer at the community centre and had to leave her two children then aged seven and 12 alone from 6.30am in the morning to get ready for school themselves. Sharon earned £177 before stoppages for a 30-hour-week in the cheese packing factory, and with the changes in her housing benefit and council tax benefit she was £9 a week better off financially. However, her health very quickly deteriorated through working in a freezing cold environment and the constant stress of leaving her children alone. After three months Sharon had to quit the job through ill health and depression. Despite Sharon's previous hope and personal sense of value she had from her position in the community, the realities of an unjust economic situation, and the consequences of damning class and gender stereotypes meant that ultimately Sharon could never really be in control of her and her children's lives.

The working class and the EU referendum: left out not left behind

Sharon's story is not unique. Margaret Thatcher's neoliberal project in the 1980s, and then New Labour's 'Third Way', followed by the 2008 banking crash and the subsequent austerity measures has actually transferred funds from the poorest to the pockets of the better-off. The richest at the top of the 1 per cent wealthiest have significantly increased their wealth. But as John Hills' (2014) research clearly shows, austerity measures have had no net effect on public funds. The economic argument for cutting social services and public goods has not been made. However, that has had little to no difference at all in public policy, which continues to find new ways in cutting our social services.

As Bourdieu argues (1986) in 'Distinction', class reproduction is not just economic but also cultural. This work is done subtly by linking moral worth to monetary worth. As Sharon found out, her position in the community as a volunteer when the economy shrank and policy changed was of no value in a society that only acknowledges value from an individual's own economic and paid endeavour. Although Sharon knew that her previous community position was of great value locally, and her treatment by the state was unfair and unjust, there was little she could do. At the same time, the people who lived in East London felt that they are not worth the land that they live on and are waiting one by one to be cleansed out, and care to your family, community, or fellow humans is deemed valueless.

The general political comment around the working-class vote to leave the EU since June 2016 has been predominantly that of 'the left behind'. This view has been articulated across the political spectrum, even by the new Prime Minister Theresa May. The week following the referendum there were thousands of column inches of opinion and commentary. Jonathan Freedland in 'The New European', a newspaper that claims to represent the 48 per cent of voters that wanted to remain in the EU described 'the left behind' as those: 'In seats that were traditionally held by Labour, in some of the run-down, hard-up towns of northern England and Wales' (Freedland, 2016). *The Guardian*'s line on this tended to focus upon the 'older left-behind' working-class voters: '[t]he mass migration from poorer EU countries that began in 2004 was something the 'left-behind' electorate never wanted, never voted for and never really accepted' (Ford, 2016).

While there is clearly some truth in this position, the 'left behind' rhetoric is somewhat simplistic, incorrect and disingenuous when one considers the depth and intensity of what has happened to agents of the working class, their communities, and their identities for over 30 years. By the mid-1980s and especially as the mines, the docks, and the factories closed, there has been a shifting process about how working-class people in the UK are known and named. Although all working-class people have seen their incomes fall, and the weakening of opportunities for their children to get on the housing ladder, find well-paid jobs, and enter into higher education, it is the 'white working class' that has become named and known as not only economically but also culturally impoverished. Chris Haylett (2000), a social geographer, wrote very perceptively almost 20 years ago that the white working class had become an embarrassing contradiction, by losing the symbolic status their colour and their class had awarded in the past and have become 'abject and white'.

The patronizing 'left behind' rhetoric actively supports this de-valued identity of the de-industrialized working class. Rather than focusing on an attempt to genuinely understand the structural nature of de-industrialization, of class inequality and prejudice, the 'left behind' rhetoric relies on the stereotypes that the poor white working class are unmodern, have no mobility and long for the past. Working-class Leave voters have borne the brunt of the commentariat's backlash, despite the larger middle-class Brexit vote (Dorling, 2016).

The working class breaking the political consensus?

As the 1945 postwar social democratic consensus appears to have ended, so has the left and right party political consensus. In Britain, this has manifested through Brexit, the conclusion of a referendum called by the Conservative Party asking the British public whether they wanted to leave or remain in the EU. The ethnographic research in working-class communities in East London and the East Midlands with Leave voters has uncovered the similarities in their reasoning in voting. The London group were an urban working-class community in a 'global', cosmopolitan, multicultural city, while the group in the East Midlands were living in a small and isolated post-industrial ex-mining town. The similarities in their reasoning around the referendum was overwhelming despite their different geographies and varied community identities. Significant commonalities existed in the ways in which both groups critically understood their social positions and the social positions of others. What emerged was a shared class anger and a shared reading of their unfair and unequal social positions. Both groups' marginalization was so significant that their democratic rejection of the UK's membership of the EU was understandable. Dismissing such a view as irrational or xenophobic betrays a lack of sociological understanding of the long-term progression of narratives and markers that class as a social formation has had over several decades (Bourdieu, 1977; Skeggs, 2000, 2004). Elites in the political classes as well as middle-class 'cosmopolitans' now seem to have lost any sensible way to interpret such narratives and markers without recourse to demonizing and sermonizing, and defaulting to corrosive narratives about a 'feckless poor' that recalls Victorian-era poverty discourses (Savage et al, 2015, p. 352).

In 2015 the Conservative Party campaigned with a manifesto that included another £12bn pounds of savings from welfare services, on top of the prior five years of austerity budgets. Leading policy scholars were at this time exploring the impact of government policies on inequality and on the delivery of services, such as health, education, adult social care, housing and employment, since the 2008 recession (see Chapter Griffiths). This research also showed that spending on housing and community amenities, including the funding to build social housing, fell by 35 per cent. At the same time, all the main central government funding streams for neighbourhood renewal were removed (Lupton et al, 2016). Those most in need of social goods and services were at the coal face of the austerity measures, and the mantra of the Conservative Party 'we are all in this together' was simply untrue. Despite this, the general election of May 2015 returned a Conservative single-party government for the first time since 1992 (Mckenzie, 2017), due to the continued weakness of a Labour Party that had been steadily losing support among its core voting demographic since the last years of Tony Blair's rule.

During the election campaign in 2015, the author interviewed the women in East London as the pre-election televised debates were taking place. As befits their economically and socially marginalized position, they showed little to no interest in these debates and in the election campaign in general. None of the women at this point intended to vote in the general election, despite the very obvious wealth inequality in this part of London. Deprived council estates are yards from the corporate offices and high-end apartment complexes of the global elite. Yet despite the obvious inequality, conversations with the group of women in East London about the political situation were not straightforward during the 2015 election campaign. They hint at a broader discourse about the exclusion of 'traditional' white working-class communities; the kind of discourse that the UK Independence Party has thrived on. When trying to explore such matters in more detail, these conversations were mostly cut short and were answered about voting in general. The women prioritized the politics that directly affected them and their families, such as the lack of housing, the shortage of places in local schools, and the inadequacies of local health service provision. The larger issue of the 2015 general election was simply not a priority, as the women in this community felt estranged from national politics despite living only three miles away from Westminster and parliament.

Conclusion

The women in this research had believed in 2015 that they have no agency, were being ignored and 'didn't matter'. They used their experiences of class struggle in order to 'pull themselves together' from their precarious lives and to try to keep going even though they acknowledged life was a constant struggle. For a brief moment during the referendum, the apathy of the British working-class electorate subsided and gave way to a howl of anger, revealing the frustration of those who had been left out of the successes and rewards that capitalism had created for a cosmopolitan middle class. The reluctance to engage in national politics had been put aside by June 2016 by the working class in order to spoil the party they had never been invited to.

The people who had taken part in this research and had voted to leave the EU did so not because they thought their lives would be better if Britain was not in the EU. They did so because they just could not stand it being the same. It is certainly unlikely that leaving the EU will have any obvious positive effects for Britain's disenfranchised urban and regional poor. Although in some sense many agents, and in particular underprivileged people, voting for Brexit have harmed their own interests, it is also very reasonable to doubt that remaining in the EU does much for these people, either. The EU, although responsible for the implementation of some important policies in Britain, such as employment relations' legislation, has contributed to the expansion of neoliberal globalization. This involves a broad set of processes that have been largely a disaster for underprivileged communities across much of the world (Perrucci and Perrucci, 2009). Despite the geographical distance of the people that were part of this research, what they all spoke about in length and with passion was having no control over their own lives and being frustrated and angry by the constraints of their agency and class position. Consequently, despite the working-class people in this research having no strong ideological connection or position in regards to the EU prior to the 2016 referendum, what they did connect to was the Leave campaign's key message which was 'take back control'.

References

Bathmaker, A., N. Ingram, R. Waller (2013) 'Higher education, social class and the mobilization of capitals: recognising and playing the game', *British Journal of Sociology of Education*, 34(5–6): pp 723–43.

Bourdieu, P. (1977) *Outline of a Theory of Practice*, Cambridge: Cambridge University Press.

Bourdieu, P. (1986) *Distinction: A critique of the social judgement of taste*, London: Routledge.

Bourdieu, P. (1999) *The Weight of the World*, London: Polity Press.

Dorling, D. (2016) 'Brexit: The decision of a divided country', *BMJ*, 2016;354:i3697: http://www.dannydorling.org/wp-content/files/dannydorling_publication_id5564.pdf.

Ford, R. (2016) 'Older 'left-behind' voters turned against a political class with values opposed to theirs', *The Guardian*, 25 June.

Frank, T. (2001) One Market Under God: Extreme Capitalism, Market Populism, and the End of Economic Development, New York: Doubleday.

Freedland, J. (2016) 'A Roar of Rage from the left behind', *The New European*, 20 July.

Haylett, C. (2000) 'Modernization, Welfare and 'Third Way' Politics: limits to theorising in 'thirds'?', *Transactions of the Institute of British Geographers*, 26(1): 43–56.

Hills, J. (2014) *Good Times, Bad Times: The Welfare Myth of Them and Us*, Bristol: Policy Press.

Hills, J. (2015) 'The Coalition's Record on Cash Transfers, Poverty and Inequality 2010–2015', *CASE – Social Policy in a Cold Climate Working Paper 11*, London: Centre for Analysis of Social Exclusion, LSE.

Hodkinson, S., P. Watt and G. Mooney (2013) 'Neoliberal housing policy: time for a critical re-appraisal', *Critical Social Policy*, 33(1): pp 3–16.

Levitas, R. (2005) *The inclusive society*, 2nd edn, London: Macmillan.

Lupton, R. et al (2016) *Social policy in a cold climate Policies and their consequences since the crisis*, Bristol: Policy Press.

Mckenzie, L. (2015) *Getting By: Estates, Class and Culture in Austerity Britain*, Bristol: Policy Press.

Mckenzie, L. (2017) 'The class politics of prejudice: Brexit and the land of no-hope and glory', *The British Journal of Sociology*, 68 (1): 265–80.

Perrucci, R. and C. C. Perrucci (2009) *America at Risk: The Crisis of Hope, Trust and Caring*, Lanham, MD: Rowman & Littlefield.

Savage, M. (2015) *Social Class in the 21st Century*, London: Penguin Books.

Savage, M., N. Cunningham, F. Devine, S. Friedman, D. Laurison, L. Mckenzie, A. Miles, H. Snee and P. Wakeling (2015) *Social Class in the 21st Century*, London: Penguin Books.

Sayer, A. (2015) *Why We Can't Afford the Rich*, Bristol: Policy Press.

Skeggs, B. (2000) *Formations of Class and Gender*, London: Sage.

Skeggs, B. (2004) *Class self and culture*, London: Routledge.

Skeggs, B. (2014) 'Values beyond value? Is anything beyond the logic of capital?', *The British Journal of Sociology*, 65(1): 1–20.

Welshman, J. (2006) *Underclass: A History of the Excluded, 1880–2000*, London: Continuum International Publishing.

3

Political Activism and Agency under Austerity and Brexit

Tom Montgomery and Maria Grasso

Introduction

The global financial crisis of 2008 and the austerity measures which followed have formed the backdrop in recent years for a reconfiguration of the political environment across Europe. This reconfiguration has been underpinned by a recognition of the polarization in society that has exposed the asymmetries of income, wealth and power in the UK. Exposed to the crisis, the UK government at the time decided to respond with an austerity agenda. Subsequently, the decision to leave the EU in 2016 has served as a crucial example for understanding the dynamics that are continuing to disrupt the political order across the globe.

This chapter looks at agency through the prism of collective action and in doing so it seeks to understand the characteristics of citizens who express their agency through membership of activist groups that are explicitly opposed to: a capitalist economy in general; public budget cuts; and groups seeking to protect the rights of women, a section of society that has been particularly exposed to the consequences of austerity policies. The chapter also looks at attitudes to the EU among members of such groups, given the argument that the vote to leave may have been an alternative expression of agency for some in the UK. This chapter therefore takes the following structure: firstly, it defines austerity; secondly, it explores how austerity has been operationalized in the UK and how austerity policies have had an uneven impact on different groups and geographies; thirdly, it builds upon the UK context and explores various expressions of agency by different groups as well as attitudes to the EU.

Understanding the contours of Austerity Britain

The word austerity has become part of the lexicon for understanding the social and political context that has shaped much of contemporary Europe following the global financial crisis of 2008 and continues to form the background to political manifestations, from movements to governments, which are reconfiguring the political landscape. However, despite its proliferation, the term austerity is often deployed without definition. This chapter relies upon the historical analysis undertaken by Blyth (2013) of the development of austerity as a 'dangerous idea' that has been fundamental for policymakers in some contexts to repackage a banking crisis as a crisis in public spending. As such, he describes austerity as a flawed project that involves 'a form of voluntary deflation in which the economy adjusts through the reduction of wages, prices and public spending to restore competitiveness, which is (supposedly) best achieved by cutting the state's budget, debts and deficits' (Blyth, 2013, p. 2).

In the UK, the aftermath of the global financial crisis was also marked by a change in government that in 2010 saw the end of a 13-year period in power for the Labour Party and the introduction of a coalition government led by the Conservative Party with the Liberal Democrats as their junior partner. This change in government was almost immediately marked by an emphasis being placed on the importance of 'deficit reduction' that has been identified as an effort to reframe the effects of the financial crisis in the UK as being the result of profligate spending by the previous Labour government (Gamble, 2014). As a consequence of the emphasis on cutting public spending as a pathway to growth, the new Coalition government identified particular government departments that were to bear the brunt of austerity. Although austerity was implemented across government spending – aside from those areas that had been 'ringfenced' such as the NHS and international aid – some areas of spending were to form a particular focus for the deepest cuts, including the Department for Work and Pensions responsible for welfare support and local government, a level of government that is involved in the front-line delivery of services (Institute for Fiscal Studies, 2015).

This chapter will return to the impact of austerity at the local level later, however, at this point it considers the consequences of austerity for the British welfare state. The cuts to spending formed the centrepiece of the welfare reform agenda pursued in the aftermath of the financial crisis by the Coalition government elected in 2010 and articulated in its policy document *Welfare in the 21st Century*, which identified concerns of a 'culture of worklessness' in some parts of the UK and thus re-energized those tropes that emphasized the problem of 'welfare dependency' (Department for Work and Pensions, 2010, p. 4). Thus, the shrinking budget of the Department of Work and Pensions was accompanied by the characterization of welfare recipients as lazy and as undeserving of public support accompanied by the operationalization of sanctions and conditionality (Watts and Fitzpatrick, 2018). Rather than deficit reduction being presented as a consequence of the failures of financial capitalism, it was recast as an individual-level problem resulting from the deficiencies of those who require support to meet their most basic needs (Wiggan, 2012). Moreover, austerity policies reflect an ideological process of the transformation of poverty from market failure to personal failure – a consistently strong trope in post-crisis Britain that has been resilient to contrary evidence.

The broad impact of austerity cannot be fully understood without recognizing the varied consequences and responses to it that emerged in the UK across sections of the population and geographies as a consequence of the deep cuts to public spending. Turning to this varied impact of austerity helps one to understand how austerity has been a key component in creating new dividing lines in contemporary British society and intensifying old ones.

To fully understand the impact of public-spending cuts in some parts of the UK it is necessary to recognize that the cuts following the crisis did not take place in a vacuum. Some parts of the UK, particularly those which in previous generations were dependent upon heavy industry for employment, have never fully recovered from the 1980s when the process of deindustrialization, that is the closure of mines, steelworks and shipbuilding, accelerated alongside the failure of the miners strikes and the long decline of working-class agency through the trade union movement (Milne, 2014). Moreover, the shift to post-Fordism in these communities has resulted in a different set of labour-market opportunities for young people, with a new generation of young workers disproportionately exposed to greater precarity through the use by employers of zero-hour contracts and the emergence of the 'gig economy'. Alongside these developments, young people in some of the most deprived communities in the UK have simultaneously been navigating a more austere welfare system that has been marked by conditionality and sanctions that have disproportionately affected young people (Watts and Fitzpatrick, 2014). Consequently, the rising number of young people using food banks in the years since austerity through welfare reform has been implemented can come as no surprise, as this new generation becomes enmeshed in a situation where they find themselves oscillating from in-work poverty to out-of-work poverty, or as some researchers have labelled it, a 'low pay, no pay cycle' (Shildrick et al, 2012).

The exposure of people, of all ages, living in disadvantaged communities, to the potential economic implications of the global financial crisis was already disproportionate given the fragility of local economies that are still grappling with the transition from heavy industry to employment that is often more insecure. However, it is in these communities that the effects of austerity through welfare reform have been the most profound. Existing research that has traced the geographical impact of austerity has identified that alongside some seaside towns in the UK, it is those communities where heavy industry has been hollowed out and where many have required welfare support that have felt the full impact of austerity as it is translated into welfare reform:

> Welfare cuts inevitably impact most in the places where claimants are concentrated. Therefore, it is no surprise that Britain's older industrial areas figure so prominently among the worst-hit places. Once more, it is places such as South Wales, the industrial North from Merseyside across to the Humber, North East England and the West of Scotland that stand out, whilst large parts of southern England around London are much less affected. (Beatty and Fothergill, 2017, p. 175)

The fallout of these cuts of course has to be addressed in some way by those who are involved in the delivery of services at the front line, such as local authorities. However, research has indicated that the burden of the cuts caused by austerity has equally fallen upon this level of government which has in many cases across the UK, but particularly in some parts of England, led to local authorities being forced to sell off assets and plunder reserves to maintain services, thus increasing inequalities between some of the poorest areas, where people may rely more heavily upon local authority services, and the more wealthier communities (Gray and Barford, 2018). In tandem with these budgetary cuts has come the problematization of those communities by policymakers revisiting narratives from the 1980s of a 'broken Britain' that was the result of family breakdown and welfare dependency, shifting the focus from policies that were exacerbating inequalities. These stigmatizing narratives have often taken a geographical form and have become manifest in sections of the UK media that have reinforced negative stereotypes of those living in communities where people are struggling to meet their basic needs (Shildrick, 2018).

Of course the stigmatization of welfare recipients is nothing new in Britain, and this reflects the continuation of a class divide in society that has been amplified in the era of austerity as the impact of the cuts enabled some policymakers to inextricably link their tropes of 'broken Britain' and moral decay with working-class communities more broadly (Hancock and Mooney, 2013) and working-class families in particular (Crossley, 2016) (see Chapter Mckenzie). Those living in working-class communities in the age of austerity have found themselves navigating the long-term impact of industrial decline, the cuts and conditionality brought by the welfare reform agenda to basic levels of support, their now underfunded local authority unable to offer assistance and a narrative from government that casts those who do access benefits as shirkers and scroungers (Garthwaite, 2011).

These forms of stigmatization have been identified as carrying a gender dimension that places women in working-class communities at a double disadvantage as they also fill the gap in terms of care roles left by austerity (Allen et al, 2014). The impact of austerity on women in the UK requires an appreciation, that despite advancements, opportunities for women are often placed at the intersection between the tax and benefit system, policies affecting the still feminized conceptions of child care and elderly care and the quality of opportunities in the labour market compared to their male counterparts (Macleavy, 2011). According to the Women's Budget Group (2018), an independent network of leading academic researchers, policy experts and trade unionists, women in the UK have as a consequence of austerity measures been faced with a 'triple whammy'.

Firstly, women are more likely to be in poverty and thus require greater welfare support and use more public services due to their labour market opportunities being affected by their role as unpaid carers. They have disproportionately comprised that part of the workforce experiencing non-standard forms of employment such as zero-hour contracts (ONS, 2018). Secondly, women make up the majority of the public-sector workforce and have therefore been more exposed to redundancies caused by cuts to public budgets. They disproportionately make up the local government workforce in the UK (in 2010 this was 75 per cent per cent) and thus have been employed at that level of governance at the sharpest edge of spending cuts (Fawcett Society,

2012). Thirdly, women often replace the care lost by public services to children, the elderly and disabled people through unpaid care roles. In the UK, women carry out 60 per cent per cent more unpaid work including adult care and child care than men (ONS, 2016). Therefore, the impact of austerity not only presents a risk to the progress towards gender equality but may represent a reversal of previous gains to women's agency.

Alongside an agenda of welfare reform and cuts to public services, particularly at the front line via local authorities, the Coalition government revisited longstanding concerns regarding immigration, including the now infamous 'go home vans' deployed in 2013 by the then Home Secretary Theresa May in communities with a historically high density of immigration that warned of illegal immigration in the area. This specific initiative has since been identified by researchers as a turning point in contemporary immigration discourses in the UK (Jones et al, 2017). The impact of pursuing a policy strategy underpinned by the creation of an explicitly 'hostile environment' for illegal immigrants has more recently been revealed through the experience of many members of the 'Windrush' generation of immigrants. Arriving in the UK between the late 1940s and early 1970s from the Caribbean many found themselves at risk of deportation and denied basic rights including healthcare and the right to work because of a lack of paperwork – some of which had been destroyed by the Home Office. Moreover, the policies and strategies that led to the scandal surrounding the treatment of the Windrush generation must also be considered when seeking to understand the rhetoric that underpinned the xenophobic populism evident in some elements of the Leave campaign during the referendum on EU membership in June 2016, crystallized in the advertisement presented by UKIP leader Nigel Farage that in terms of immigration the UK was at a 'breaking point'.

In fact, in terms of actual breaking points, it is the nexus of austerity and Brexit that has raised a fundamental question around the constitutional future of the UK. The vote to leave the EU having received only minority support in both Scotland and Northern Ireland has served to reanimate calls for a second Scottish independence referendum and simultaneously calls from Sinn Féin for a poll on Irish unity at a point when the question of the Irish border has cast a long shadow over the Brexit strategy of the UK government. Alongside these developments the austerity policies driven by Westminster have been met with condemnation by the Welsh government, Sinn Féin and even in some cases (for example, the so called bedroom tax) mitigation by the SNP led Scottish government who have sought to construct a vision of an independent Scotland in social democratic terms (Wiggan, 2017).

Austerity and agency in Brexit Britain

Austerity cannot be extracted from its social, economic and political contexts and this also extends to the turbulence that has come to characterize the political landscape in the UK. Against the background of the financial crisis, cuts to public services and an intensification of the dividing lines between sections of the population more exposed to declining incomes as well as the entrenchment of the geographies of inequality (see Chapter Cochrane), the UK has been further divided since 2016 by the vote to leave the EU. It is in this context that researchers have begun to debate if Brexit is at least in part a consequence of sections of the UK population feeling 'left behind', especially those living in the former industrial heartlands (Becker et al, 2017).

This chapter draws on unique survey data and examines agency, or lack thereof, through the prism of citizens' actions in times of crisis. The analysis of agency through the survey data is embedded in a context in which the capitalist system and the financial sector have come under increased scrutiny, in which austerity has exposed the geographical nature of inequalities in the UK, and in which women have been disproportionately impacted by austerity measures. Capturing the full spectrum of reactions to austerity from other voices, such as trade unions and civil society organizations, many of whom were vocal in their opposition to austerity measures which impacted upon particular groups (for example, young people, disabled people, migrants, refugees and asylum seekers), is beyond the scope of this chapter. To analyze agency through collective action in an era of austerity (Bailey et al, 2018), the chapter examines membership of groups that are specifically opposed to the capitalist system and the public budget cuts that were implemented following the global financial crisis (Della Porta, 2015) as well as members of those groups which seek to protect the rights of women (Bassel and Emejulu, 2017). The chapter looks at participation in these groups as a means of agency against austerity and the hardship that has accompanied it, against capitalism more broadly as a system and agency in the promotion of gender equality. In view of those arguments that the Brexit referendum may have offered some form of agency to those living in communities most exposed to austerity and the excesses of capitalism, this chapter also looks at attitudes towards EU.

Findings

The survey data for the UK (N approx. 2,000) was collected during the Horizon 2020 EU-funded project TransSOL 'European paths to transnational solidarity at times of crisis: Conditions, forms, role-models and policy responses' (grant agreement: 649435). First, the analysis examines patterns of activism across three activist groups (anti-capitalist organizations, anti-austerity organizations and feminist organizations) by focusing on how they vary by gender, geography and social class. In a second step, the analysis turns to attitudes towards the EU, looking specifically at whether people participating in these three different activist organizations feel that membership of the EU is good for employment.

Gender

Women are slightly more active in anti-capitalist and feminist organizations but slightly less active in anti-austerity organizations. The survey found that 8.5 per cent per cent are active in anti-capitalist organizations compared to 8 per cent per cent of men; 7.4 per cent per cent are active in anti-austerity organizations compared to 7.8 per cent per cent of men; and 9.3 per cent per cent are active in feminist or women's rights organizations compared to 7.5 per cent per cent of men. Thus, the findings indicate that despite the disproportionate impact of the financial crisis and austerity on women in the UK, there are only very small gender differences in participation among anti-capitalist and anti-authority organizations and slightly wider ones for the feminist organizations.

Geography

Given that austerity has impacted some regions more than others, particularly in the North of England and the industrial heartlands, it is reasonable to expect that levels of engagement in anti-capitalist, anti-cuts and feminist groups should be higher in these areas.

However, the findings reveal that around 7.2 per cent of respondents belong to or volunteer with anti-capitalist groups in the North of England, 8.1 per cent in the Midlands and East of England, 6.0 per cent in the South of England, 16.5 per cent in London, 7.3 per cent in Wales, 6.0 per cent in Scotland, 6.5 per cent in Northern Ireland, and 8.3 per cent in the UK overall.

With respect to anti-austerity groups, 7.3 per cent are active in the North of England, 7.1 per cent in the Midlands and East of England, 6.3 per cent in the South of England, 13.6 per cent in London, 5.2 per cent in Wales, 6.6 per cent in Scotland, 4.4 per cent in Northern Ireland, and 7.6 per cent in the UK overall.

As for feminist groups, about 7 per cent are active in the North of England, 8.1 per cent in the Midlands and East of England, 6.4 per cent in the South of England, 16.9 per cent in London, 5.2 per cent in Wales, 8.2 per cent in Scotland, 6.5 per cent in Northern Ireland, and 8.4 per cent in the UK overall.

Regional patterns thus show that London stands out as the region or nation with higher levels of activism across the three types of organizations. Moreover, activism is not as high in the North as one might expect given the impact of austerity in this region. While the findings suggest that participation in such organizations is skewed towards London, in regions and constituent nations outside the capital, agency may manifest itself in different ways and the vote for Brexit could have been one such avenue. Nevertheless, in some parts of the UK, such as Northern Ireland and Scotland, constitutional questions can offer another route for citizens to express discontent with policies emanating from Westminster that have driven forward austerity measures.

Social class

With respect to social class, the analysis examined differences by the occupation of the chief wage earner to examine the profile of activists across the three groups.

With anti-capitalist groups, around 9.6 per cent belong or are active members from professional or higher technical sectors, 9.9 per cent from managerial or senior administrator sectors, 6.9 per cent from clerical professions, 18.5 per cent from sales or services, 5.6 per cent are foremen or supervisors, 4.6 per cent are skilled manual workers, 5.6 per cent are semi-skilled workers and 6.5 per cent belong to other occupations.

With anti-cuts organizations, around 8 per cent belong to or are active members from professional or higher technical sectors, 9 per cent from managerial or senior administrator sectors, 6 per cent from clerical professions, 16.8 per cent from sales or services, 5.6 per cent are foremen or supervisors, 4.6 per cent are skilled manual workers, 6.4 per cent are semi-skilled workers and 6.5 per cent from other occupations.

With feminist organizations, around 9.6 per cent belong to or are active members from professional or higher technical sectors, 10.3 per cent from managerial or senior administrator sectors, 6.9 per cent from clerical professions, 18.5 per cent from sales or services, 5.5 per cent are foremen or supervisors, 4.5 per cent are skilled manual workers, 6.8 per cent are semi-skilled workers and 5.1 per cent from other occupations.

Patterns by class suggest that individuals from households in which the chief wage earner belongs to the sales or services class tend to be the most likely to be involved across each of the three types of organizations. Processes of deindustrialization have marked a shift in the labour market from manufacturing to the sales and service sector. Various changes may be contributing to politicizing new social bases with low pay and insecure employment. Given the context within which such activism takes place, it is important to consider the perspectives of those participating across each of the three groups on the impact of EU membership on the UK labour market.

Attitudes to the EU

This chapter looks at attitudes towards the EU by examining a question about the expected effect on jobs if the UK were outside the EU.

Among those involved in anti-capitalist organizations, most felt that leaving the EU would have a negative impact: 45.2 per cent among members and 41.5 per cent among active participants. Yet a sizeable minority hold the opposing view that Brexit would be positive for employment: 23.2 per cent among members and 39.5 per cent among active participants. Smaller percentages believe it would make no difference either way: 20.4 per cent among members and 13.2 per cent among active participants.

In contrast, among those involved in anti-austerity organizations, most thought that being outside the EU would be positive for employment: 46.3 per cent among active participants held this view. Only 35.7 per cent among the activists thought that Brexit would be bad for jobs, and 15.9 per cent that it would make no difference. Whereas within members of anti-austerity organizations, that is those less actively involved in these organizations, most believed Brexit would be negative for the labour market (46.7 per cent), fewer that it would be good for employment (25.2 per cent) and 18.5 per cent that it would make no difference either way.

Among those in feminist or women's organizations, there is a similar pattern to that from the anti-austerity organizations with active participants feeling that leaving the EU would be good for jobs (45.4

per cent), a lower proportion of 36.7 per cent thinking that it would be bad, and 15.2 per cent believing that it would make no difference. Among members less active in these organizations, more feel it would be bad (43.3 per cent), fewer that it would be good (26.3 per cent), and only 16.4 per cent that it would make no difference.

What these findings indicate is ambivalence among activists in the UK with respect to some of the claims surrounding the Brexit vote. The patterns emerging from the data suggest that activists are split over the question of whether EU membership is good or bad for employment. Some of the questions surrounding Brexit in this sense appear to cut across members of activist organizations that share similar goals and are generally opposed to inequalities in UK society.

Conclusion

At the outset, this chapter identified that much of the contemporary political context is shaped by the experiences of austerity and how these experiences have contributed towards deepening the divisions in British society, divisions exemplified by the EU referendum.

Research indicates that austerity has had a divergent impact in terms of gender, region and class. As such, the chapter set out to understand to what extent groups on the front line of the impact of austerity expressed their discontent with the status quo, specifically, through the activism in anti-capitalist, anti-austerity and feminist organizations.

The findings indicate that among those who have engaged in these organizations there are only small differences in levels of activism in terms of gender, despite the impact of austerity falling heavily upon the shoulders of women. It is worth reflecting on the earlier part of this chapter regarding the 'triple whammy' that women have faced during austerity, and recognize both the barriers that women may face in terms of political participation and that the negative effects of austerity on gender equality also decrease the potential for greater political activism.

Despite the fact that the impact of austerity has a geographical aspect (see Chapter Cochrane), with the hardest-hit areas often, though not exclusively, being found in deindustrialized communities in the North of England, Wales and Scotland, the findings indicated that the highest levels of activism in these groups were to be found in London. This is likely to be for a series of reasons – for example the greater opportunities for mobilization and activism within greater city centres or the profile of activists. It could thus be that communities outside the capital may be more likely to find other forms of agency to express their discontent and the vote to leave the European Union may have been one such avenue.

There is potential for some movements to rely on certain professional sectors: those located in sections of the labour market where insecurity and low pay have become the norm appear to be more engaged in the organizations examined here. As precarious labour markets and the 'gig economy' further evolve, different aspects of class and new cleavages with respect to aspects of precariatization could emerge as key factors for political mobilization, although such mobilization may also depend on the responsiveness of activist organizations and trade unions to converting discontent into political action.

Building upon a contextual awareness of the crisis, austerity and inequalities that have come to the fore in a divided Brexit Britain, the empirical analysis in this chapter offers an insight into how agency could be manifest across particular organizations: anti-capitalist organizations, anti-austerity organizations and feminist organizations. These groups may reflect some of the key challenges facing many citizens and communities across the UK. Yet, political activism is unevenly distributed across key categories of geography, class and to a lesser extent, gender. Those involved in the investigated activist groups were also divided on the issue of EU membership and its effect on employment. Therefore, in order to understand who is exercising agency in Brexit Britain it is necessary to focus not only on the divisions in collective action of citizens but also on how geography, class, gender and attitudes to the European Union shape the membership and activism of such organizations.

References

Allen, K., I. Tyler and S. De Benedictis (2014) 'Thinking with 'White Dee': the gender politics of 'austerity porn'', *Sociological Research Online*, 19(3): 1–7.

Bailey, D. J., M. Clua-Losada, N. Huke, O. Ribera-Almandoz and K. Rogers (2018) 'Challenging the age of austerity: Disruptive agency after the global economic crisis', *Comparative European Politics*, 16(1): 9–31.

Bassel, L. and A. Emejulu (2017) *Minority Women and Austerity: Survival and Resistance in France and Britain*, Bristol: Policy Press.

Beatty, C. and S. Fothergill (2017) 'The impact on welfare and public finances of job loss in industrial Britain' *Regional Studies, Regional Science*, 4(1): 161–80.

Becker, S. O., T. Fetzer and D. Novy (2017) 'Who voted for Brexit? A comprehensive district-level analysis' *Economic Policy*, 32(92): 601–50.

Blyth, M. (2013) *Austerity: The history of a dangerous idea*, Oxford: Oxford University Press.

Crossley, S. (2016) 'Realising the (troubled) family, crafting the neoliberal state', *Families, Relationships and Societies*, 5(2): 263–79.

Della Porta, D. (2015) *Social movements in times of austerity: bringing capitalism back into protest analysis*, John Wiley & Sons.

Department for Work and Pensions (2010), *Consultation responses to 21st Century Welfare*, gov.uk: https://assets.publishing.service.gov.uk/government/uploads/system/uploads/attachment_data/file/181144/21st-century-welfare-response.pdf.

Fawcett Society (2012) *The impact of austerity on women*, https://www.fawcettsociety.org.uk/the-impact-of-austerity-on-women.

Gamble, A. (2014) 'Austerity as Statecraft', *Parliamentary affairs: A journal of representative politics*, 68(1): 42–57.

Garthwaite, K. (2011) "The language of shirkers and scroungers?' Talking about illness, disability and coalition welfare reform' *Disability & Society*, 26(3): 369–72.

Gray, M. and A. Barford (2018) 'The depths of the cuts: the uneven geography of local government austerity' *Cambridge Journal of Regions, Economy and Society*, 11(3): 541–63.

Hancock, L. and G. Mooney (2013) 'Welfare Ghettos" and the 'Broken Society': Territorial Stigmatization in the Contemporary UK', *Housing, Theory and Society*, 30(1): 46–64.

Institute for Fiscal Studies (2015) *Recent cuts to public spending*, https://www.ifs.org.uk/tools_and_resources/fiscal_facts/public_spending_survey/cuts_to_public_spending.

Jones, H., Y. Gunaratnam, G. Bhattacharyya, W. Davies, S. Dhaliwal, K. Forkert and R. Saltus (2017) *Go home?: The politics of immigration controversies*. Manchester: Manchester University Press.

MacLeavy, J. (2011) 'A 'new politics' of austerity, workfare and gender? The UK coalition government's welfare reform proposals', *Cambridge journal of regions, economy and society*, 4(3): 355–67.

Milne, S. (2014) The enemy within: The secret war against the miners, London: Verso.

ONS (2016) *Women shoulder the responsibility of 'unpaid work'*, Office for National Statistics, 10 November.

ONS (2018) *Contracts that do not guarantee a minimum number of hours: April 2018*, Office for National Statistics, 23 April.

Shildrick, T. (2018) *Poverty propaganda: Exploring the myths*, Bristol: Policy Press.

Shildrick, T., R. MacDonald, C. Webster and K. Garthwaite (2012) *Poverty and insecurity: life in low-pay, no-pay Britain*, Bristol: Policy Press.

Watts, B. and S. Fitzpatrick (2014) *Young Adults Hit Hardest by Benefit Sanctions*, Welfare Conditionality: www.welfareconditionality.ac.uk/2014/09/young-adults-hit-hardest-bybenefit-sanctions/.

Watts, B. and S. Fitzpatrick (2018) *Welfare Conditionality*, Abingdon: Routledge.

Wiggan, J. (2012) 'Telling stories of 21st century welfare: The UK Coalition government and the neo-liberal discourse of worklessness and dependence', *Critical Social Policy*, 32(3): 383–405.

Wiggan, J. (2017) 'Contesting the austerity and "welfare reform" narrative of the UK Government: Forging a social democratic imaginary in Scotland', *International Journal of Sociology and Social Policy*, 37(11–12): 639–54.

Women's Budget Group (2018) *The impact of austerity on women in the UK*, https://wbg.org.uk/resources/the-impact-of-austerity-on-women/.

4

Culture Matters: Cuts and Resistance

Ingrid von Rosenberg

Introduction

As 'culture' is a slippery term it seems useful to define what is meant by the 'cultural sector' on which this chapter focuses. In Cultural Studies, 'culture' as a rule 'indicates a particular way of life, whether of a people, a period or group [...].' (Williams, 1976, p. 80). Yet Raymond Williams, initiator of this use, also defined another meaning of the noun: 'the works and practices of intellectual and especially artistic activity. This seems often now the most widespread use; culture is music, literature, painting and sculpture, theatre and film' (Williams, 1976, p. 80).

This chapter examines the cuts which the Conservative Liberal-Democrat Coalition (2010–15) and the following two Conservative governments have administered to culture in this narrower but 'most widespread use'. It will assess their consequences for British society and appraise the effectiveness of the resistance put up by various agents and actors. The field of education will be included as far as the teaching of music and the various arts are concerned.

Compared to the havoc austerity politics has wreaked on the income and life chances of the weakest members of society – for example the disabled, single mothers and large families – cutbacks in the cultural sector may seem a luxury concern. Yet the author hopes to show how the cuts to culture have also been disastrous for society as they further disadvantage the poor, with crippling effects on future generations, and endanger Britain's rich cultural mix.

Financial sources for cultural activities in the UK

The financial means for culture in the UK come from a variety of sources: ticket sales, commercial activities of cultural institutions, private sponsors and – the biggest share – from state expenditure, boosted by Lottery money since the mid-1990s and – until now – complemented by grants from various EU funds. State support, including Lottery money, is channelled through several bodies. In England, the Department for Culture, Media and Sport (DCMS) funds 43 non-departmental public bodies directly, among them the Arts Council England (ACE), the British Library and 15 national museums including the British Museum, the Tate, The Science Museum Group and the National Gallery. ACE, in its turn, supports many other cultural institutions in England (theatres, operas, museums, galleries, cultural organizations, individual artists) following the 'arm's length principle'. The Shakespeare Company, for instance, received 23 per cent of its 2017 budget through ACE; the Royal Opera House 20 per cent. Since devolution in 1999, culture in Scotland, Wales and Northern Ireland is part of the devolved powers and state support there is channelled through Creative Scotland, the Arts Council of Wales and the Arts Council of Northern Ireland. The second most important funders have for a long time been the local authorities which are funded by the respective governments, in England through the Department for Communities and Local Government (DCLG). They are responsible for regional and local public libraries, local museums and theatres and youth services.

Although the government investment in the cultural sector in the UK has long been one of the lowest in Europe, amounting to only 0.6 per cent of GDP compared to the EU average of 1 per cent, the two most important mediators of financial support have lost a considerable part of their income since 2010. Arts Council England, which had enjoyed a substantial increase under New Labour from £180m to £453m, (Gardner, 2015) lost about 30 per cent of its state aid for the period of 2010–13 and a further 5 per cent in the following three years, which could, however, be partly compensated for by an increased share of Lottery money, amounting in 2018 to about £70m per year. Creative Scotland's state aid, granted by the Scottish Government, fell from £48.3m in 2010/11 to £40.3m in 2016/17, and Arts Council of Wales, supported by the Welsh Government, had to cope with an

18 per cent drop between 2011 and 2017, also partly compensated by Lottery money, while the Arts Council of Northern Ireland was faced with an even sharper 38 per cent drop in state aid between 2013 and 2018, with less Lottery money available to compensate for the loss. Among the local authorities those in England were worst hit by cuts: they lost over 40 per cent of state funds (about £16bn) between 2010 and 2016, Scotland and Wales only about half this much. The devolved governments, though themselves receiving reduced grants from Westminster, made different decisions regarding austerity than England, and Scotland and Wales have buffered the worst effects for local government by, for instance, allowing a rise in council tax up to 3 per cent (Gray and Barford, 2018, p. 546). As a consequence local governments in England had to reduce their spending on services between 2009 and 2017 by 24 per cent, but those in Scotland by 'only' 11.5 per cent and in Wales by 12 per cent (p. 554). As most of the government funds allocated to local authorities are no longer ring-fenced, individual councils have to decide how to distribute the scarce resources – poor chances for culture as discretionary spending in competition with statutory obligations. The governments of Wales and Scotland have tried to protect local authorities and the arts as best they could, for several reasons. Most important may be the traditionally great store both nations have set by culture as an important pillar to national identity: the ruling parties, SNP in Scotland and Labour in Wales, both following a social-democratic rather than a conservative agenda, apparently feel pledged to hold up this tradition even in the face of scarce resources. An additional practical reason may be the fact that there are fewer rich citizens than in England, whom the government could expect to sponsor cultural activities. An example of the Scottish government's basic willingness to support culture was a decision taken in January 2018: when Creative Scotland was expecting a further 30 per cent cut, the government stepped in with a £6.6m increase to maintain the arts funding at £99m over three years. Nevertheless, the cuts to culture have been serious throughout the whole UK and have far-reaching consequences. This has aroused opposition, not surprisingly strongest in England, which is examined in detail in this chapter.

The main justification given by the government for its austerity measures, including the cuts to culture, was the huge deficit, falsely blamed on the outgoing Labour government for its 'irresponsible' spending policy. In fact, both the Labour government and the Coalition that followed increased spending in order to save British banks in the worldwide financial crisis. Thus the true reasons for austerity are found elsewhere: in the Conservative political agenda.

Combatants in the conflict about culture

The Conservative actors, their view of the state and their agenda for cultural policy

The deeper reasons for the current conflict about financial state-support for culture lie in differing views of two important issues: the role of the state in relation to its citizens and the meaning, purpose and use of culture. To assess the respective motives and the amount of power in the hands of the various parties involved, the concept of agency seems a helpful instrument. The author's use of it is based mostly on the theoretical work of Anthony Giddens, Margaret S. Archer, Laura M. Ahearn and John Clarke. Ahearn provides a useful 'provisional definition': 'Agency refers to the socioculturally mediated capacity to act' (Ahearn, 2001, p. 112). In the current conflict about culture one can identify two very unequally powered groups facing each other: on the one side there are the politicians of the ruling Conservative Party, their voters as well as the loyal state employees. They are, according to a distinction of different types of agency defined by Ahearn (Ahearn, 2001, p. 113), 'agents of power'– they hold the 'whip hand'. On the other side there is a heterogeneous alliance of 'agents of resistance', who, though at a disadvantage in the current balance of power, are driven by strong convictions and the hope to bring about change. Both groups are motivated – or in the words of John Clarke 'animated' – by 'multiple contexts' of diverse origin. Clarke argues that 'contexts are not the background against which the action takes place', but are 'constitutive of the action', 'animate actions'. They are never single but plural: 'Any particular action has multiple contexts – spatial, social, political, cultural, economic, organizational and so on' (Clarke, 2013, pp 22–4). Multiple contexts can even include 'contradictory logics of action', which may lead to 'unstable or incoherent forms of agency' (p. 30).

In his vision of the Big Society, proclaimed before he came to power, David Cameron formulated an aim that to his adherents may have sounded idealistic: 'So we will take power away from the central state and give it to individuals' (Cameron, 2009). He promised to curb the influence of the state, which to the Conservatives' mind had grown disproportionately under Labour (into 'Big State'), and appealed to people to no longer 'turn to officials, local authorities or central government' for help, but 'instead to feel both free and powerful enough to help themselves and their own communities' (Cameron, 2010). In terms of the theory of agency one can detect in this and similar statements the imprint of one dominating 'context' motivating the ruling Conservative actors: the ideology of neo-liberalism, advancing worldwide since the 1980s. Stuart Hall – polemically – explains:

> However anachronistic it might seem, neo-liberalism is grounded in the idea of the 'free, possessive individual'. It sees the state as tyrannical and oppressive. The state must never govern society [...], regulate a free-market society or interfere with the God-given right to make profit and amass personal wealth. [...] the state – and the welfare state in particular – is the arch enemy of freedom. State-led 'social engineering' must never prevail over corporate and private interests. (Hall, 2011, p. 706)

In the same article, Hall identified three more 'contexts' of Conservative agency (which subsequently helped to bring about the vote for Brexit): nationalism, traditionalism and racism. 'Even today, the market/free enterprise/private property discourse persists cheek by jowl with older conservative attachments to nation, racial homogeneity, Empire and tradition' (Hall, 2011, p. 613).

These 'plural contexts'– and one might add as a further one, an elitist upper-class bias in Conservative thinking – have 'animated' the governments' actions, including the unleashing of severe cuts to culture, though many public statements have drawn on very different discourses. Thus the 57-page-long *Culture White Paper*, published in 2016, was full of democratic-sounding intentions such as: 'This white paper [...] seeks to spread the gift of our arts, heritage and culture to more people and communities across the country and abroad and free the creative genius that can make a better world for all' (DCMS, 2016, p. 6).

Such lip service to communal and individual needs has not prevented the government from rigorously cutting support for culture. So, if Cameron and the party made much of the freedom and power of the individual in their vision of a 'Big Society', their intention was not to increase more people's chances to enjoy 'the quality of life activities' (Hall, 2011, p. 24), but to appeal to the citizens to take over many of the tasks and costs so far shouldered by the state. The *Culture White Paper* towards the end becomes very clear on that point: 'The government believes that there is scope for cultural organizations to benefit further from philanthropy and private donations and to make greater use of non-grant funding including commercial revenues' (DCMS, 2016, p. 50).

In Theresa May's election manifesto of 2017 any democratic soft-soaping is skipped, and culture figures only marginally, short references scattered over the text covering in total no more than one page out of 84. What resounds strongly in the few snippets is the nationalistic aspect: 'The UK is home to some of the finest cultural institutions in the world. We will continue to promote those institutions and ensure they have the resources they need to amplify Britain's voice on the world stage and as global force for good' (*Conservative Party Manifesto*, 2017, p. 39). Other references stress the economic interest: promises are made to improve conditions for the creative industries (p. 78).

Excursus: the 'creative industries'

The 'creative industries' concept is one of the very few of New Labour ideas which the Tories willingly embraced. Discussed since the 1970s by both cultural theorists and practitioners, it was introduced to British politics by Tony Blair's government in 1997. It was born from the combination of two motivations: the democratic wish to give more recognition to commercially produced art (film, TV, pop music, etc.), to which broader sections of society than just the educated elite contributed, and the insight that the field had become economically important, providing jobs and contributing considerably to GDP – a good example of a somewhat contradictory 'multi-contextual animation' of a political action. The creative industries were defined as: 'Industries based on individual creativity, skill and talent with the potential to create wealth and jobs through intellectual property.' Of the 15 fields listed in 1997 seven had traditionally been recognized as cultural activities (music, art, architecture, performing arts, crafts, design and designer fashion), three belonged to the field of distribution and marketing (advertising, antique markets and publishing), three to the media (film and video, TV and radio) and two to the new area of information technology (software and computer services) (Flew, 2012, p. 10). When the Blair government first defined the sector, it employed 1.4 m people and generated an estimated £60bn per year, about 5 per cent of GDP. Government policies for the creative industries included tax relief (for film, videogames, etc.), direct financial support of individuals and projects as well as the regulation of copyright. Considering the economic potential of the sector, it is not surprising that the Tories should have continued supporting it. In a 2016 speech, Cameron praised the creative industries for growing three times faster than any other sector, generating £80bn per year, and announced a new initiative called Creative Entrepreneurs, to help young people start their own business. In 2018 the sector had risen to a record height of £101.5bn, creating 3.12 m jobs.

The agents of resistance and their political and cultural motivations

The attitudes and position of Labour

The loose alliance resisting the Conservative attack on culture consists of heterogeneous agents and actors including the Labour Party, the Green Party, territorial parties in Scotland, Wales and Northern Ireland, local government members, local citizen groups, charities, journalists, celebrities and other critical citizens.

As the Labour Party is not in power, it does not presently have the agency to transform national cultural policy. Even where a local authority is run by Labour, it is endowed with only the shadow of agency because, being subject to the government's austerity policy, it can only try to distribute its limited resources wisely. Party members as citizens, however, can and do engage in public resistance. In this they are animated by the context of Labour's traditionally democratic attitude to culture, dating back to the 19th century, when cultural reformers such as William Morris hoped to improve social equality by bringing the 'sweetness and light' of culture (Matthew Arnold's term) into the life of the masses (cf. Hesmondhalgh et al, 2015). Though the national party, when in power after the Second World War and in the 1960s and 1970s, tended to treat cultural affairs as marginal, some Labour-run local authorities pledged themselves seriously to this democratic ideal, above all the Greater London Council (GLC) in the 1980s: it strongly promoted small co-operative organizations and created new opportunities for black and Asian British cultural activities – for which it was punished with abolition by the next Conservative government. When New Labour came to power in 1997, it picked up the party's traditional commitment to democratize culture, but also took into account that the field had come strongly under the influence of capitalism. Thus, typical for its Third Way politics, New Labour combined a democratic agenda with economic considerations: expenditure was increased to allow more people access to culture (by investment in education, free entrance to museums etc.), but also the 'creative industries' were discovered. As was mentioned, since devolution, the Labour parties in Wales and Scotland as well as the SNP have endeavoured to continue this policy. Though the national party after its defeat in 2010 paid little attention to cultural affairs, Jeremy Corbyn, party leader since 2015, has rediscovered the field's political potential. While also promising more money for the creative industries, Corbyn, in speeches, articles and the election manifestos of 2015 and 2017, has stressed the spiritual importance of culture, outlining a programme which would in the first place 'support people in leading more enjoyable and fulfilling lives' (quoted in Wilkinson, 2015). In the Labour Party manifesto of 2017, this was spelled out in plans to end the cuts to local authorities, to improve cultural infrastructure, to give more support to the arts outside London and to promote arts and music in schools.

Civil agents of resistance and their motivations

Apart from personal fears of job loss or income reduction, the various civil agents of resistance seem to be inspired by two main lines of thought: one is the political context of communal commitment in the Labour tradition, the other is the context of idealist-humanist concern for the possibilities of individual development. Sharon Heal, director of the Museums Association, combined both arguments, concern for the individual and the collective: 'Our museums play a vital role at the heart of the community. They preserve our heritage, provide life-long learning and improve our well-being' (quoted in Brennan, 2015).

Protest actions have ranged from numerous small spontaneous initiatives to petitions by celebrities and long-running campaigns organized by agents and actors from various professions and civil interest groups. An impressive early example of notables protesting was an open letter to the Cultural Secretary Jeremy Hunt of 1 October 2010 signed by more than 100 artists, including 19 Turner prize winners and other famous artists such as David Hockney, Yinka Shonibare and Tracy Emin. The protest was organized by Save the Arts, a big national campaigning group of 2,000 individuals and art organizations. A Scottish activity was an open letter by Nicola Solomon on behalf of the 700 Scottish members of the national Society of Authors to the Scottish Secretary for Finance in 2017 asking to ensure continued financial support for Scotland's renowned literary programmes. A further nationwide activity is the 'Don't Stop the Music' campaign, which targets the reduction of art and music teaching in schools (see next section). Started by pianist James Rhodes, it is now co-ordinated by the Incorporated Society of Musicians and the Music Industries Association.

Apart from such political actions, a growing number of charities and individuals have practically engaged as volunteers in community services no longer funded by the state, in museums and galleries, but above all in libraries and youth clubs, gradually realizing the idea of a Big Society.

The facts: exemplary sectors hit by the cuts and counter measures

National institutions

Austerity has hit both big national and small local institutions, yet the flagships of British culture, most of them located in London and receiving their state support through ACE, have suffered relatively little. The Royal Opera House got away with a 2.2 per cent cut of its grant in 2010, which it managed to balance by fundraising, commercial activities and high ticket sales. In 2017 state aid amounted to only 20 per cent of the Opera's income, but it lost a further 3 per cent in 2018/19. The National Theatre and the Royal Shakespeare Company both lost 6.7 per cent earlier on and had to cope with 3 per cent more cuts in 2018/19. But the English National Opera (ENO) lost 30 per cent of its support in 2014, the chorus being hit hardest: it was reduced in numbers, the remaining contracts were shortened and salaries reduced. As a result of reshuffling the portfolio in 2017, the ENO's funding was been raised again to £12.38m per year. Less lucky were staff members of the National Gallery, who in 2015 closed down departments and demonstrated spectacularly in Trafalgar Square against the planned outsourcing of certain visitor services to the commercial company Securitas – but the plans were realized. The DCMS-funded national institutions in England had to take an average cut of 20 per cent since 2010, while governments of Scotland and Wales, by contrast, have managed to keep support for their national institutions such as national galleries and museums almost level since 2009.

Regional institutions: museums, theatres, libraries, youth clubs, schools

One big group of institutions severely affected by austerity measures are the regional and local museums and galleries, financed by the local authorities. More and more of them can no longer hold up the principle of free entry introduced by New Labour. In England, where the councils lost £100m between 2006 and 2017, many local museums had to reduce opening hours and can no longer acquire new objects. 55 have closed since 2010, most of them in the North and Midlands, with further closures expected. Others closed departments or have imposed charges, and some are even selling exhibits: the sale of a 4,000-year-old Egyptian statue in Northampton in 2014 was a much discussed first. Yorkshire and Lancashire seem to be struck particularly hard. Yorkshire has had to cope with a 69 per cent loss, and Lancashire's budget was reduced from £1.3m to £100,000. Even museums which are of particular significance for the local community's identity have been affected. The Helmshore Mills Textile Museum in Rossendale, one of the last memorials of the cotton industry once dominant in the area, was mothballed in 2016. After a public petition the County Council reopened it in 2018, but only on weekends during the next two summers. Yet the Light Infantry Museum in Durham, an iconic venue remembering the national service of Durham citizens in the wars since 1881, was closed for good in April 2018.

Theatres in the regions are also having a hard time. Newcastle is an extreme example: in 2013 the city announced it would have to reduce its budget for culture by 100 per cent, though later, after much protest and negotiations, it softened the cuts to 50 per cent. The Live Theatre, an experimental company originally producing new drama addressing a working-class audience, had to accept a 70 per cent loss, while the venerable Theatre Royal, founded in 1837, lost all its funds. Both survived by their own efforts, for instance by including more popular entertainment in their programmes.

Libraries, once a pride of British cultural policy, have been particularly vulnerable. In March 2016 the BBC Data Journalism Team published alarming figures: as a consequence of a 16 per cent reduction in library funding between 2012 and 2016, some 343 libraries were closed down nationwide with 8,000 jobs lost. Meanwhile the savaging has gone on: 478 were closed by December 2017 and 130 more in 2018 with further 712 full-time employees dismissed. Even some of the 660 highly esteemed Carnegie libraries, erected in the UK between 1883 and 1919 with generous grants from Scottish-born American steel millionaire Andrew Carnegie, many of them listed buildings, have not been spared. In libraries still working, opening hours have been slashed and stocks reduced and in many cases volunteers have taken over the services: in 2018 their number had risen to 51,394. Observers believe that the 'main plank of government policy towards libraries is to shift them into the voluntary sector' (Kean, 2016). The number of 'community-run libraries' has rocketed from ten in 2010 to 500 in 2017. Of course, the loss of professional expertise has meant a decline in standards, and, in part as a result, visitor numbers have fallen, from almost 300 million in 2011/2012 to 233 million in 2018 (Kean, 2016; and Cain, 2018). It is especially sad that book loans to children have gone down, in some cities by more than 30 per cent since 2011 (Harris, 2017). Numerous passionate protest campaigns, often supported by prominent writers including Zadie Smith, Poet Laureate Carol Ann Duffy, the former National Poet of Wales Gwyneth Lewis and J. K. Rowling in Scotland, have had no effect.

The cuts in local government expenditure that affect the young seem the most damaging because of the negative effects on their future. Besides losing easy access to books, young people have faced further reductions: between 2010 and 2016, youth service budgets were cut by £387m so that 600 youth clubs across the UK with 139,000 places were forced to close, robbing thousands of – in most cases poor – young people of creative or sportive activities in their free time. A third alarming development is the severe reduction of music and arts teaching in schools. New Labour had put special store by boosting music education in schools, raising funding from 2007 on by £332m and starting several successful initiatives such as Creative Partnerships, which since 2002 brought artists of all kinds to work with teachers in 5,000 schools in England, Sing Up, Wider Opportunities (for ensemble teaching) and In Harmony. Creative Partnerships was stopped in 2011 and the funding of Sing Up seriously slashed. The 123 so-called Music Education Hubs, established by the government in England in 2012, in which several organizations work together, have not been able to compensate the reduced chances for poorer children as their funds – one third from the DCMS, the rest from local authorities, charitable and private sources (Department of Education, 2011, pp 27–8) – have not reached the expected levels. As a result, the hubs cannot pay and keep qualified staff (Musicians Union, 2015).

A DCMS survey of state-maintained schools in England in 2014 showed that after-school classes for music, drama and dance had been reduced, but the decline in regular teaching time had even more devastating effects. The Warwick Commission, set up in November 2013 to value the role of culture in British society, stressed the importance of creative subjects for developing 'enterprise and creative achievement' needed in many kinds of professions. But in their final report published in 2015 they had to deplore that the number of arts teachers, drama teachers, design and technology teachers had fallen by 8 per cent to 11 per cent since 2010. As a consequence, GCSE numbers for creative subjects had dropped drastically, for example in craft-related subjects by 25 per cent, in drama by 23 per cent and in design and technical subjects by even 50 per cent (Warwick Commission, 2015, pp 44–5, 47). Meanwhile the decline in creative subject GCSE entries has continued: compared to 2010, by 2018 participation had fallen in dance by 45 per cent, in drama by 29 per cent, in music by 23 per cent, in design and technology by 57 per cent, in performing arts by 63 per cent (Cultural Learning Alliance, 2018).

The government's disregard for creative subjects has been callously confirmed by the latest version of the English Baccalaureate (EBacc), last updated January 2019, which is relevant for England, Wales and Northern Ireland while Scotland operates its own system of qualification. In this influential list of GCSE subjects recommended to improve the chance of university access, a combination of English language and literature, maths, the sciences, geography or (!) history and one (!) foreign language is suggested, but music and the arts are ignored. A large group of artists, writers and other intellectuals published a petition in *The Guardian* in May 2018 calling on the government to reverse its decision which would 'seriously damage the future of many young people.' The threatening abolition of arts and music teaching in schools does, however, not only reduce the life prospects of pupils, who cannot afford private tuition, but the creative industries, so highly valued in all parts of the country for its economic power, will also be affected – they may soon be faced with a serious recruiting problem.

Assessment and outlook

Assessing the current state in the ongoing battle over cuts in the cultural sector, the Conservatives have undoubtedly been victorious. Theresa May has continued the austerity politics of her Conservative predecessor. Though she announced £80m funding for youth projects in England in 2016 (perhaps to repair the worst damages), this measure has been effectively neutralized by the announcement of a further £1.3bn funding cut (36 per cent) to local governments for 2019/20 (Local Government Association, 2018). Labour is not in a position to bring about a fundamental change. Despite their passionate and loud public protest and massive voluntary engagement the civil agents of resistance have also not been able to make much difference to the deplorable situation. So only small improvements can be expected.

In the field of the arts a new policy launched by ACE under the chairmanship of Nicholas Serota has brought some positive changes by reallocating the meagre funds available, which promise relief to specially disadvantaged groups: in the portfolio for 2018–022 more money was allocated to 98 smaller organizations outside London, and the number of 'diversity-led' (female, disabled, LGBT or BAME) organizations supported has grown considerably from 183 to 351. Also seven library organizations and 72 museums were added (Arts Professional, 2018).

Despite such modest improvements, prospects for the cultural sector in Britain generally do not look positive in the near future, for in addition to the continuing austerity impact, there is an elephant in the room: the Brexit decision. If Brexit is realized, one thing is certain: many cultural activities will suffer. There are serious financial worries: the government, having to face large payments to Brussels and the forecast damage to the UK economy, will tighten the reins even more. Additionally, experts fear rising costs for cooperation across borders as well as the loss of grants from European sources such as Creative Europe, the European Regional Fund, Erasmus, etc. At the moment Creative Europe alone supports the cultural and audiovisual sector in the UK with €18.4m annually. According to a survey ordered by ACE, a majority of 992 stakeholders expect even greater damage from limited freedom of movement in Europe (ICMUnlimited, 2017). Sectors including dance, music, film, TV and the visual arts rely strongly on an uninhibited collaboration with European partners. The House of Lords, apparently more concerned about culture than the government, has pleaded strongly for 'reciprocal preferential treatment' of EU and British citizens rather than applying the same restrictions as to third-country nationals and, in the case of failure, has suggested a number of special rules for cultural workers such as short-term permits for Europeans to travel to the UK, permit-free arrangements for festivals and multi-country touring visas for British citizens (House of Lords, 2018). One can only hope that the many people working in the cultural field for the benefit of British society will not lose heart in the face of the destructive developments which Conservative actors have set in motion.

References

Ahearn, L. M. (2001) 'Language and agency', *Annual Review of Anthropology*, 30: 109–37.

Arts Professional (2018) 'Arts funding: 183 new NPOs as largest organizations take 3% cut', https://www.artsprofessional.co.uk/news/arts-funding-183-new-npos-largest-organisations-take-3-cut.

Brennan, C. (2015) 'Art cuts deaden our regions', *The Guardian*, 13 December.

Cain, S. (2018) 'Nearly 130 public libraries closed across Britain in the last year', *The Guardian*, 7 December.

Cameron, D. (2009) 'The Big Society', *Speech*, 10 November: https://conservative-speeches.sayit.mysociety.org/speech/601246.

Cameron, D. (2010) 'Big Society Speech', *gov.uk*, 19 July: https://www.gov.uk/government/speeches/big-society-speech.

Clarke, J. (2013) 'Contexts: forms of agency and action', in C. Pollitt (ed.) *Context in public policy and management: The missing link?*, Cheltenham: Edward Edgar, pp 22–34.

Conservative Party Manifesto: Forward together (2017), https://www.conservatives.com/manifesto.

Cultural Learning Alliance (CLA) (2018) 'Further decline in arts GCSE and A level entries', https://culturallearningalliance.org.uk/further-decline-in-arts-gcse-and-a-level-entries.

Department for Digital, Culture, Media and Sport [DCMS] (2016) *The Culture White Paper*, gov.uk.

Department of Education (2011) *The importance of music: a national plan for music education*, gov.uk.

Flew, T. (2012) *The creative industries: Culture and policy*, London: Sage.

Gardner, C. (2015) 'Election 2015. A vote for the arts', *sinfinimusic.com*: http://www.sinfinimusic.com/uk/features/other-features/uk-politics.

Gray, M. and A. Barford (2018) 'The depth of the cuts: the uneven geography of local government austerity', *Cambridge Journal of Regions, Economy and Society*, 11(3): 541–63.

Hall, S. (2011) 'The neo-liberal revolution', *Cultural Studies*, 25(6): 705–28.

Harris, J. (2017) 'The Tories are savaging libraries – and closing the book on social mobility', *The Guardian*, 15 December.

Hesmondhalgh, D. et al (2015) *Culture, economy and politics. The case of New Labour*, Houndsmill: Palgrave Macmillan.

House of Lords, European Union Commission (2018) 'Brexit: movement of people in the cultural sector', *19th Report of Session 2017–19*, 26 July.

ICMUnlimited (2017) 'Impact of Brexit on the arts and culture sector', *A report by ICM and SQW on behalf of Arts Council England*, 20 February, London: Unlimited House.

Kean, D. (2016) 'UK library budgets fall by 25 m in a year', *The Guardian*, 8 December.

Local Government Association (2018) 'Local services face further £1.3 billion government funding cut in 2019/20.' *Report*, 1 October.

5

Agents and Agency in the Face of Austerity and Brexit Uncertainty: the Case of Legal Aid

Steven Truxal

Introduction

An 'age of austerity' – a term used previously only to describe the UK austerity programmes in the years immediately following the First and Second World Wars – was cited as the answer to what Prime Minister David Cameron called 'the age of irresponsibility'. The task, he said, was to 'identify wasteful and unnecessary public spending' (2009). The UK's 'fiscal crisis' created space for the re-birth of austerity politics (see O'Connor, 1973), and the (re-)framing of policy discourses, such as fiscal responsibility aligned to the new predicament (Prince, 2001). Referring to UK public services, Clarke would call this particular context 'the financial crisis of the state and fiscalization of policy discourses' (2005, p. 213).

A rise in austerity politics can generally be said to incite new government policies which impact upon our daily lives. In 'Austerity Britain', the contested policies that cut legal aid funding and court system financing threaten justice and the rule of law, which are the very foundations of the legal systems in England and Wales, Scotland and Northern Ireland. The UK's legal systems are admired and respected worldwide for their strength and robustness. This good reputation is now at risk of decline, owing to the situation in England and Wales, as the case study presented in this chapter recognizes. Thus, it is necessary firstly to identify and then to critically analyze policies that affect law and justice, the impacts of such policies and resistance to them. The growing body of literature on austerity policies which scope wide-ranging areas of public life has identified a worrying trend: the clear reversal of policies designed to be enabling and inclusive into policies which constrain and exclude.

Offered as a case study of the wider debate on austerity-through-policy in Britain, this chapter reviews legal aid reform, which previously has been described as 'discount justice' in other common law jurisdictions, as now threatening England and Wales as well (see Baum, 1979; Greenberg and Cherney, 2017). Particular focus is given to the impacts, or likely impacts, austerity policies have on the availability of legal aid, on the one hand for civil disputes involving citizens – including family, employment and immigration matters linked to the UK's exit from the European Union; and on the other for criminal cases. In light of Brexit uncertainty, the quantum of future public spending on justice is uncertain to boot. Taken together, austerity and uncertainty lead us to query whether the judicial system in England and Wales is in crisis, and to identify the impacts of and resistance to legal aid cuts.

This chapter will provide details on changes to legal aid and justice financing in England and Wales, and policy reversals, government justifications for changes, and the response of agents (citizens) on the one hand, and professional actors (lawyers) on the other. This is proposed as a basis for the chapter's reflective narrative on the risk of 'discount justice' in Britain, declining faith in justice and the current state of the judicial system in England and Wales. As the debate is contextualised by the relationship between austerity and agency, this chapter also considers the relationship between austerity and agency in economic, legal and social contexts. The aim is to think contextually as a means to study the forms of agency that arise where the act (or omission) is giving and receiving legal advice (or not).

Legal aid, its reform and a system in crisis

Article 40 of the celebrated bill of rights, the *Magna Carta Libertatum*, states: 'To no one will we sell, to no one will we refuse or delay, right or justice' (1215). It is widely accepted that the public's right to legal advice is a long-standing cornerstone of the UK judicial systems. The public's right of access to the courts has also long been recognized as a constitutional right in the UK. In addition, the provision of assistance to members of the public who cannot afford legal representation, 'legal aid', can be traced as far back as the Tudor and Stuart eras (Brookes, 2017). Thus, the right of individuals as citizens to receive legal advice and adequate representation are fundamental aspects of the UK judicial systems.

The contemporary legal aid system has its foundations in the work of the Rushcliffe Committee, which was established by the Coalition government in 1944. At the end of the Second World War in 1945, the Committee reported on what would become the crucial four pillars of the new, postwar welfare state: The National Health Service (NHS), universal housing, state security benefits and universal education. Notably, legal aid was not among them. The Rushcliffe Committee did recommend and the postwar Labour Government accept, however, that new legislation in the field of legal aid should be proposed. The government published a White Paper in 1948, in which it set out a new objective: 'to provide legal advice for those of slender means and resources, so that no one would be financially unable to prosecute a just and reasonable claim or defend a legal right; and to allow counsel and solicitors to be remunerated for their services' (Brookes, 2017, p. 5). This in turn led to the enactment of the Legal Aid and Advice Act 1949, under which legal aid was to be made available in available in 'all courts and tribunals where lawyers normally appeared for private clients. Eligibility should be extended to those of small or moderate means, and above a free limit there should be a sliding scale of contributions' (Brookes, 2017, p. 5).

The costs associated with the administration of the legal aid system increased significantly in the decades that followed, with 'unprecedented rises in cost' documented from about the mid-1980s and onwards. While the rising costs solicited responses from governments to amend rules relating to eligibility, and to restructure the provision of criminal legal aid, the most significant changes have transpired after the 2008 global financial crisis, when the relevant budgets have been consistently and incrementally reduced due to austerity measures. This can be evidenced by direct cuts to the justice budget: 'In 2010, the Ministry of Justice controlled a £10.9bn budget to administer the courts, legal aid, prisons and probation service. By 2017–18 the budget was down to £7.6bn; for 2019–20 the budget is projected to be £6.3bn ... a fall of more than 40 per cent' (Croft and Thompson, 2018b).

There have also been major changes made as to the designated responsible bodies and oversight structures for the provision of legal aid. For instance, the Legal Aid Board, which was founded in 1949, holding over half a century's mandate, was dismantled and 'replaced' by the Legal Services Commission in 2000. This was a modification by way of the Access to Justice Act 1999. The Legal Services Commission was established as a non-departmental public body, which funded the Civil Legal Advice Service. The Legal Services Commission was then abolished under the Legal Aid, Sentencing and Punishment of Offenders Act 2012 (LAPSO) and replaced with a new body, the Legal Aid Agency, which continues to exist today as an executive agency of the Ministry of Justice (MOJ). Notable here is the change in status from non-departmental public body to executive agency; this means its management and budget is separate from that of the MOJ. It is nonetheless of interest to recognize some consistency within the Agency even if six different justice secretaries have sat at the MOJ's helm over the past eight years or so.

LAPSO, which came into force in 2013, also reversed the previous position under the Access to Justice Act 1999, whereby civil legal aid was available for any matter not specifically excluded. Some types of cases were taken out of the scope for legal aid funding altogether; the legislation provides that cases are not eligible for funding unless they are of a specified type (James and Forbess, 2011). According to Croft and Thompson (2018b), LAPSO 'removed aid for entire areas of civil disputes overnight ... taking divorce [which was the original impetus for contemporary legal aid cases] and child custody, immigration, parts of debt and housing, employment and welfare benefit out of the legal aid net'. Owing to such sweeping changes, it is perhaps not surprising that the LAPSO legislation has come under significant scrutiny owing to its real effect on the public and access to justice. 'Many law firms across the country have given up their provision of various legal aid services entirely because it is so unprofitable' (Croft and Thompson, 2018b). This has yielded a new phenomenon: parties representing themselves.

At the same time, there has been a push to resolve family disputes through alternative dispute resolution (ADR) mechanisms, such as mediation, whereby diverting such disputes, parties to the dispute and the associated expenditures in time and financial cost, away from the courtroom. Increasingly, ADR is adopted in other jurisdictions as a non-adversarial precursor or pre-requisite to resolution of family disputes by litigation. The idea is that ADR should fill the gaps following cuts to legal aid budgets for civil disputes. Although ADR may be less expensive and more expedient than following traditional litigation in the courts, this depends on the complexity of the case and willingness of the parties to agree to this alternative route.

In the face of Brexit, and the feeling of uncertainty this has created for the future of immigrants to the UK from the European Economic

Area and beyond, the number of difficult legal questions around immigration status, employment and settlement rights is rising. In 2018, the Law Society, which represents solicitors in England and Wales, claimed Britain's legal aid system to be 'broken' following the release of statistics by the MOJ. The figures revealed, alarmingly, that only three individuals received legal aid to challenge their immigration status in 2016, compared with 22,000 in 2012 (Croft, 2018). Following implementation of LAPSO, non-asylum related cases are excluded from eligibility for legal aid. Voluntary work (so-called pro bono legal advice) offered by lawyers, community organizations and law schools are helping parties to disputes that are no longer eligible for legal aid and who are unable to afford legal representation otherwise, though time and resources are limited.

While legal aid is still available for criminal cases, the income threshold has been reduced for defendants seeking legal aid advice. According to Andrew Walker QC, chair of the Bar Council of England and Wales, 'The simple effect [of LAPSO] is that people are not able to secure the advice and representation they need to make sure that we are getting the right outcome in every case' (Croft and Thompson, 2018b). Therefore, it is argued that, with the fundamental rights to legal advice and adequate representation at risk of becoming less or not at all accessible, the foundations of justice are crumbling. If this is so, then the UK justice systems are indeed in crisis – but with respect to whom?

Agency and the agents: lawyers and citizens

The challenges presented by austerity and Brexit in the context of declining justice have been set out in the previous section. It is necessary now to identify the agents within the classical agency matrix arising where civil and criminal legal aid and other advice and representation contracts are made between government, advisers and legal representatives, and the public (citizens). At the same time, citizen disengagement may be witnessed. Seemingly, this is owing to frustration over restrictions on agency, where 'agency' is accepted as the freedom and capacity to perform an act or omission, consciously and intentionally (Hay, 2002, p. 94). In a legal sense, agency is created where one party acts on behalf of another, called the principal, with his consent. An agent in law, whether citizen or professional actor (lawyer), has the authority to act – and to bind the principal. This is interesting to elaborate upon as regards the current topic of legal aid as lawyers may be seen as acting for citizens, on their instruction, and as independent from the state. As Clarke (2013, pp 19–20) puts it: 'Front-line workers – and those at other organizational tiers – are rarely 'just' workers'. Yet lawyers are also agents of a particular 'social zone' as regards social class and certain freedoms and availability of options when choosing to act. The next section will provide some brief remarks on 'agency', and then move on to consider the relationship between austerity and agency with reference to legal actors (striking lawyers) and agents (disruptive citizens).

Agency

The notion of 'agency' and 'agent' and theories of agency are not uniform across all disciplines; in fact, they can be quite different. This chapter recognizes that the relationship between austerity and agents – the focus of which here are lawyers as professional actors distinguished from citizens as agents – could be examined in different disciplinary spaces: political science, economics, law and sociology. In the interest of providing clarity, and to defend the complexity of the subject of legal aid cuts in the context of austerity and Brexit, this section provides a brief account on each.

While theories of agency emerged in political science and economics at about the same time, agency theory in economics developed rapidly (see Mitnick, 1973; Ross, 1973). Shapiro suggests that agency in political science 'borrows heavily from the economics paradigm rather than the more sociological conception' (2005, p. 271). She goes on to clarify that '[p]rincipals delegate to agents the authority to carry out their political preferences. However, the goals of principals and agents may conflict and, because of asymmetries of information, principals cannot be sure that agents are carrying out their will' (p. 271). The spectrum of agents and actors in the political science space includes citizens, nation states, elected officials, lawmakers, courts, and so on. Shapiro identifies that

> [p]olitical principals also face problems of adverse selection, moral hazard, and agent opportunism. So principals contrive incentives to align agent interests with their own and undertake monitoring of agent behavior, activities that create agency costs […] The literature also considers the matter of agency costs; when they are too high, principals may decide not to squander resources on them. (Shapiro, 2005, pp 271–2; see also Banfield, 1975; Mitnick, 1998)

Relevant to this chapter's focus on legal aid cuts, political science gives more attention than economics to the role of sanctions (for example budget cuts). Principals in this instance are 'in the driving seat', so to speak.

In law, agency is

> the fiduciary relationship which exists between two persons, one of whom expressly or impliedly assents that the other should act on his behalf so as to affect his relations with third parties, and the other of whom similarly manifests assent so to act or so acts pursuant to the manifestation [...]. (American Law Institute, 2006)

Therefore, the law of agency addresses the legal consequences of consensual relationships. A principal can never be entirely sure what act or omission his agent makes. None the less, the relationship is one of trust. In a legal sense, agency theory may therefore provide a framework for the provision of, in keeping with the thrust of this chapter, what are or have traditionally been government-funded (advice) services; alternatively, it may be a means to legitimize what are in reality only cuts to funding (Reynolds, 1997).

Lawyers

Before discussing lawyers, the role and importance of other advice providers must be given due consideration. Alongside volunteer advice organizations, government also 'contracts out' service delivery to different advice organizations as providers. Examples include Citizens Advice Bureaux, debt advice agencies, employment tribunal advice, and benefits, disability and housing services. While it is widely recognized that as individual demand for advice services outstrips supply, advice agencies are even more seriously challenged in this age of austerity. As Evans puts it: 'We know that scantly resourced services struggle to meet demand, and that economic "austerity" has delivered a double blow to those seeking advice, stripping away much-needed services whilst also adding to the problems of the advice seekers, afflicted with poverty, worklessness, debt and homelessness' (2017, p. 23).

To paint a picture of how austerity has affected advice organizations, Kirwan et al (2017) provide a series of useful case studies and reflections on the challenges experienced by advisors and advisees in austerity, which could also serve as powerful evidence of the unhealthy state of affairs for advice agencies. Reflecting on the case studies, Clarke remarks: 'The future is perilous, both for those who would use Citizens Advice and for the service itself. The experience of constantly striving to do more with less is not sustainable - either for the organizations or the people who work in them' (2017, p. 162). For advisers themselves, the typical problem of 'mediating professions' should also be considered (see Johnson, 1973). The work of advisers and other front-line public services 'is always framed by the potentially conflicting demands of their organization (and the state policies it enacts) and those of public/users/clients of the service' (Clarke, 2013, p. 30).

In 'Austerity Britain', the frustration of lawyers – solicitors and barristers – is not without cause. It has also been widely publicized. In February 2014, the government announced plans to cut the number of contracts for duty solicitor work in magistrates' courts and police stations from 1,600 to 525, a reduction of about 67% (see BBC Q&A Legal Aid Challenges, 2013). Twice barristers have taken to the streets in major protests in 2014 and again in April 2018, striking in the fight for legal aid (Croft and Thompson, 2018a). In protest, criminal barristers have also refused to take new legal aid cases (see Dearden, 2018). These calls for strike and decisions not to take on casework are troubling, particularly for a group typically adverse to strike action. With that said, Bailey et al observe that 'a corresponding increase in the presence of refusal-prone materialists is perhaps best illustrated by a number of groups that are typically averse to strike activity beginning to adopt conventional strike action. This includes actions by barristers, lawyers, probation officers, midwives and junior doctors' (2018, p. 19). Thus, the legal aid cuts have yielded disengagement by lawyers by way of protests and strikes. This reveals a new instance of disruptive agency within what is a rather unexpected space. The decision by criminal barristers to refuse to take on new legal aid cases demonstrates a separate instance of disruptive agency. This rebellious dissent – if it may be termed that – leaves citizens feeling disempowered while barristers may feel more empowered to bring about change by way of their collective agency. While no doubt the intentions of criminal barristers are entirely good, this rebellious act may spur further, more obvious forms of dissent in society. These actions provide evidence of actors exercising resistance to the reversal of policies relating to the provision of legal aid schemes. A greater number of voices demand to be heard on this matter, which represents social protest – and subsequent legal challenge to make a difference to the lives of the affected.

Austerity policies have not gone without legal challenge either. For instance, the London Criminal Courts Solicitors' Association and the

Criminal Law Solicitors' Association brought legal challenge against the cuts, vis-à-vis an application for judicial review, in September 2014. The applicants argued that the cuts are ideologically driven and would push the courts and justice system to 'breaking point'. The judge overturned the change to legal aid. In the High Court ruling it was held that the government's consultation process had failed to let lawyers comment on two reports and was 'unfair as to result in illegality' (International Legal Aid Group, 2014). The case was appealed to the Court of Appeal, which ruled in 2017 that the LAPSO system did not have capacity to fill the gaps following removal of the previous legal aid scheme and that safeguards should have been put in place to ensure prisoners could engage in decisions and processes related to their treatment. While the Ministry of Justice initially stated that the ruling would be appealed to the Supreme Court, this was later dropped.

In August 2018, the High Court ruled that cuts to legal aid fees for lawyers representing criminal suspects at trial were illegal. The challenge against the government policy was brought by the Law Society relating to the Advocates' Graduated Fee Scheme (AGFS). While at the time of writing it is unclear if this decision will be appealed, the ruling demonstrates the dissatisfaction with government austerity policies on legal aid vis-à-vis legal representatives and the independent judiciary. Thus, the frustration of advisers and lawyers as manifested through different levels of disengagement surely reveal widening cracks in the UK judicial systems. As government excludes ever more types of disputes from the scope of legal aid, it is tantamount to calling into question the availability of access to justice to those citizens less fortunate in society, thus limiting their individual agency considerably. Challenges to new government policies that trade their origins in austerity politics come under increased scrutiny – within solicitor firms, barrister chambers, in the street and in the courts and advice centres.

Citizens

As posited by Lerch et al, 'individual agency is a core cultural ideological theme in today's world' (2017, p. 39). Agency in social science is the capacity of individuals to act independently and to make their own free choices. This is combined with availability of options or means to achieve intended ends (see Kockelmann, 2007). Lerch et al argue that '[i]ndividuals become endowed with a growing range of rights, stemming not just from their national states but also universally, from greatly expanded notions of their inherent entitlement to justice and equality' (2017, p. 39; see also Therborn, 2000; Skrentny, 2009; Stacy, 2009). If agency means power or control, the cuts in legal services affect citizens and individual agency. Particularly affected are those citizens who are determined by lower social and economic class unable to afford the cost of advice services and legal representation, if required. Agents are thus unable to make their own free choices and feel disempowered as a result; and their decisions are therefore limited by structural determinations. And ultimately, the realities may be devastatingly life-changing for someone who has legal questions or legal charges against them, and does not benefit from access to advice or legal representation.

One must not turn a blind eye to the risks associated with declining faith in justice among citizens which are brought about by direct constraints on individual agency in a sociological sense; take for example 'disruptive agency' (Bailey et al, 2018). Indeed, there are plenty of examples of disruptive agency flowing from the relationships between austerity and agency. A feeling of disempowerment leads to disengagement, and possibly rebellious dissent. In the UK geography, '[p]erhaps the most visible instance during which everyday forms of disengagement transformed into more open forms of dissent and rebellion came with the 2011 London (and then national) riots. In the words of one of the rioters, 'We hate the police, hate the government, got no opportunities ...' (Lewis et al, 2011, p. 20; quoted in Bailey et al, 2018, p. 19; see also Kawalerowicz and Biggs, 2015). Bearing in mind that protestors may be arrested and charged with disturbing the peace, at least, the narrative returns full circle to the rights of citizens to receive legal advice and adequate representation. In the light of austerity, these 'rights' may not be enforceable – either because eligible citizens cannot find a lawyer to advise or barrister to represent them in court; lawyers and barristers are disengaged professional actors – or citizens ineligible for legal aid feel powerless. And so, agents are disempowered, again. In this structural context, some things become 'unthinkable, impossible, irrelevant, undesirable and unnecessary' (Clark, 2013, p. 24) – and therefore agents become more disengaged, more disruptive, and crying out for someone to listen.

It is worth noting that, '[a]gents – being embodied social actors – may bring other contexts with them into the context of action or practice' (Clarke, 2013, p. 30). The examples provided in this chapter give some insight into actions or practices of agents as social actors. These acts are difficult to foretell, however, as 'agency is simultaneously underdetermined in the sense that how it is enacted/performed cannot be predicted in advance' (Clarke, 2013, p. 31). We do not always know why one agent performs in a different way to another. With that said, the forms of agency identified in this chapter contain the possibility of 'acting up or acting out, or just acting' (Clarke, 2013, p. 31). This leads us to the final 'act' of this chapter: Brexit.

If agency is 'contextually unstable', then as Clarke posits: 'Intercontextuality provides a means of pointing to the unpredictably productive intersections of different contexts that enable specific forms of agent, types of agency and action' (Clarke, 2013, pp 31–2). The opportunity (for some) to exercise the right to vote in the national referendum on UK membership of the EU was given on 23 June 2016. A majority of 51.89% eligible voters gave 'No' to the question of: 'Should the United Kingdom remain a member of the European Union?'

At the time of writing, Brexit is expected to bring with it a raft of immediate upsets and uncertainty, and longer-term rifts in society. No matter which box an agent ticked on the referendum ballot paper, agency achieves, through the exercise of power or resistance where both raise new feelings of empowerment and engagement, the aim of 'making a difference'. In turn, the difference this engagement makes may impact on agents and the structural contexts around them seen as conditioning their position. Perhaps a link can be made between the cuts in justice funding and the attitudes and understandings which gave rise to the Brexit vote. There is certainly a need for further research in this area.

The general pressures on citizen advice are now multiplied by the known and also the yet uncertain challenges of Brexit, which risks upsetting, as Clarke puts it, 'the collective infrastructure of being able to think and behave in significant ways' (2017, p. 162). The changes described in this chapter to the provision of citizen advice services, as compounded by lack of legal aid support and the unknown future environment following Brexit, are performed at what Clarke would likely call 'a dangerous moment, when the wider dynamics of social and economic dislocation create dangerous times for citizens and citizenly conduct' (2017, p. 162).

Conclusion

This chapter has explored cuts to legal aid in England and Wales as a case study of the re-occurring British 'age of austerity' following the 2008–9 global financial crisis. Over the past decade, the UK government has delivered sweeping changes to eligibility of citizens for the provision of legal aid, the overall justice budget underpinning such support, and a series of great administrative changes to 'responsible' oversight bodies. These unhappy events weaken citizens by reducing or altogether removing the availability of legal advice and representation to those who may need it. Academically, these events create a useful window through which to explore the relationship between austerity and agency, and the impact on professional actors – advisers, lawyers, barristers – on the one hand, and agents – citizens – on the other; noting that professional actors may and do also seek to exercise collective agency, such as organizing strikes.

Acts of resistance are intensified in austerity. Ponder this hypothetical scenario: in 2013, an underperforming company dismisses their employee. The former employee seeks to challenge the unfair dismissal as claimant through the employment tribunal, which is costly in terms of a fee payable by the claimant to bring the claim and the cost of legal advice and representation. A lawyer is ready to assist the citizen, but changes to legal aid mean the citizen is no longer eligible. The citizen feels disempowered; success is unthinkable, impossible. In 2016, Brexit offers an opportunity for empowerment, to make a change. The lawyer feels disempowered, disengaged, resistant. Austerity and Brexit, and particularly where the two intersect, play out as impacts on citizen and lawyer and become catalysts for disengagement, resistance, protest, strike and rebellious dissent – disruptive agency. And then? Discount justice and Brexit divisions?

References

American Law Institute (2006) *Restatement of the Law – Agency, Restatement (Third) on Agency*, Philadelphia: American Law Institute.

Banfield, E. C. (1975) 'Corruption as a feature of governmental organization', *Journal of Law and Economics,* 18(3): 587–605.

Bailey, D. J., M. Clua-Losada, N. Huke, O. Ribera Almandoz and K. Rogers (2018) 'Challenging the age of austerity: Disruptive agency after the global economic crisis', *Comparative European Politics,* 16(1): 9–31.

Baum, D. J. (1979) *Discount justice: The Canadian criminal justice system*, Toronto: Burns and MacEachern.

BBC News (2013) *Q&A Legal Aid Challenges*, bbc.com.

Brookes, S.H. (2017) 'The History of Legal Aid 1945–2010', *Bach Commission on Access to Justice: Appendix 6*: https://www.fabians.org.uk/wp-content/uploads/2017/09/Bach-Commission-Appendix-6-F-1.pdf.

Cameron, D. (2009) 'The age of austerity', *Conservative Party Speech*, 26 April 2009.

Clarke, J. (2005) 'Performing for the Public: Doubt, Desire, and the Evaluation of Public Services', in P. Du Gay (ed.) *The Values of Bureaucracy*, Oxford: Oxford University Press.

Clarke, J. (2013) 'Contexts: forms of agency and action', in C. Pollitt (ed.) *Context in Public Policy and Management: The Missing Link?*, Cheltenham: Edward Elgar.

Clarke, J. (2017) 'Reflections on Advising in Austerity', in S. Kirwan (ed.) *Advising in austerity: Reflections on challenging times for advice agencies*, Bristol: Polity Press.

Croft J. (2018) 'Lawyers attack legal aid cuts that hit migrants', *Financial Times*, 1 May.

Croft, J. and B. Thompson (2018a) 'Chaos in UK courts as protests by lawyers leave clients undefended', *Financial Times*, 19 April.

Croft, J. and B. Thompson (2018b) 'Justice for all? Inside the legal aid crisis', *Financial Times*, 7 September.

Dearden, L. (2018) 'Lawyers call for strike over 'relentless legal aid cuts'', *The Independent*, 29 March.

Evans, S. (2017) 'A Reflection on Case Study One: The Barriers to Accessing Advice', in S. Kirwan (ed.) *Advising in austerity: Reflections on challenging times for advice agencies*, Bristol: Polity Press.

Greenberg, M. D. and S. Cherney (2017) *Discount Justice State Court Belt-Tightening in an Era of Fiscal Austerity*, Santa Monica, California: Rand Corporation.

Hay, C. (2002) *Political Analysis: A Critical Introduction*, Basingstoke: Palgrave.

International Legal Aid Group (2014) *Editorial No. 33*.

Jackson, S. (2011) *Social Works: Performing Art, Supporting Publics*, London: Routledge.

James, D. and A. Forbess (2011) 'Rights, Welfare and Law. Legal Aid Advocacy', in *Austerity Britain*, London School of Economics E-Prints.

Johnson, T. (1973) *Professions and Power*, London: Macmillan.

Kawalerowicz, J. and M. Biggs (2015) 'Anarchy in the UK: Economic deprivation, social disorganization, and political grievances in the London Riot of 2011', *Social Forces*, 94(2): 673–98.

Kirwan, S. (ed.) (2017) *Advising in austerity: Reflections on challenging times for advice agencies*, Bristol: Polity Press.

Kockelmann, P. (2007) 'Agency: The Relation Between Meaning, Power and Knowledge', *Current Anthropology*, 48(3): 375–401.

Lerch, J. et al (2017) 'The rise of individual agency in conceptions of society: Textbooks worldwide, 1950–2011', *International Sociology*, 32(1): 38–60.

Mitnick, B. M. (1973) 'Fiduciary responsibility and public policy: the theory of agency and some consequences', Paper presented at 69th Annual Meeting of American Political Science Association, New Orleans.

Mitnick, B. M. (1998) 'Agency theory', in R. E. Freeman and P. H. Werhane (eds) *The Blackwell Encyclopedic Dictionary of Business Ethics*, Malden: Blackwell.

O'Connor, J. (1973) *The Fiscal Crisis of the State*, New York: St. Martin's Press.

Prince, M. (2001) 'How social is social policy? Fiscal and market discourse in North American welfare states', *Social Policy and Administration*, 35(1): 2–13.

Reynolds, S. (1997) 'Contracting for Chaos', *Alternative Law Journal*, 22(1): 22.

Ross, S. A. (1973) 'The economic theory of agency: the principal's problem', *American Economic Review*, 63(2): 134–9.

Shapiro, S. (2005) 'Agency Theory', *Annual Review of Sociology*, 31: 263–84.

Skrentny, J. D. (2009) *The Minority Rights Revolution*, Cambridge, MA: Harvard University Press.

Stacy, H. (2009) *Human Rights for the 21st Century: Sovereignty, Civil Society, Culture*, Stanford, CA: Stanford University Press.

Therborn, G. (2000) 'Globalizations, dimensions, historical waves, regional effects, normative governance', *International Sociology*, 15(2): 151–79.

PART II

The Politics and Discourse of Brexit

6

The Economy of Brexit: Performance, Interests and Agency

Carlo Morelli

Introduction

The Brexit referendum, as a project to resolve the internal political conflicts within the British Conservative Party, has been a political misjudgement of monumental proportions. Historical comparisons are thin on the ground but the political crisis, within the Whigs and the Liberal Party, arising from the repeal of the Corn Laws in the 19th century is one of the few historical precedents on such a scale in English history. Unlike the Corn Law repeal, however, the Brexit debate occurs in an era in which the British economy is no longer a rising global power, but instead the reverse, with its world economic importance increasingly under question. The British economy has experienced a long-run relative economic decline and falling international competitiveness with the replacement of manufacturing sectors by a broad-based service sector. Manufacturing now accounts for under 20 per cent of GDP, and services account for 70 per cent. This has implications for European and global economic integration and hence economic policy. Thus, the parallel noted here with debates over the Corn Laws lie not simply with their relevance as a moment of political crisis but that sharp economic change shaped future economic policy. Consequently, there is a need to examine the economic importance Brexit has for the wider economy as a moment of economic transition, articulated through a debate over Britain's future trading relationships.

Lukács' (1990) concept of class consciousness identifying the importance of agency is an important tool in this respect, suggesting that 'praxis' represents the political articulation of collective consciousness arising from the specific sectoral position of differing class interests. The chapter demonstrates how differing elements of British business not only have divergent interests in Brexit but that these differences arise from their position in the economy. This is not to suggest we can simply reduce political interests to economic interests; rather, it is to suggest that it is the dominant interests within each economic sector that plays a disproportionate role in determining policy and outlook for these sectors.

In taking case studies of Brexit, divergent interests can be identified and agency and praxis examined. This chapter examines debates regarding the potential effect Brexit will have on the economy and, in particular, specific areas of the economy in which international trade plays an especially important role. It thus focuses on Brexit in relation to agriculture, financial services and internationally traded manufactured goods as three examples of sectoral interests.

A second element of the chapter is to continue with the analysis of the economic impact of the Brexit debate by looking at the social consequences of these economic transitions. Here, it seeks to examine the potential impact of Brexit on austerity and poverty in society. While a clear area of contention focused upon the UK government's ability to fund social welfare, the shape of welfare policy in a post-Brexit economy is not known. Remarkably, debates between Labour's vision for welfare under Jeremy Corbyn and those of the Conservative Party exist largely independent from the Brexit debate itself and are not connected with the final outcome of Brexit. Similarly, whereas the free movement of labour is a further area of contention, wider immigration policy, including the EU's 'Fortress Europe' approach, Theresa May's 'hostile environment' policy (see Chapter Forkert) and the 'Windrush' scandal, have not been prominent in the Brexit debate. Indeed, the most recent announcements suggest, at least in the short term, a continuing close alignment with existing migration policy for European nationals.

The chapter seeks to utilize agency and praxis in the area of welfare and poverty, as a means to understand linkages between Brexit and austerity. This is not to reduce agency to economic determinism but to identify economic interests as a dominant influence in debates over social welfare. Despite the awakening of political discourse and political engagement during the Scottish independence referendum of 2014 or the mass rallies during Corbyn's election campaign in 2017, the ability of the working class to engage as an organised collective in the Brexit debate failed to materialize. Agency and praxis within this context are therefore understood in the lack of ability of the wider population to influence the Brexit debate during and after the referendum.

State and capital

Since the third quarter of the 20th century the concept of relative economic decline was uniformly accepted as a characteristic of British capitalist development throughout the 20th century. While highly divergent policy conclusions exist for resolving this relative decline, the role of government in the development of industrial policy is a common emphasis. Interventionist Keynesian governments through the 1950s and 1960s focused upon promoting the 'white hot heat of technology' as a means of accelerating research in innovation and reorganization in the private sector. By the 1980s, this had given way to neoliberal market-led approaches, such as those identified by Olson (1982), who proposed shock therapies and the destruction of what was termed 'distributional coalitions'. Markets are suggested to facilitate a firm's decision making in the promotion of efficiency, while removing social welfare would incentivize labour to adjusting its wage demands or risk unemployment. In contrast to Keynesian and neoliberal approaches, Marxist interpretations have located the limitations of British capitalism's ability to raise its rate of profit, in relation to newer more dynamic centres of capital accumulation, as the central explanation for relative economic decline. British capitalism, within this framework, pioneered the development of globalization strategies by increasing the ability of British-owned oligopolistic and monopolistic firms' to extract profits under colonial control rather than focusing upon national development within the British economy (Roberts, 2016). While the 18th-century Navigation Acts had provided early forms of monopoly control for British trading firms such as the West and East India companies, imperial preference in the 20th century continued to grant privileged status to British business under Empire and later Commonwealth markets. British capitalism specialized in activities within the world economy rather than its own national economy for the accumulation of value.

For Marxists, late 20th-century finance and manufacturing interests combined together to develop innovative mechanisms for the accumulation of capital on a global scale (Harman, 2009). In contrast to the neoliberal and Keynesian perspectives, according to which finance capital was divorced and parasitical on manufacturing capital,

Marxist approaches emphasize their mutuality and inter-relationships. While the period from the 1970s to the 2000s was one of decline for manufacturing industry, finance capital grew and prospered as returns on finance deriving from global expansion grew rapidly.

The growing importance of financial capital has underpinned the scale of the 2008 financial crash (Varoufakis, 2016). In the context of transitions within economies, debates over Brexit have emerged. Brexit should therefore be understood not as an isolated debate over short-term trade relationships but as an issue shaping the long-term future direction of the British economy. Rather than solving divisions within the Conservative Party, Brexit has exacerbated them and moved the debate beyond the party. Brexit has become a debate over the extent to which future economic growth is a function of global markets, regional trading blocs and national economic development. This has created uncertainty and risks for business throughout the UK, which will have consequences for decades.

There have been demands for the UK to leave the EU since the UK's entry in 1973 (then the EEC) – traditionally a view of the left hostile to supranational structures of economic liberalism. Anti-EU arguments have also been commonplace among the right of British politics, ranging from fascist organizations, such as the National Front, the British National Party, to the far right UK Independence Party (UKIP) and parts of the Conservative Party. As Prime Minister, David Cameron's appeal to his party's discontented right was intended to marginalize their influence. His premiership had developed approaches contrary to the xenophobic ideologies within his government. Cameron's economic and socially liberal approach to the rehabilitation of the Conservative Party from its reputation as the 'nasty party' were all inimical to the right of the party. The 2016 EU referendum was the attempt to maintain unity within the Conservative Party. Since losing the EU referendum to the Leave campaign, differences between the Conservative Party and British business over EU membership have become ever more strained leading to significant questions over the future direction of British businesses.

Within Brexit we can observe the differences in the policy outcomes across landed, manufacturing and financial interests. The ending of the Common Fisheries and Agricultural Policies, concern over passporting rights for financial services and attempts to entice Nissan to maintain their investments in car manufacturing are examples of the particular influence business has over government policy. Such a focus seeks to recognize that the management of divergent sets of, often competing and contradictory, economic interests within the structure of a nation state gives rise to complex outcomes. Here, agency exercised by business and government actors in the determination of the state policy becomes relevant. This is now examined against the UK's departure from the EU and in the context of a globalized, capitalist economy.

Agriculture, financial services and manufacturing

The development of a post-Brexit solution through which British economic development can be separated from that of a wider European economy involves competition between the interests of national and international capital. Examining the sector specific technical notices of the UK government and of the EU provides a snapshot of the diverging approaches (Department for Exiting the European Union, 2018). Up to October 2018, some 105 technical papers had been published by the UK Department for Exiting the European Union covering 21 separate areas of regulation. Of these, 40 per cent dealt with regulation in just three areas of business: *Labelling Products and Making Them Safe*, *Importing and Exporting* and finally *Meeting Business Regulations*. On the part of the European Commission (2018), 75 separate preparedness notices cover 13 separate areas of which 51 per cent deal with the three most significant areas of *Health and Food Safety*, *Internal Market*, *Industry*, *Entrepreneurship and SMEs*, and *Mobility and Transport*. Collectively, the papers represent an indication of the extent to which alternative arrangements in the continuation of trade are required as the British and the European economies are diverging.

Agriculture

Food regulation continues to be a major area of cross-border regulatory consideration with the European single market. Significant limitations on the cross-border movement of food products are evident in the technical notices. While landed interests vary considerably across the EU, predominated by small-scale family farming, the ownership of agriculture in Britain is the most concentrated within the EU (El-Agraa, table 9.2, p. 190). Food regulation and transport highlight the differences in the nature of British and European agriculture. Within Europe, the common external tariff in the food industry protects small-scale producers from external competition. Brexit from the Common Agriculture Policy may initially provide a competitive advantage for British agriculture, arising from its higher level of concentration, and result in the capture of a greater market share for larger producers as smaller producers have less access to EU subsidies.

However, Brexit in this sector may potentially undermine even the concentrated, low-cost production sector within British agriculture. Lowering of environmental standards, for example by allowing the usage of chlorine washing of chicken products or an extensive use of antibiotics in beef production, enables producers in the United States to benefit from their significantly larger economies of scale. Thus, future trade agreements with economies outside the EU invariably present risks to British agricultural producers. EU agricultural policy also protects European producers through the imposition of tariffs on agricultural imports from third countries. This has historically restricted the processing of agricultural raw material, such as olive oil, coffee or coca, within developing countries and limited their export to unprocessed commodities. Global free trade agreements for a post-Brexit agriculture inevitably challenge the continuation of tariff ramping restrictions on the import of processed agricultural goods.

These contradictory tendencies within the agricultural sector are reflected in surveys of farmers by the National Farmers Union (NFU) (2016), which concluded that the 'NFU Council resolves that on the balance of existing evidence available to us at present, the interests of farmers are best served by our continuing membership of the European Union' (NFU, 2016).

Financial services

International financial services, including foreign exchange, asset management and insurance contracts, are largely absent from the technical notices of either the British government or the EU. This is due to the extensive international linkages and permissive regulatory environment in which global financial institutions operate within Britain. London, as a centre for internationally traded financial services, has a leading role not simply in European but global financial transactions. As with agriculture, Brexit restricts the extent to which European regulation can be imposed. Unlike agriculture, however, this would not necessitate a restriction on British-based firms' participation in networks of globally integrated financial transactions. In the course of the post-2008 financial crisis, calls for further regulation of international finance intensified and EU directives and regulations increased the monitoring and reporting requirements on financial institutions. Both the Regulation (EU) 575/2013 on prudential requirements for credit institutions and investment firms and Directive 2013/36/EU on capital requirements (Capital Requirements Directive IV) seek to define and limit the extent to which financial institutions may undertake riskier and more speculative activities.

Yet the City of London and the British financial service industry continue to operate in a regulatory environment in which oversight is benign. Britain has continued to act as an attractive centre for the location of international financial institutions. Extensive offshore tax jurisdictions run as British dependencies and thus remain outside of the EU regulatory framework. The prominence of London in the 'Panama papers' and in the £180bn money laundering scandal of the London-based Danske Bank provide only two examples of a benign regulatory framework.

The Brexit-supporting economist David Blake (2018) notes that London is a dominant monopolistic centre for a wide range of financial transactions, responsible for some 40 per cent of Europe's assets under management; including 85 per cent of assets held by European hedge funds, a market share of 60 per cent of capital market transactions, 78 per cent of European foreign exchange trading, and 74 per cent of its derivatives trading. These are global institutions which advocate low regulatory oversight. Brexit for the financial services sector offers opportunities to resist greater regulatory control over non-EU transactions while possibly retaining the ability to engage in EU-based operations. Thus shortly after the decision to leave, banks and financial institutions operating within the City of London started to establish new subsidiaries in the EU to facilitate passporting or equivalence arrangements for European operations while retaining their operations within the City of London for non-EU activities. Jacob Rees-Mogg MP, leading campaigner for Brexit within the Conservative Party, for instance is partner in Somerset Capital Management, which has established operations in Dublin and Luxembourg to continue its European operations after Brexit.

Manufacturing goods

A final example of the impact of Brexit are internationally traded manufactured goods. The car industry in particular, a recent success in attracting foreign direct investment into the British economy, faces significant disruption to its supply chains. British warehousing organizations report record occupancy rates, and manufacturers of physical goods built up stock levels in the expectation that supply chains will lengthen as border checks and the processing of documentation increases.

Global manufacturers located in Britain have wanted to operate within the single market or at least the customs union. The Japanese manufacturers Toyota and Nissan have sought assurances to exempt the car industry from any new customs arrangements in post-Brexit Britain. Nissan's announcement to withdraw its investment in the next generation cars in Sunderland revealed that the British government had offered multimillion pound subsidies to limit the damage on their complex supply chains. For internationally integrated manufacturing interests whose supply chains involve international transportation networks, Brexit is a thread to their transaction, logistics and warehousing costs. Economies of scale within internationally traded manufacturing provide little benefit from an increasing influence within a small post-Brexit national market. To them, a larger integrated advanced market for consumers is all important. As Mike Hawes, Chief Executive of the Society of Motor Manufacturers and Traders identified:

> Leaving the EU, our biggest and most important trading partner, without a deal and without a transition period to cushion the blow would put this sector and jobs at immediate risk. 'No deal' must be avoided at all costs. Business needs certainty so we now need politicians to do everything to prevent irreversible damage to this vital sector. (SMMT, 2019)

Agency and praxis in business

These three examples demonstrate the differing potential impacts of Brexit on internationally trading sectors, demonstrating that the British economy is not represented by a singular identifiable interest group. Rather, it consists of a collection of competing and often conflicting interests. Both dominant views and agency nevertheless emerge as a result of an institutional hegemony created by particular interests in capital accumulation. Britain's pre-eminent role in the development of global finance capital encourages the development of government policies aligned with the interests of the most powerful sector of the British economy. Business elites with interests in agriculture may benefit from a restricted access of EU producers to their domestic market. Yet, as new trade agreements emerge, they lose out to lower cost production from major international exporters of agricultural goods.

International manufacturing interests face greater disruption in their globalized supply chains, and higher networking and coordination costs, as warehousing and logistical operations are redesigned. At the same time, the domestic market for manufacturing interests is unable to provide a sufficiently large market to ensure minimum efficient economies of scale. Here, manufacturers' agency requires an alteration of their systems to ensure either a greater focus upon national production, or leaving the UK and locating elsewhere within the European single market.

Government policy needs to balance competing interests and develop an interventionist industrial policy, as manufacturing capital requires support to access developed consumer markets in a post-Brexit economy. In agriculture, a replacement of EU subsidies is required to continue the development of a managed agricultural industry. Government policy towards international financial services, in contrast, seeks to resist further regulation of market activity. However, the dominance of financial services risks rendering the British state unable to provide support when a new financial crisis emerges. Iceland's experience of the 2008 financial crisis warns of the potential problems for an individual national government that cannot rely on coordinated European wide state intervention.

Working-class agency in Brexit Britain

The explanation in this chapter utilizes an understanding underpinned by the concepts of agency and praxis. An economic analysis also includes an interpretation of agency and praxis of the working class within the Brexit debates. The geographic pattern of Remain and Leave votes across the UK (see Chapter Cochrane) indicates that a singular uniform explanation for voting patterns is unlikely to capture the multifaceted elements of the referendum's outcome. Nevertheless, to examine working-class agency and praxis, this chapters turns to the impact of policy changes for the working population. In the following, austerity and poverty are means by which the interconnection of agency and class can be examined within the British working class.

British society has polarized around questions of inequality and poverty in similar ways to other advanced economies. The rise of far right and far left political formations are simply the party-political embodiment of a crisis that has emerged from the collapse of the centre ground within liberal democracies. Thomas Piketty's (2014) extensive study of income and wealth inequality in advanced economies demonstrates the impact of a higher return to asset wealth in contrast to returns to labour income through employment. Similar work by Milanovic (2016) identified the emergence of an 'elephant curve' depicting income inequality globally spanning an era of two decades from 1988. Milanovic demonstrates that the newly emerging working classes of the developing world, at the rear of the elephant, are rapidly catching up with the working classes of the developed world. In the developed world, those with middle incomes, along the back of the elephant, have seen stagnant and falling incomes, whilst the global business elites benefit from exceptional rises in income, as the elephant's trunk rises inexorably upwards towards the sky.

The impact of austerity policies in the UK is perhaps demonstrated most profoundly at the aggregate level of population life expectancy. Recent government data for life expectancy (ONS, 2018) shows a marked slowdown in the general upwards trend since 2011. Large scale public health improvements through sanitation, universal provision of health care, education and rising living standards have been associated with long-term trends towards rising life expectancy throughout the 20th century. However, just ten years after the collapse of Lehman Brothers, triggering austerity, the impact on life expectancy has already become detectable (Domantas, 2018). The rising tide of inequality, however, impacts on agency differentially, affecting popular attitudes towards government and economic policy (Varoufakis, 2016).

The evident decline in living standards and the socio-economic impact of austerity identified by Milanovic (2016), Piketty (2014) and Wilkinson and Pickett (2009) marked a sharp break from the ideological framework in which policy formation around austerity and poverty had been conceptualized. The growth of inequality and poverty under neoliberal economic policies was justified by a rhetoric of a return to individualism, the weakening social support from the state and a shift away from concepts of social security towards concepts of welfare. The ideology of conditionality, distinguishing between deserving and non-deserving recipients, has then increasingly been the central focus of welfare reform (see Chapter Forkert). This was in contrast to the emergence of universality and social solidarity underpinning the welfare state that emerged in the middle of the 20th century. As a consequence, free at the point of delivery principles in the health system are increasingly undermined by the introduction of additional payments and, still more draconian, checks on citizenship prior to treatment within the National Health Service.

Unlike the response of sector-specific businesses, working-class responses to Brexit are shaped by the lasting environment of austerity. According to Lukács, agency leads to active engagement of praxis. Working class influence on Brexit, however, is less evident in shaping government policy, making it the object rather than the subject of the Brexit debate (Lukács, 1990, pp 46–82). This lack of agency often makes it difficult to ascribe motivation within the working class within the apparently contradictory examples of working class agency over Brexit. The revival of left-wing ideas within the Labour Party under Jeremy Corbyn witnessed in the 2017 and 2019 general election campaigns had a strong social-liberal focus, similar to those in the earlier 2014 Scottish independence referendum. The Brexit referendum in 2016, in contrast, was ostensibly driven by insular, xenophobic demands of 'taking back control' and 'controlling our borders', and has typically been portrayed as the antithesis of Corbynism or demands for Scottish independence. Yet, there are much greater similarities between the three phenomena than is commonly considered. The Scottish referendum, Corbyn's electoral success and the Brexit referendum can all be seen as evidence of working-class agency in the face of an alienation towards government policies. The idea of 'taking back control' expresses a frustration with the absence of action to counter the impacts of austerity, poverty and inequality. This suggests that in their rejection of the status quo and support for Brexit, the 'left-out' working class (see Chapter Mckenzie) nevertheless exercise agency, or, in Bourdieu's (2000) terminology, 'acts of resistance'.

The key differences between the Scottish referendum and Corbynism with the Brexit referendum lies in the strong social movements which were evident in the former but lacking in the latter. Support for the Scottish National Party around the referendum and Corbynism in England were often associated with geographies of deprivation (see Chapter Cochrane). Similar geographical patterns can be found in the votes for Scottish independence and Brexit. The post-industrial Scottish city of Dundee provides one such example (Morelli, 2014). Dundee, a city with some of the highest levels of deprivation in the UK and with longstanding Labour Party and Communist Party traditions, became known as the YES city for supporting independence. At the same time, some 30 per cent of Yes voters in the Scottish independence referendum also voted for Leave in the EU referendum.

Conclusion

This chapter started from the perspective that Brexit was a political articulation of divergent business interests of large-scale oligopolistic and monopolistic business, which the outcome of the referendum has exacerbated and brought into sharper focus. Within the British economy, however, Brexit has come to be dominated by the sectoral interests of international aspects of finance capital embodied within the City of London. In contrast, agency within the working class has largely been absent in the Brexit debates despite demands for greater social provision.

To return to the question of how the rate of profit and austerity are linked, austerity has failed to resolve the structural difficulties of persistent low rates of profit. Despite holding down living standards to such a degree that life expectancy trends have stalled, the rate of profit for British capitalism remains low and productivity growth stubbornly weak. Investment decisions of manufacturing focused corporations themselves are being further undermined by Brexit exacerbating already low productivity growth. At the same time, as the EU referendum has shown, those who have suffered most from austerity are increasingly antagonistic to the dominant ideology of contemporary governance and respond with 'acts of resistance'.

References

Alvaredo, F., L. Chancel, T. Piketty, E. Saez and G. Zucman (2017) 'The elephant curve of global inequality and growth', *Working Paper,* December, World Inequality Lab.

Anderson, P. (1976) *Considerations on Western Marxism*, London: Verso.

Barnett, C. (1986) *The Audit of War: The Illusion and Reality of Britain as a Great Nation*, London: Macmillan.

Blackledge, P. (2004) *Perry Anderson, Marxism, and the New Left*, London: Merlin Press.

Blake, D. (2018) 'The City of London is strong enough to go it alone post-Brexit.' *Financial News*: https://www.fnlondon.com/articles/the-city-is-strong-enough-to-go-it-alone-post-brexit-20180606.

Bourdieu, P. (2000) *Acts of Resistance: Against the New Myths of Our Time*, Cambridge: Polity Press.

Department for Exiting the European Union (2018) *How to prepare if the UK leaves the EU with no deal. Guidance on how to prepare for Brexit if there's no deal*, Gov.uk: https://www.gov.uk/government/collections/how-to-prepare-if-the-uk-leaves-the-eu-with-no-deal.

El-Agraa A. M. (1990) 'The Common Agricultural Policy', in A. M. El-Agraa *Economics of the European Community* (3rd edn), Hemel Hampstead: Philip Allen, pp 187–217.

European Commission (2018), *Preparedness Notices*: https://ec.europa.eu/info/brexit/brexit-preparedness_en.

Harman, C. (2009) *Zombie Capitalism: Global crisis and the relevance of Marx*, London: Bookmarks.

Jasilionis, D. (2018) 'Reversals in life expectancy in high income countries?', *British Medical Journal*, 2018;362:k3399.

Lukács, G. (1990) *History and Class Consciousness*, London: Merlin Press.

Milanovic, B. (2016) *Global Inequality: A New Approach for the Age of Globalization,* Cambridge, MA: Harvard University Press.

Morelli, C. J. (2014) 'The Dutch disease: the role of industrial policy for industrial transformation – the case of the jute industry', *International Journal of Management Concepts and Philosophy*, 8(2/3): 156–87.

Nairn, T. (1981) 'The crisis of the British state', *New Left Review*, I(130).

National Farmers Union (2016) 'NFU Council agrees resolution on the EU referendum', *NFU Online*: https://www.nfuonline.com/news/latest-news/nfu-council-agrees-the-following-resolution-on-the/.

Olson, M. (1982) *The Rise and Decline of Nations: Economic Growth, Stagflation, and Social Rigidities*, New York: Yale University Press.

ONS (2018) *Changing trends in mortality: an international comparison: 2000 to 2016*, HMSO: Office of National Statistics.

Piketty, T. (2014) *Capital in the Twenty-First Century*, Cambridge, MA: Harvard University Press.

Roberts, M. (2016) *The Long Depression: How it happened, why it happened and what happens next*, Chicago: Haymarket.

SMMT (2019) *SMMT Statement on Brexit*, 15 January: https://www.smmt.co.uk/2019/01/smmt-statement-on-brexit-vote/.

Varoufakis, Y. (2016) *And the Weak Suffer What They Must?: Europe's Crisis and America's Economic Future,* London: The Bodley Head.

Wilkinson, R. and K. Pickett (2009) *The Spirit Level: Why more equal societies almost always do better*, London: Allen Lane.

7

Brexit Populism: Disenfranchisement and Agency

Marius Guderjan and Adrian Wilding

Introduction

Britain in a time of Brexit is a 'hotbed' of populist politics. Traditional party-political cleavages and the familiar spectrum of public debate have given way to a cross-party focus on the narrow issues of immigration, border control and sovereignty. Political opinion in England and Wales now shows increasing scepticism towards globalization and multiculturalism and a rise in nationalist and even xenophobic sentiment. Where Eurosceptics long sat on the political side lines, there is now a conscious sharing of Eurosceptic ideas by the main Westminster parties and the brazen use of populist rhetoric.

Though the current disruption of UK politics did not arise out of the blue, what concerns us particularly as political scientists is that Brexit Britain exposes the vulnerability of a multicultural civil society and a nominally liberal-democratic polity to subversion by a small but vociferous populist party. How was it possible for Britain, in particular for England, to slide into populism and for nationalist and xenophobic voices to become mainstream?

Brexit is a highly ambivalent phenomenon, one containing both rational and irrational elements. The rational element lies in its expression of legitimate discontent with social inequality, social exclusion and reduced life chances – for this reason the slogan 'take back control' rings true for so many. Indeed, an economic, political and cultural disenfranchisement of citizens dating back decades but exacerbated by recent government austerity policies is a key reason why populist ideas are gaining ground. The irrational element of Brexit lies in the very exploitation of this discontent by populist politicians and media for nationalist and secessionist ends. In these circumstances *agency* – the basic human need for self-determination – takes distorted forms.

This chapter puts agency at the heart of an understanding of Brexit Britain by showing ways in which the Leave vote is a misguided expression of dissatisfaction with the political, economic and social order. Brexit reveals – in estranged form – a widespread desire of a considerable number of citizens for deeper democratic responsiveness and for a recovery of political, economic and cultural agency. Agency is thus at the core of Brexit populism in two respects: it is fundamental to citizens' desire to 'take back control' which Leave voters exhibited and it is the reason why populism cannot fulfil that desire. This is so because only where individuals are able to act co-operatively rather than in antagonism and enmity (the enmity populism promotes) can they freely develop their collective potential and take autonomous, rational decisions, that is be agents in the full sense.

Agency and disenfranchisement

Agency is defined by Anthony Giddens in the following terms:

> To be able to 'act otherwise' means being able to intervene in the world, or to restrain from such intervention, with the effect of influencing a specific process or state of affairs. [...] Action depends on the capability of the individual to 'make a difference' to a pre-existing state of affairs or course of events. An agent ceases to be such if he or she loses the capability to 'make a difference', that is, to exercise some sort of power. (1984, p. 14)

The EU referendum, it seems, was just such an opportunity for individuals to 'act otherwise' and to 'make a difference'. As Wright explains:

> There are many lessons from the referendum, but a clear one is that many people now feel that they have little or no control over their lives. There is a sense of powerlessness that mocks the self-governing promise of democracy. In this context, the EU referendum seemed to offer an

opportunity to reclaim lost power over our laws, over our rulers, over our borders that was eagerly taken, despite the authoritative warnings about the dire economic consequences of doing so. (2017, p. 191)

The 'sense of powerlessness' Wright refers to can be traced back to a structure of socio-economic inequality and reduced life-chances which the established political parties have either been unable to change or have exacerbated. As Edmiston has argued:

Individuals may be notionally recognized as full and equal citizens of a given polity; however, they may also systematically lack the material, political and cultural resources necessary to exercise or attain their rights as citizens. [...] In turn, the uneven exercise of political agency shapes the configuration of citizenship and inequality. Importantly, this political agency should be understood as extending well beyond the conventional confines or representative democracy. [...] Within the context of rising structural inequality, the prevailing conditions of unequal citizenship have the capacity to serve the interests and ideals of those with the greatest social, economic or political agency. (2018, pp 8–9)

What Wright calls 'powerlessness' and Edmiston 'a lack of resources to exercise or attain rights' the authors term the *disenfranchisement* of citizens, a process that has economic, political and cultural dimensions. Disenfranchisement refers to a set of disintegrative dynamics encompassing alienation, powerlessness, fragmentation, uncertainty and what in German is called *Entmündigung*. Crucial here is that it involves a real or perceived loss of agency. Employing the concept of disenfranchisement makes it possible to understand voters' intentions, strategies, and opportunity costs when supporting the populist politics of the Leave campaign. Of course, the Leave constituency was and is socially diverse, coming from a range of socio-economic, demographic and geographical backgrounds. In particular, it is important to make sense of the split between the vote in rural and urban England and the fact that Leave voters form a minority in Scotland and Northern Ireland, all of which suggest there was more to the EU referendum than an irrational 'protest vote' and that a serious engagement with voters' lives, hopes, fears and self-understanding is needed.

Economic disenfranchisement

In England in particular, the EU referendum brought to light deep economic cleavages and a widespread sense of voters feeling 'left behind' by the development of the European single market and its 'four freedoms'. It saw statistically significant correlations between educational attainment, poverty, unemployment and the likelihood of voting Brexit: some of the poorest areas of England displayed particularly high support for Leave (Evans and Menon, 2017, pp 76–7). Such economic disenfranchisement results from an increasing gap between rich and poor, a 'squeeze' of the middle classes, and a reduction in public welfare. Though employment levels in the UK are officially high, a growing mass of 'working poor' remain dependent on a low (and sometimes circumvented) national minimum wage and on 'zero-hours contracts', creating a precarious workforce unable to share in wider social wealth. Austerity policies implemented by the Conservative government since 2010 have exacerbated these trends.

A comprehensive report by the Institute for Public Policy Research (2018) highlights how, despite record employment levels, a large part of the British population is stuck in precarious jobs and faces stagnant or falling living standards. The Gini Coefficient shows the UK to be one of the most unequal countries in Western Europe, with high levels of poverty and debt, evident in the massive growth of food banks in recent years (see Chapters Grasso and Montgomery, and Morelli). A deepening of inequality as a result of austerity policies has meant the further social exclusion and stigmatization of underprivileged groups, along with a shift from a participatory to a market-based, individualized model of citizenship (Cummins, 2018). Studies have shown that people who suffer most from austerity policies find it hardest to mobilize and develop lasting forms of collective action to defend their social rights, and tend instead to engage with short-term political issues (Edmiston, 2018, p. 143). In this context a one-off vote in a referendum surely provided a tempting opportunity to enact remedial change. Nevertheless, the correlation between poverty and the Leave vote does not hold universally. Scotland was an important exception: there, even areas of high poverty and unemployment saw clear majorities for Remain, suggesting that other factors are in play.

Political disenfranchisement

The vote to leave the EU was driven primarily by domestic rather than foreign politics. For a large number of voters (the EU referendum turnout was 72 per cent), many of whom were irregular voters (the turnout for the general elections in 2015 was 66.1 per cent), the Brexit referendum seems to have been an opportunity to give the political establishment 'a kick'. And though it is tempting thereby to dismiss the referendum result as an uninformed protest vote there is clearly more going on in voters' open disaffection with their representatives and their anger about a political 'elite'.

Disaffection with representatives and 'the establishment' has long been a feature of British politics. Numerous studies confirm a long-term decline in trust in politicians and mainstream parties, a phenomenon known as 'anti-politics' (cf. Stoker, 2011; Jennings et al, 2016). Citizens who believe their actions have a real impact are more likely to participate in political processes, whereas distrust tends on average to lead to disengagement (Dermondy et al, 2010, pp 422–4). Certainly this appears to be one explanation for the growth of right-wing populism in England and Wales. As Ford and Goodwin (2014, p. 270) have suggested, the UK Independence Party, which led the Leave campaign, 'are a first home for angry disaffected working-class Britons of all political backgrounds, who have lost faith in a political system that ceased to represent them long ago.'

The Westminster model of democracy with its majoritarian structure and system of disproportional representation is another cause of anti-political sentiment, producing electoral outcomes which 'large minorities of voters regard ... as illegitimate and distorted, since they rarely match votes shares' (Dunleavy, 2016). British politics has traditionally been a top–down and power-hoarding practice often unresponsive to and distant from citizens' needs. Devolution may have revived politics at the level of the nations but the 'reserve powers' mean Westminster retains the final say on decisive issues, alienating voters at the periphery. For commentators such as Wright the Brexit referendum has worsened rather than improved the state of British democracy:

> Britain's democracy has many real virtues, but its lack of a democratic moment, with its consequent failure to develop a vibrant culture of democratic citizenship, continues to mark its political life. [...] What this means is that we need to pay far more attention to the quality of democracy in Britain. The reason why the EU referendum campaign was such a depressing spectacle was that it reflected the worst aspect of our political culture. (2017, p. 195)

Cultural disenfranchisement

The referendum also exposed deep cultural cleavages in British society. Symptomatic of the referendum debate was a sharp divide between voters with outward-looking, multicultural and cosmopolitan views and those who orientate strongly towards a 'British' (or more often 'English') nation that – so they believe – is losing its cultural identity and sovereignty. As it happens, many Leave voters were not poor but 'middle class': in demographic terms they tended to be white, elderly and living in rural southern England – individuals who cannot really be classified as globalization's 'losers'. Yet the perception as well as the reality of disenfranchisement is important here: individuals who feel a status loss in comparison with others may develop a sense of being 'left behind'.

This paradox of the middle-class perception of being 'left behind' can best be understood as a sense of being sidelined by rapid social and cultural change (Evans and Menon, 2017, p. 84). In recent studies, a majority of English, particularly older cohorts, report feeling their country has 'changed in recent times beyond recognition' (Goodhart, 2017, p. 2). They perceive a wide array of 'threats to their national identity, values and ways of life' (Goodwin and Heath, 2016, p. 325). Certainly referendum campaigning saw a remarkable resurgence of ideas of national sovereignty and long-dormant discourses around the British empire. It seems that many voters feel disorientated by the speed of current social and cultural change and are finding comfort in the 'imagined community' (Anderson, 1983) of national identity.

Agency and populism

Populism is both value-laden and notoriously difficult to define. One key problem is that it implies a normality within democratic systems which populism destabilizes. But if populism is used to name any political movement, party or personality deviating from the democratic norm, no matter how wide that deviation, it becomes not merely a 'fuzzy concept' but may downplay the specificity of the right-wing movements which are the predominant form populism takes today. Current debates tend to present populism as an irritating deviation from a stable, well-functioning parliamentary democracy; in methodological terms, they court a functionalism that may allow critical analysis of the exception but not of the norm.

Populism as a 'thick' ideology

Considering the wide range of different political movements and politicians that have been labelled populist, it is clear that populism rests not on a specific political philosophy or theory but on its relationship to other ideologies. For many scholars, populism is at best a 'thin' ideology that lacks core values and so cannot be analyzed primarily in terms of its content. As their ideas and aims serve the pragmatic purposes of mobilizing support rather than forming cohesive ideological visions, populists tend to be chameleon-like and populism more of a style than an ideology.

Populists themselves typically adopt a narrow or single-issue focus or borrow from other ideologies. Without such 'thickening out', populism itself is 'colourless and can be of the left and of the right' (Jagers and Walgrave, 2007, p. 323). One common populist idea, for instance, is the call for direct participation of 'the people' in decision-making. In itself this idea could point to the right or left, and the possibility that a popular will exists for more participation and more say in British politics should not be dismissed out of hand. Indeed there are occasions where populist-style grassroots mobilizations 'generate formidable power, bringing down a regime; more rarely, they sometime manage to make a fresh start and to lay the foundations of a lasting political community' (Canovan, 2004, p. 252). Similarly, anti-elitism, a typical trait of populism, could normally be considered a 'healthy' element of democracy itself, and there is hardly any party or politician who does not appeal to 'the people'.

A more helpful insight from the literature is the distinction between 'inclusive' and 'exclusive' populism. Whereas 'inclusive' populists seek to overcome social domination by a small but powerful elite, 'exclusive populists' understand 'the people' as an ethnically or culturally homogeneous group whose identity is threatened by others (especially minorities). This distinction has the further merit of chiming with common-sense understandings of a left-right political spectrum: while both left- and right-wing populists present themselves as fighting for the people against an elite, the right mobilizes not only 'upwards' but more often 'downwards', stigmatizing particular social groups (usually of a lower status) such as ethnic or religious minorities and immigrants (Filc, 2011, p. 223). Whereas left-wing populists focus on socio-economic issues and inclusion (March, 2017, p. 285), Brexit populism often displays an illiberal face, particularly on such issues as nationalism, immigration, welfare and crime.

In the 1980s, cultural theorists Stuart Hall and Martin Jacques (1983) spoke of 'authoritarian populism', referring to the strong-arm governance that emerged under Margaret Thatcher's leadership. A discourse of 'law and order' and a privileging of 'security' over freedom were key parts of its ideological lexicon, often translating into calls for constraints on immigration and the mainstreaming of a repressive and disciplinary political culture. To this extent, immigration has long been an issue on the UK political agenda. What is novel in the present conjuncture is the success of a relatively small right-wing party in putting the issue at the centre of political debate. In the Brexit referendum, the cross-party Leave campaign all but adopted UKIP policy, nurturing and exploiting a hostile climate for immigrants particularly from Eastern Europe and the Middle East, but also non-white communities whose members have lived in the UK for generations.

It would be misleading, however, to reduce Brexit populism to a simple 'native vs. immigrant' divide. Older generations of British immigrants also tend statistically to support quotas on further immigration (the 'drawbridge' mentality). Nonetheless, rabble-rousing by populist politicians seriously aggravated the situation during referendum campaigning, with the result that many UK immigrants now report feeling acutely aware of their outsider status (see Chapters Forkert, and Nowicka).

For immigrants in the UK, the EU referendum has already limited their ability to live the lives they were used to. Not only are their longstanding rights now under threat; they suffer a range of ongoing discriminatory practices. They have become members of an 'out-group' confronted by an 'in-group' to whom populist politics is addressed. Shortly after the vote there were numerous reports across England of verbal abuse of immigrants, xenophobic social media commentary, the distribution of anti-migrant leaflets and physical attacks on Muslims and members of the black and Asian community. In the first week after the referendum, police reported 331 hate crimes, five times the weekly average. Emblematic of the violence latent in Brexit populism was the murder of Jo Cox, a pro-Remain MP, by a far right-extremist shouting "This is for Britain!".

At the same time as the agency of an out-group is constrained, that of the in-group is seemingly nurtured. By claiming to fight for those 'left behind' by globalization, Brexit populism raises hopes of reversing perceived losses of privilege and status. Such populist promises are dangerously misleading, though, and are only superficially driven by their professed aims. This becomes clearer when looking at the 'thin' ideology of Brexit populism.

Populism as a 'thin' ideology

The notion of a 'thin-centred ideology' addresses populists' lack of a comprehensive vision for 'the full spectrum of socio-political problems that the grand ideological families have customarily sought to provide' (Freeden, 2017, p. 2). So it is useful to view populism primarily as a specific strategy, method or communication style, one that can be exploited by political parties and media from across the political spectrum. Drawing on analyses of populism from a range of scholars, including Margaret Canovan (2004), Paul Taggart (2004), Benjamin Moffit and Simon Tormey (2014), and Michael Freeden (2017), one can identify a number of common stylistic elements that are not necessarily populist in themselves but become so in combination with other ideas.

A commonplace in populist rhetoric is an appeal to 'the people' against the political 'establishment', against a political 'caste' that has supposedly 'let the people down'. Populist politicians often present themselves as 'outsiders' who nevertheless know what 'the people' want, tending to deny the validity of the knowledge of experts, bureaucrats, technocrats, representatives and journalists. Against a background of increasing 'stylization' and 'mediatization' of politics, populism is particularly effective in attracting support through performance. Its proponents rely on drastically simplified communication and rhetorical tropes, such as political incorrectness, colloquialisms and disruption to distinguish themselves from the perceived unemotional and technocratic language of the political mainstream. Above all, populism addresses emotions, thriving on the perception of crisis, exploiting fears of immigration, economic recession and moral decay, presenting itself as a remedial agent for change and renewal.

It is not hard to see these strategies, methods and rhetorical tropes at work in the Brexit campaign and its aftermath. The Leave campaign was built on a drastic simplification of complex political issues and intensified use of rhetoric and misleading information. Thus UKIP famously warned of '15 million Turkish citizens coming to the UK', despite the fact that Turkey is not an EU member and any possible accession is a long way off. Leave's most contentious claim, splashed on the side of a bus, that the UK 'sends the EU £350 million a week', money that could be used to fund the NHS, likewise proved a salient issue with voters. It showed the power of a political debate permeated by half-truths and so-called fake news, whose rapid spread was clearly aided by social media. Shortly after their win, Leave campaigners distanced themselves from the £350m claim, along with their promises to stem immigration, their function apparently having been achieved.

In his victory speech in the early morning hours of 24 June 2016, UKIP's leader Nigel Farage can be seen 'summoning' a people – a unified British identity – and an enemy – multinationals, banks and a corrupt political elite:

> This, if the predictions now are right, this will be a victory for real people, a victory for ordinary people, a victory for decent people. We have fought against the multinationals, we have fought against the big merchant banks, we have fought against big politics, we have fought against lies, corruption and deceit. (BBC, 2016)

In the referendum's aftermath, populism has in turn shaped the debate about the *kind* of Brexit the government wants. Here a 'metropolitan-cosmopolitan elite' seeking to frustrate the 'will of the British people for Brexit' has been added to the list of enemies. Theresa May's speech at the Conservative Party conference in October 2016 was revealing in this regard:

> But today, too many people in positions of power behave as though they have more in common with international elites than with the people down the road, the people they employ, the people they pass in the street. But if you believe you're a citizen of the world, you're a citizen of nowhere. You don't understand what the very word 'citizenship' means. [...] Just listen to the way a lot of politicians and commentators talk about the public. They find your patriotism distasteful, your concerns about immigration parochial, your views about crime illiberal, your attachment to your job security inconvenient. (2016)

May, like Farage, draws upon a populist repertoire and drastically simplifies the issues around Brexit into a friend–foe divide. In a contradiction typical of populists, she inveighs against both a liberal press and commentariat as well as the very elites who traditionally support her party. In populist style, she terms the referendum result the 'will of the people', despite the very narrow majority for Leave, de-legitimizing the 48 per cent who voted Remain. Indeed since the vote, a largely pro-Brexit UK press has explicitly stigmatized the 48 per cent as 'Remoaners' while May's Conservative government has sought to block parliamentary debate on the terms of Brexit, citing the direct democracy of the referendum over the very representative system that elected them. Boris Johnson, who replaced May as Prime Minister in July 2019, was elected by about 90,000 members of the Conservative party – hardly 'the people'. In office, he continued to pursue his political agenda with drastic rhetoric and political incorrectness, and appointed a hardline right-wing cabinet. His uncompromising intentions became obvious when he sought to steamroller a No-Deal Brexit through Parliament by 'proroguing' the House and withdrawing the whip from any MPs (even former cabinet ministers) who opposed him. Brexit, it appears, has upended the traditional balance of parliamentary power and even threatened a constitutional crisis.

Brexit populism and the irony of agency

In his discussion of agency, Giddens (1984, pp 12–13) highlighted that though individuals reflect upon their actions, they are not necessarily aware of all the consequences of their actions. For instance, seemingly irrational actions may serve a social purpose and seemingly rational actions may have perverse effects. The Brexit vote was in large part driven by an active desire to overcome disenfranchisement. Yet an analysis of both thick and thin ideologies indicates that populists are unlikely to re-establish agency in any lasting way. The participation and direct democracy they promote seem not to be ends in themselves but mere means to the end of withdrawing the UK from the EU. The Leave campaign can only superficially be understood as mobilizing 'the people' against 'the elite' but, more worryingly, has cultivated an authoritarian and backward-looking ideology which has emboldened and enabled the spread of xenophobic views amongst the British population.

One germ of truth in populist arguments is that politics, British politics included, is often an elite vocation. But Brexit populism is no grassroots phenomenon, nor is it a deliberative or inclusive exercise. It is a continuation of elitism by other means: 'When Brexit populists repetitively voiced their mantra "take back control", it was "control" on their terms, not on the terms of those whose concerns they claimed to express, concerns that rankle at a much more fundamental level than the fear of immigration and the obsession with sovereignty' (Freeden, 2017, p. 5). Grassroots politics could be a means for British citizens to regain their agency. But such a politics must fundamentally challenge the structure of economic and political power which has disenfranchized them. The same applies to the political instrument of the referendum, as Eleftheriadis (2017, p. 187) has put it: 'Direct democracy, which limits decision to a one-off choice between two pre-selected alternatives, prevents full deliberation on the available options. Cutting off deliberation is the same thing as cutting off representation.' A referendum could, in theory, be a laudable exercise in direct democracy and participation, but it requires freely available impartial information and – on such a complex issue as the virtues or vices of EU membership and the precise future relationship to have with the EU – more than a simple binary question.

Conclusion

The rise of right-wing populism in the UK, especially in England, stems from a multi-layered and intertwined set of factors that can be termed disenfranchisement. Populism's appeal can be understood as the perversion of a desire to 'take back control' from economic, political and cultural structures which, over decades, have disempowered individuals and evoked a sense of injustice. The populist promise to fight the establishment and satisfy the various (and often contradictory) needs of neglected voters thus has a powerful and unifying appeal. Understanding the Brexit vote in this manner involves taking voters' concerns seriously though not simply at face value. While the authors have not condemned populism *per se*, they have underlined the threat that today's right-wing populism presents to a pluralist and multicultural civil society. It is highly unlikely that the disenfranchisement and lack of agency which Brexit populism exploits will be solved by a populist politics.

As the political and economic difficulties of leaving the EU become more and more evident, polls show considerable public reservation towards Brexit (particularly in Scotland and Northern Ireland) and regrets about the populist turn. Scotland may hold a key to Brexit's political dynamics. Since the EU referendum, Scotland has generated a decidedly more cosmopolitan debate on Europe, cultural identity, and migration, than that in England. While the Westminster-Holyrood divide appears on one level as a conflict between English and Scottish nationalisms, the Independence cause in Scotland is currently disproving the prejudice of it being a straightforwardly insular, tribal and backward-looking movement. It is, as McGarvey and Stewart (2016, p. 62) put it, 'less about the cultural superiority traditionally associated with nationalist movements, and far more to do with political empowerment. It forged a tenet of [...] 'civic' nationalism – a diverse and forward-thinking ideology, premised on the vision of Scotland as an open and equal society' with a European and global identity.

With Boris Johnson's move into 10 Downing Street populism has continued to dominate British politics. Outside of the Westminster bubble, however, there are signs of renewed and wide-reaching grassroots participation. Young people in particular have started to pose questions of political scientists' diagnosis of 'anti-politics'. The 2017 general election saw young British voters turn out in unprecedented numbers, as if to atone for their absence from the referendum. Social movements, such as 'Fridays for Future' and 'Extinction Rebellion', have brought tens of thousands of new political actors to the streets to protest the government's failure to tackle climate change. At present UK citizens seem increasingly prepared to broaden the terms of political debate and to place agency centre-stage. It remains to be seen whether these new developments can fundamentally challenge the populist turn.

References

Anderson, B. (1983) *Imagined Communities. Reflections on the Origin and Spread of Nationalism*, London: Verso.

BBC (2016) 'Nigel Farage says Leave win marks UK "independence day"', *BBC EU Referendum*, 24 June 2016.

Canovan, M. (2004) 'Populism for Political Theorists?', *Journal of Political Ideologies*, 9(3): 241–52.

Cummins, I. (ed.) (2018) *Poverty, inequality and social work: The impact of neoliberalism and austerity politics on welfare provision*, Bristol: Policy Press.

Dermody, J., S. Hamner-Lloyd and R. Scullion (2010) 'Young People and Voting Behaviour: Alienated youth and (or) an interested and critical citizenry?', *European Journal of Marketing*, 44(3/4): 421–35.

Dunleavy, P. (2016) 'How democratic is the UK's 'Westminster Plurality Rule' electoral system?', *Democratic Audit UK*, 11 January: http://www.democraticaudit.com/2016/01/11/how-democratic-is-the-uks-westminster-plurality-rule-electoral-system/.

Edmiston, D. (ed.) (2018) *Welfare, inequality and social citizenship: Deprivation and affluence in Austerity Britain*, Bristol: Policy Press.

Eleftheriadis, P. (2017) 'Constitutional Illegitimacy over Brexit', *The Political Quarterly*, 88(2): 182–8.

Evans, G. and A. Menon (eds) (2017) *Brexit and British Politics*, Cambridge: Polity Press.

Filc, D. (2011) 'Post-populism: explaining neo-liberal populism through the habitus', *Journal of Political Ideologies*, 16(2): 221–38.

Ford, R. and M. Goodwin (eds) (2014) *Revolt on the Right: Explaining support for the radical right in Britain*, London: Routledge.

Freeden, M. (2017) 'After the Brexit Referendum: revisiting populism as an ideology', *Journal of Political Ideologies*, 22(1): 1–11.

Giddens, A. (ed.) (1984) *The Constitution of Society. Outline of the Theory of Structuration*, (1997 reprint), Cambridge: Polity Press.

Goodhart, M. (ed.) (2017) *The Road to Somewhere: The Populist Revolt and the Future of Politics, London*: Hurst & Company.

Goodwin, M. and O. Heath (2016) 'The 2016 Referendum, Brexit and the Left Behind: An Aggregate-level Analysis of the Result', *The Political Quarterly*, 87(3): 323–32.

Hall, S. and M. Jacques (eds) (1983) *The Politics of Thatcherism*, London: Lawrence & Wishart.

Institute for Public Policy Research (2018) 'Prosperity and Justice: A Plan for the New Economy', *The Final Report of the IPPR Commission on Economic Justice*, Cambridge: Polity Press.

Jagers, J. and S. Walgrave (2007) 'Populism as political communication style: An empirical study of political parties' discourse in Belgium', *European Journal of Political Research*, 46(3): 319–45.

Jennings, W., G. Stoker and J. Twyman (2016) 'The Dimensions and Impact of Political Discontent in Britain', *Parliamentary Affairs*, 69(4): 876–900.

March, L. (2017) 'Left and right populism compared: *The British case*', *The British Journal of Politics and International Relations*, 19(2): 282–303.

May, T. (2016) 'Theresa May's conference speech in full', *The Telegraph*, 5 October.

McGarvey, N. and F. Stewart (2016) 'European, not British? Scottish Nationalism and the EU Referendum', in M. Guderjan (ed.) *The Future of the UK: Between Internal and External Divisions*, Berlin: Centre for British Studies, pp 59–70.

Moffit, B. and S. Tormey (2014) 'Rethinking Populism: Politics, Mediatisation and Political Style', *Political Studies*, 62(2): 381–97.

Stoker, G. (2011) 'Anti-Politics in Britain', in R. Heffernan, P. Cowley and C. Hay (eds) *Developments in British Politics*, 9, London: Palgrave Macmillan, pp 152–73.

Taggart, P. (2004) 'Populism and representative politics in contemporary Europe', *Journal of Political Ideologies*, 9(3): 269–88.

Wright, T. (2017) 'Democracy in Britain: Retrospect and Prospect', *The Political Quarterly*, 88(2): 189–97.

8

A Sovereign People? Political Fantasy and Governmental Time in the Pursuit of Brexit

John Clarke

> May faced a choice between a fantasy Brexit, designed only to gratify a minority who are immune to gratification, and real Brexits that require compromise on every side. It wasn't an appealing decision, but nor was it a hard one. (Behr, 2018)

There has been an outpouring of journalistic and academic writing that has used the idea of fantasy to describe and critique Brexit (see, for example, Gearty, 2016; Nawratek, 2017; Newbigin, 2017; Eaglestone, 2018; Shariatmardi, 2018). It has been one widely used figure through which to address both the political leadership (of the campaign to leave and of the Conservative Party in government) and the popular support for Leave. Much of the time, 'fantasy' has been deployed as an image driven by liberal scepticism – denoting the apparently ill-informed, misguided and potentially disastrous project of leaving the EU. It has been frequently expressed in the image of searching for 'unicorns' as a way of registering the triumph of fantasy and desire over rationality (for example, Rigby, 2019). It is not the aim here to treat fantasy in these terms, as marking a politics that is explicitly or implicitly contrasted with hard-headed realism or rational political decision-making. Too much of the debate around Brexit has found it convenient to dismiss the vote to leave in such terms. However, this does not mean abandoning the idea of fantasy: this chapter is more interested in how fantasy may be a productive way of thinking about processes of political articulation and mobilization – offering a means of addressing projections and promises that find political purchase. The chapter certainly does not assume that only the Leave campaign traded in affective politics that involved the use of collective fantasies: the campaign to remain was dubbed 'Project Fear' by the Leave campaign for good reason, and contrasted the projected economic misery outside the EU with images of other empowered (largely consumerist) futures for UK citizens should they make the 'reasonable' choice.

In the context of Brexit, then, one might pay attention to specific aspects of political-cultural fantasy work that project a double dynamic of loss and restoration; examples of what Paul Gilroy has described as melancholia, borrowing and adapting the term from Freud to explore the postcolonial condition in Britain. He suggests that the condition of postcolonial melancholia results from the country's refusal to face up to the end of an empire that was foundational for its economic, social and political arrangements. Rather than the collective culture working through this sense of loss, Britain refuses to address both the history of empire (except as a mercantilist and a civilizing project) and the implications of its loss. Instead, he argues, Britain is trapped in a collective pathology which manifests itself in mood swings that switch from 'racist violence [as] an easy means to 'purify' and re-homogenize the nation' that is sometimes the condition for 'shame-faced tides of self-scrutiny and self-loathing', to 'outbursts of manic euphoria' of national celebration (Gilroy, 2004, p. 102). As Gary Younge (2016) among others has claimed, this long history is intertwined with the promise of Brexit: the restoration of (imperial) greatness, the celebration of a sovereign nation and the recovery of a lost 'way of life'.

This chapter explores the central place that ideas of British sovereignty played in the referendum campaign and its aftermath. In particular, it shows how the conception of the nation as a sovereign people was central to the political mobilization through the promise to 'take back control' and how this idea has persisted as a key reference point for continuing conflicts over Brexit. This promise to 'take back control' acted as a representation of *collective agency*, evoking an idea of restoring power to the people in a variety of ways. This has formed a potent but troubling coupling of fantasy (as a mode of political mobilization) and agency, making the projection of collective agency vital for the political alignments that the campaign to leave the EU constructed. Subsequently, the chapter examines the disjuncture that emerged between the distinctive populist temporality of the Leave campaign (the promise of immediate liberation) and the return of governmental temporality (the long march through the institutions). In doing so, it draws on and develops Taguieff's (2007) insight that populist political discourse suspends time in favour of a continuous present. By contrast, the negotiation of Brexit has restored different temporalities (of negotiation, of constitutional reform, of parliamentary debate and more). In this process, the fantasy of the sovereign people and Brexit as an expression of collective agency has continued to play a central role in the paranoid denunciation of delay, doubt and dissent.

A sovereign people?

The political conflict over the UK's membership of the EU articulated around the 2016 referendum was dominated by questions of sovereignty, particularly the Leave campaign's desire to bring about a restoration of political sovereignty from Brussels to Westminster. Sovereignty has emerged as a contemporary keyword in response to the dynamics of its displacement, rearrangement and disciplining by transnational dynamics, most evidently those driven by neo-liberal globalization. Wendy Brown has argued that:

> While it is no news that nation-state sovereignty is challenged by global movements of capital and the growing power of transnational legal, economic and political institutions, the other forces are less often recognized as part of political sovereignty's undoing. These include the political rationalities of neoliberalism, transnational moral and legal discourses, along with activations of power related to, but not reducible to capital – those that traffic under the sign of culture, ideology and religion. Meanwhile forces sustaining or shoring up nation-state sovereignty are few and tend to be backward looking – for example, nationalism, despotism and imperialism. (Brown, 2010, pp 22–3)

Nation states have occupied a critical place as the creators and guarantors of the political, social and cultural conditions for neo-liberalization and renewed capital accumulation: constructing consent, policing emergent crises and managing contradictions (even while dismembering particular state apparatuses). At the core of this process has been the welfare state and Claus Offe's famous contradiction: 'The contradiction is that while capitalism cannot co-exist *with*, neither can it exist *without*, the welfare state' (1984, p. 153; emphasis in the original).

We have seen forty years of constant innovation – varieties of welfare reform and state reform – attempting to resolve this contradiction, often creating new welfare apparatuses that are more disciplinary. Such reforms have developed models of 'corporate welfare' while making social welfare increasingly anti-social (responsibilizing welfare, 'do-it-yourself' welfare and welfare as surveillance and scrutiny). Despite this, the contradiction persists, not least because of the glaring failures of neo-liberalization, including growing inequality, social dislocation and the inability to meet the most basic human needs. As recent national-populist political movements have understood, people still look to nation states to provide support and well-being, even if these movements have constructed those desires in nationalist/nativist terms – welfare for 'our people'.

As a result, it is not surprising that so many current political projects – including Brexit – deal in this hyphenated complexity, offering to rescue both the nation-as-people and the nation-as-state. These restorationist promises centre on a strange combination of 'sovereignty' and the 'way of life' associated with the people that underpins the commitment to 'make X great again'. These contemporary nationalisms come in different forms and imagine the rearrangement of the nation's relationship to the global in different ways. Some claim to step out of the circuits of neoliberal globalization by renegotiating the terms of membership or trade (such as Trump's trade wars and attacks on multilateral institutions such as the United Nations and International Criminal Court, for example). Others (Modi's Hindu nationalism, for instance) seek an expanded place in the global economy. The UK's Conservative government has offered a vision of a post-Brexit UK that would transcend the narrow confines of Europe by leading a new era of global free trade:

> A truly Global Britain is possible, and it is in sight. And it should be no surprise that it is. Because we are the fifth biggest economy in the world. Since 2010 we have grown faster than any economy in the G7. And we attract a fifth of all foreign investment in the EU. We are the biggest foreign investor in the United States. We have more Nobel Laureates than any country outside America. We have the best intelligence services in the world, a military that can project its power around the globe, and friendships, partnerships and alliances in every continent. We have the greatest soft power in the world, we sit in exactly the right

time zone for global trade, and our language is the language of the world. (May, 2016)

Such projections of the post-Brexit future emerge in the contradictions of the fraught location occupied by the nation-state in the interstices of neo-liberal globalization. They combine past, present and future in unsettling ways, locating past greatness alongside present debilitation and future triumph.

Wendy Brown's analysis connects the experience of 'waning sovereignty' with the rise of 'walled states' and while the UK may not be engaged in the project of wall building, the withdrawal from the EU was demanded in familiar terms – notably the capacity to control 'our own borders'. Sovereignty, as Gordon has argued, occupied a central but confusing place in the Leave campaign, involving a conflation of 'internal' sovereignty aspects (the constitutional location of sovereignty in parliament) and 'external' forms (the UK's capacity to act as a state 'engaged in supranational and international systems and relationships') (2016, p. 335). Such confusions have been politically and governmentally consequential in arguments about the proper location of sovereignty and about the composition of the nation, not least in relation to the border between the UK and the Republic of Ireland (and the EU). The chapter will come back to these issues later, but here it is important to draw a distinction between expert knowledge about constitutional questions and the political imagining of sovereignty as a site in which national virility and popular agency are condensed. Sovereignty in this sense is the bearer of potent fantasies about power – and powerful fantasies about potency.

Imagining agency: 'Take back control'

It may be productive to focus on one particular aspect of political-cultural fantasy that concerns the issue of agency – the central Brexit promise of 'taking back control'. This promise was central to the campaign and to its capacity to mobilize a wide constituency of disaffected groups (see Jeremy Gilbert on 'disaffected consent', 2015). As the author has argued elsewhere, the Leave campaign was able to articulate a variety of disaffections and senses of loss (Clarke, 2019). These include the economic dislocation of de-industrialization (starting in the early 1980s); the cultural dislocation of the 'way of life' premised on full male employment in Fordist capitalism, in which work, family and the state (especially the welfare state) were articulated in what are now cast as 'traditional' ways (see, for example, Williams, 1989; Jessop, 1993; Clarke, 2013). Tzouvala suggests that the profound sense of *loss* can also be understood as a distinctively neoliberal 'structure of feeling' (even as it draws on multiple sources): 'this real sense of "loss of control" is not only linked to the transfer of decision-making to supranational bodies, but also a direct consequence of the inherent logic of neoliberalism' (2017, p. 122). Disaffections also involve the postcolonial melancholia noted earlier, in which that 'way of life' was bound up in intimate ways with a profoundly racialized sense of Britishness, and, perhaps more importantly, Englishness. In the moment of Brexit, the United Kingdom, Great Britain, Britishness and Englishness performed endless substitutions, with the precise reference slipping and sliding. Frustrations also piled up around a sense of being ignored by the political classes, intensified by the willingness of those leaders to distribute misery through post-2008 austerity policies (see Chapters Montgomery and Grasso, Mckenzie, and Morelli). Equally significant were the multiple feelings of loss and displacement associated with social and political and cultural changes associated with a range of 'equality' projects – around gender, sexuality and race. It is no coincidence that older white men in England and Wales were at the core of the 'rage' expressed in the Vote Leave campaign.

David Cameron's ill-advised choice to propose a referendum on the EU encountered this maelstrom of disaffections – the decision itself a perverse confirmation of how 'out of touch' Westminster's political classes had become. The political form of the referendum loosened established political affiliations and simplified matters into the binary Yes/No vote. It created the possibility of these disaffections finding a voice. More precisely, the Leave campaign offered a very selective voicing of disaffection, ventriloquizing some varieties and ignoring or silencing others, particularly those about the degradation of waged work, the de-socialization of public life, and the diminished capacity of the state to protect and support those in need. What 'taking back control' signified was the possibility of a form of collective agency – seized on by those who felt themselves 'powerless' in political terms. Insa Koch (2017) has argued that the referendum was 'a chance to reject government tout court and to say no to a system of representative democracy that many have come to experience in punitive terms'. At the heart of the Brexit question, then, is this fantastic projection of individual and collective agency – the sense that control could be taken back, could be exercised and could be brandished in the faces of those who – in some form or another – had taken control away from 'us'. In these ways, the Leave campaign – and its potent slogan – offered a prospect of political agency: the chance to act effectively to bring about change and to redress grievances. The long and profoundly disenchanting rule of neo-liberalizing governments of whatever party alienated many from formal political processes, as measured in declining electoral turnout and party membership. As William Davis (2016) has argued, the slogan itself was central to this promise of agency:

> In this context, the slogan 'take back control' was a piece of political genius. It worked on every level between the macroeconomic and the psychoanalytic. Think of what it means on an individual level to rediscover *control*. To be a person without control (for instance to suffer incontinence or a facial tick) is to be the butt of cruel jokes, to be potentially embarrassed in public. It potentially reduces one's independence. What was so clever about the language of the Leave campaign was that it spoke directly to this feeling of inadequacy and embarrassment, then promised to eradicate it. The promise had nothing to do with economics or policy, but everything to do with the psychological allure of autonomy and self-respect. Farrage's [sic] political strategy was to take seriously communities who'd otherwise been taken for granted for much of the past 50 years.

While the fantasy of individual and collective agency is encapsulated in the very act of 'taking', the other two terms of the promise, 'back' and 'control', are more ambiguous. Many of the issues that swirled around the moment of Brexit have never been the subject of popular, nor even parliamentary, control. Most evidently missing from the list of liberal democracy's sites of citizen or popular control is economic democracy: the state of the UK economy (and its uneven social consequences) has haunted every discussion of Brexit but the question of control remained mute. How was control to be exercised over the City of London and the flows of finance capital, or the 'British' car industry (largely foreign-owned) or even those generators of the 'new economy', such as Amazon, Uber and the like? Equally, if 'taking *back*' implied a history of power exercised by the people, then this is a rather idiosyncratic reading of British history, in which both the economy and the state have proved remarkably resistant to popular control. In a rather different way, the question of the sites, forms and effectiveness of 'control' has become increasingly tangled in the aftermath of the referendum. Instead, it might be useful to consider the fantasy of agency promised in the referendum as one of those characteristic 'magical solutions' to which popular politics – and popular culture – have been prone.

The concept of magical solutions has played a significant role in cultural studies: for example, in Hall and Jefferson (1976), the idea was used to talk about youth subcultures wrestling with pressing contradictions in working-class experience but being only able to find resolutions to them in the realm of the symbolic. In the case of Brexit, the promised resolution to the accumulating experiences of disempowerment, disaffection and despair may also have failed to materially resolve the problems of control. The one-shot exercise of agency in the referendum vote has, so far, proved frustrating in many registers, generating both renewed despair and unleashing new waves of frustration and anger among *both* Brexiteers and Remainers.

Making Brexit mean Brexit? Time, space and sovereignty

When the result of the referendum was confirmed, Nigel Farage celebrated by describing it as the UK's 'Independence Day': 'We have broken free from a failing political union. We have managed, the little people, the ordinary people who have ignored all the threats that have come from big business and big politics and it has been a huge, amazing exercise in democracy' (Nigel Farage, 24 June 2016). However, it has been a difficult – and as yet unfinished – transition to independence, echoing difficulties that other independence projects have previously encountered. The attempt to make Brexit come true in practice has occurred at the uncomfortable intersection of two very different types of temporality. On the one hand, the promise of Brexit was articulated in what Pierre-André Taguieff has described as the distinctive temporality of populism, in which historical time is replaced by a continuous and immediate present, embodied in a promise to efface 'any distance between all desires and their realisation' (2007, p. 16; the author's translation). Here we can see the temporality of Farage's proclaimed 'Independence Day' and the recurring insistence that Brexit must be delivered, no matter what obstacles might appear.

On the other hand, there has been a return to what might be called 'political-governmental time' in which treaties need to be remade, negotiations need to be conducted, economic and political relationships need to be reconstructed and timetables, schedules and plans need to be established. Suddenly, the promise of immediate liberation became enmeshed in the different temporality of institutional or governmental politics. Moving from the Brexit vote to Britain's departure from the EU has involved dismantling existing institutionalized formations, embedded in treaties, maps, legislation, governmental ordering, sets of habituated relationships, practices and places, and forms of affiliation and attachment. Brexit required the enactment and instantiation of the desired new order in the same registers of institutionalization and normalization.

All of these insert a form of historical time between the referendum vote and the materialization of the decision in a new ordering of things. Time, in this sense, is intrinsic to the worlds of policy and politics, even though it may also be used as a device for the management of policy and politics (Pollitt, 2008). Frustrated Brexiteers have recurrently accused 'enemies of the people' of using time (delay, blocking, foot-dragging, etc.) as a means to deflect, or at least delay, the UK's exit from the EU. This may well be true, but the populist desire for immediate consummation seems ill-equipped to deal with political-governmental time – and points to a landscape of further disaffection. In the process, it might be noted, the central populist ideas of 'the people' shrinks to include only those who voted to leave: the true believers, the real people (see Chapter Guderjan and Wilding).

The efforts to make Brexit materialize have produced new *disorders* of space, scale and sovereignty as multiple social, political, governmental and constitutional problems have emerged. In this context, this chapter will only touch on the question of how united the United Kingdom might be, which is picked upon in other contributions to this volume. The UK has always been a complex political and constitutional formation that combines four political-cultural spaces: England, Wales, Northern Ireland and Scotland. In the last twenty years, that formation became more complicated through power-sharing arrangements in the north of Ireland which softened the border between the North and the Republic of Ireland, and through the creation of forms of devolved government in Scotland and Wales.

Brexit has unsettled the spatial and scalar arrangements of the UK in several ways. First, it marked a degree of political-cultural separation between England and Wales on the one hand where majorities voted Leave, and Scotland and Northern Ireland which both supported Remain. The effects of these divisions have been visible in discontent about the perceived effects of English dominance of the UK (see Chapter Stolz). The spatial and scalar problems of maintaining a union become more complex still in the case of Northern Ireland (see Chapter Birrell and Carmichael). One outcome of the peace process in the 1990s was the erasure of the former 'hard border' between the North and the Republic (see, for example, Gilmore, 2017). All three governments involved, the UK, the Republic of Ireland and the parties of the Northern Ireland Assembly, have been reluctant to restore a 'hard border' between the UK and the EU. Yet control of 'our borders' forms a central promise of the Leave campaign's imagining of sovereignty.

It is, indeed, the issue of sovereignty that has proved most disorderly after Brexit. The referendum produced much political turmoil, not least in contests over the leadership of the Conservative, Labour and UKIP parties. The Conservative Party in government found itself the inheritor of the result and its new leader, Theresa May, announced that 'Brexit means Brexit' in the face of political disaffection within her own party, as well as within parliament more widely. The government would act, she insisted, to trigger Article 50 (the legal device to begin disentangling the UK and the EU), but this announcement produced a constitutional conflict about the form and location of sovereignty. This came to centre on whether it was the government or parliament that could trigger Article 50, with the Prime Minister insisting that it was the government's choice while many MPs and legal commentators argued that it was a decision for parliament.

In a dramatic intervention, an entrepreneur, philanthropist and activist, Gina Miller, led a campaign that sought a judicial review of this issue. The Supreme Court adjudicated in 2017 that constitutional sovereignty (in the capacity to trigger the Article dissociating the UK from the EU) was embodied in parliament – a decision that led to accusations of treason against both the judges and those who brought the case – notably the evidently 'unBritish' Gina Miller. Miller attracted much hostility. She was subjected to death and rape threats, castigated as a member of the liberal/cosmopolitan London elite and attacked for not being British, despite holding British citizenship, not least from the 4th Viscount St Davids:

> Rhodri Philipps, the 4th Viscount St Davids, was jailed on July 13 for writing a number of racially and abusive posts [sic] on Facebook. One post read: "£5,000 for the first person to 'accidentally' run over this bloody troublesome first generation immigrant." Philipps, of Knightsbridge, central London, also called her a "f---ing boat jumper" four days after Ms Miller, 52, won a landmark High Court challenge against the Government. (*The Telegraph*, 2017)

Meanwhile, the three judges who made the ruling were denounced as 'enemies of the people', who were thwarting the popular will. In one of the more constitutionally accurate, if politically puzzling, twists, they were also criticized for being 'unelected'.

Much of this attack was led by sections of the tabloid press, who have identified a rich stream of popular rage to be tapped in the fantasy of 'sovereignty'. The singularity of Brexit – 'Brexit means Brexit' – is passionately defended as the 'Will of the People' and this is articulated in the same populist/anti-elitist register developed in the campaign. This 'muscular populism' denounces any attempt to undermine the 'popular will' in a recurrently racist and misogynistic repertoire. It deploys a repertoire of vitalist masculine tropes: inviting opponents to 'stop whining', 'suck it up', 'grow some balls' and so on. Those identified by the tabloid press as the 'Remoaners' are pictured as willing to try any ploy to defeat, delay or deflect the decision to leave. In this process, the governmental complexity of locating and enacting sovereignty is trumped by the clarion declaration that 'we won'.

The negotiation of governmental complexity (and governmental time) against this populist simplification and its temporality remains a central site of contestation – and one of the terrains of potential political mobilization. Different temporalities thus form one strand of the complexities of the long drawn out moment of Brexit, wonderfully summarized by Bob Jessop in the following:

> Brexit is so polyvalent a notion and so complex a process that its present meaning is hard to define and its future trajectory hard to discern. Over the next two to three years, we are likely to observe a process akin to a three-dimensional chess game with many participants and even more stakeholders playing according to uncertain rules open to contested renegotiation. (Jessop, 2017, p. 129)

Beyond fantasy: collective agency and the problem of politics

Treating the promise to 'take back control' as a fantasy of collective agency is linked to the question of political futures and to the issue of how the felt 'loss of control' has been and might be mobilized. Gerbaudo has posed this question in terms of how the return of sovereignty returns issues of collective power to the political agenda: 'The return *en auge* of the question of sovereignty in current political debates bespeaks the profound crisis of neoliberalism, and the way its agony and the connected opening of a post-neoliberal horizon, is reviving demands for collective control over politics and society' (Gerbaudo, 2016). While accepting his framing of the question, this chapter suggests two possible – and diametrically opposed – lines of potential development. The first builds on the current right-wing mobilizations of power and control, linking them to regressive and exclusivist notions of sovereignty in which the search to restore past powers – and glories – is the dominant framing. The problematic dynamic of these moves concerns the likely frustrations, failures and unfulfilled promises of such programmes, possibly intensifying the senses of loss. This might be fertile ground for a new anti-politics in which the people come to feel betrayed or abandoned by another political leadership, confirming their disaffection from politics all over again. Neither resentful immobilization nor the potential search for a 'strong man' who claims to transcend politics are attractive prospects.

The alternative is the development of a progressive politics of popular sovereignty that took the search for collective power and control seriously – and extended its reach into the hitherto insulated or resistant domains of society, not least the economy. Attending to economic exclusion, dispossession and its unevenly distributed effects (from private wealth to degraded public services) might be a terrain on which a longer term politics of democratic agency might be developed whose range could extend well beyond the economic, transforming the institutionalized systems of power and inequality in the process. It might even bring about an expansive and inclusive conception of 'the people' and the popular.

Acknowledgements

I am grateful to the organizers of the initial workshop for the invitation to take part and for the subsequent request to write this chapter. I am also grateful to Janet Newman for her comments on an earlier draft, without which it would be much worse.

References

Behr, R. (2018) 'May is chasing a fantasists' Brexit. She must change course now', *The Guardian*, 23 April.

Brown, W. (2010) *Walled States, Waning Sovereignty*, New York: Zone Books.

Clarke, J. (2013) 'Widersprüche des heutigen Wohlfahrtsstaates' (Contradictions of the welfare state today), *Sozialwissenschaftliche Literatur Rundschau*, 67: 68–81.

Clarke, J, (2019) 'A sense of loss? Unsettled attachments in the current conjuncture,' *New Formations*, 98–97: 132–46.

Davies, W. (2016) *Thoughts on the Sociology of Brexit*, http://www.perc.org.uk/project_posts/thoughts-on-the-sociology-of-brexit/.

Eaglestone, R. (ed.) (2018) *Brexit and Literature*, London: Routledge.

Gearty, C. (2016) *On Fantasy Island: Britain, Europe, and Human Rights*, Oxford: Oxford University Press.

Gerbaudo, P. (2016) *Post-neoliberalism and the politics of sovereignty*, https://www.opendemocracy.net/paolo-gerbaudo/post-neoliberalism-and-politics-of-sovereignty.

Gilbert, J. (2015) 'Disaffected consent: that post-democratic feeling', *Soundings: a Journal of Politics and Culture*, 60: 29–41.

Gilmore, A. (2017) 'Hard Borders of the Mind: Brexit, Northern Ireland and the Good Friday Agreement', *European Council on Foreign Relations*, 13 April: http://www.ecfr.eu/article/commentary_hard_borders_of_the_mind_brexit_northern_ireland_and_the_7273.

Gilroy, P. (2004) *Postcolonial Melancholia*, New York, Columbia University Press.

Gordon, M. (2016) 'The UK's Sovereignty Situation: Brexit, Bewilderment and Beyond…', *King's Law Journal*, 27(3): 333–43.

Hall, S. and T. Jefferson (eds) (1976) *Resistance through Rituals: Youth subcultures in Postwar Britain*, London: Routledge (originally published as *Working Papers in Cultural Studies 6/7*).

Jessop, B. (1993) 'Towards a Schumpeterian Workfare State? Preliminary remarks on post-Fordist political economy', *Studies in Political Economy*, 40: 7–39.

Jessop, B. (2017) 'The Organic Crisis of the British State: Putting Brexit in its Place'. *Globalizations*, 14(12): 133–41.

Koch, I. (2017) 'What's in a vote? Brexit beyond culture wars', *American Ethnologist*: http://onlinelibrary.wiley.com/doi/10.1111/amet.12472/full.

May, T. (2016) 'Britain after Brexit: a Vision of a Global Britain', *Speech to Conservative Party Conference*, 2 October: https://www.politicshome.com/news/uk/political-parties/conservative-party/news/79517/read-full-theresa-mays-conservative.

Nawratek, K. (2017) 'Lonely Island in Big World: Brexit as Imperial Fantasy', *Aspen Review*, 03: https://www.aspenreview.com/article/2017/lonely-island-big-world-brexit-imperial-fantasy/.

Newbigin, E. (2017) *Brexit, nostalgia and the Great British Fantasy*, https://eprints.soas.ac.uk/25232/1/newbigin-opendemocracy.net-brexit-nostalgia-and-the-great-british-fantasy.pdf.

Offe, C. (1984) *Contradictions of the Welfare State*, edited by John Keane, London: Hutchinson.

Pollitt, C. (2008) *Time, Policy, Management: Governing with the Past*, Oxford: Oxford University Press.

Rigby, B. (2019) 'Sky Views: Tories inhabit a fantasy world of Brexit unicorns and magic money trees', *Sky News*, 3 July: https://news.sky.com/story/sky-views-tories-inhabit-a-fantasy-world-of-brexit-unicorns-and-magic-money-trees-11755613.

Shariatmardi, D. (2018) 'The EU is right to say that Britain is 'chasing a fantasy'. That's all Brexit ever was', *The Guardian*, 25 May.

Taguieff, P. A. (2007) *L'Illusion Populiste*, Manchecourt: Editions Flammarion (1st edn, 2002).

The *Telegraph* (2017) 'Viscount jailed for Facebook threat against Gina Miller abandons appeal', *The Telegraph*, 28 August.

Tzouvala, N. (2017) 'Chronicle of a Death Foretold? Thinking About Sovereignty, Expertise and Neoliberalism in the Light of Brexit', *German Law Review*, 17: Brexit Special Supplement, 117–24.

Williams, F. (1989) *Social Policy: A Critical Introduction*, Cambridge: Polity Press.

Younge, G. (2016) 'Brexit: a disaster decades in the making', The *Guardian*, 30 June.

9

'Not an International Health Service': Xenophobia, Brexit and the Restoration of National Sovereignty

Kirsten Forkert

The chapter begins with the question about how both agency and loss of agency are constructed within the context of the 'hostile environment' approach to immigration, and in the lead-up to the Brexit vote, where immigrants' use of the National Health Service (NHS) and more generally the welfare state became a contested site. This chapter explores how immigrants' use of healthcare was produced as a problem in need of policy intervention and harsh rhetoric. It will explain how new forms of agency (specifically the outsourcing of immigration controls), and new forms of obligation were created by a hostile environment. The chapter also examines claims for agency that had been lost (control over who can or cannot access public services) which are presented as in need of recuperation. In conceptualizing agency, the chapter uses John Clarke's theorization of agency in relation to contexts animating actions (2013). Clarke asks how contexts 'make things thinkable (in Foucault's sense), possible, relevant, desirable and necessary' or might 'produce the obverse effects (making some things unthinkable, impossible, irrelevant, undesirable and unnecessary)' (2013, p. 24). Contexts shape how we might '[imagine] the problem', 'provide languages for naming the problem and frame the sorts of remedial action or solution that might be seen as reasonable to pursue' (2013, p. 24).

The contexts discussed in this chapter are neoliberal rationality, austerity and xenophobic, populist politics, and the synergies between them will be explored. The chapter examines how, through neoliberal reforms, the welfare state was transformed according to the principles of competition, individual consumer choice and conditional entitlement to benefits. This transformation has had the effect of undermining any (already limited) principles and practices of universalism and has rendered social solidarity unimaginable and unthinkable. The introduction of conditionality also rehabilitated some Victorian-era moralizing arguments about the undeserving poor. These developments have led to a situation where, within the context of 'Austerity Britain', the necessity of public sector cuts is largely accepted, and it is assumed that people are competing over a limited pool of scarce resources. The marginalization of social solidarity and collective agency means that alternative responses are not seriously considered. Instead, dominant political rhetoric redirects anger away from decisions to make cuts towards resentment towards 'problem populations'. These 'problem populations' (particularly immigrants and unemployed people) are positioned as abusing the system and taking resources away from those who need and deserve them. The most obvious and immediate response, according to this line of thinking, is to implement securitarian policies which prevent the 'problem populations' from accessing public services. The example also shows how easily common-sense intuitive links can be made between neoliberal rationality, austerity and populist politics, as well as how these contexts work together to render social solidarity unthinkable.

The figure of the 'health tourist', with its associations of cosmopolitanism and frivolity, is central to the framing of immigrants as abusers of the welfare state, and in justifying denying them access. This reflects the current climate of populist politics, and especially the principle that particular sections of society represent the 'pure public' and that others matter less (Müller, 2016). While some of the politicians quoted in this chapter (such as Theresa May or Jeremy Hunt) are from mainstream rather than far right political parties, their comments reflect attempts to opportunistically pander to anti-immigrant populist politics, particularly in the lead-up to the Brexit vote. This should serve as a warning about the degree of influence of populist ideas beyond the limited electoral success of parties such as UKIP. Populism plays an important role in framing particular situations as a problem. As 'health tourism' is only a problem for voters who are concerned about the level of immigration and who might potentially vote for populist parties, the fact that it is taken so seriously by mainstream political parties shows how this particular section of voters matters more than others (in other words, they are taken as representative of the public), and that the rights of others can be undermined to assuage these concerns.

The chapter will first discuss recent developments which restrict access to healthcare and other public services for non-European citizens in the UK and how these normalize everyday borders within the welfare state. This will be followed by an exploration of 'health tourism' as a policy problem, and how characterizing immigrants as tourists appeals to populist politics and stokes public resentment. These developments will then be contextualized as the latest phase of the neoliberalization of the welfare state: specifically, the reframing of healthcare and welfare in terms of competition and individual consumer choice and conditionality, undermining any already limited principles of universality. This makes it easier to position certain sections of society as undeserving abusers of the system and to justify securitization measures which block their access. Following this, the role of these developments within the lead-up to the Brexit vote will be examined, and how EU citizens also became framed as tourists. The chapter will conclude by calling for social solidarity to be made more readily thinkable and conceivable.

The hostile environment and the securitization of the welfare state

The Immigration Act 2014, the then Home Secretary Theresa May stated, was intended to create a 'hostile environment' for irregular immigrants (Kircup and Winnett, 2012). One of the measures of this act was to require immigrants other than asylum seekers staying in the UK for more than six months to pay a healthcare levy of £200 per year in addition to their visa fees, despite already paying for the NHS through taxes and National Insurance contributions in the same way as UK citizens. The measure was promised to raise £200m to pay for the NHS. Also central to the hostile environment was the requirement for NHS staff as well as other public sector workers and citizens to check the immigration status of people using hospitals and other public services, with those whose papers were not in order being subject to charges. This had the effect of making people reluctant to seek medical attention for fear that they would be turned over to the authorities.

This represents the latest development in the outsourcing of immigration controls and harsh rhetoric which originally began under the New Labour administration. In 2007, former Home Secretary John Reid said that he would make the UK "constrained and uncomfortable" for undocumented migrants (BBC, 2007), introducing the requirement for employers to check employees' papers at regular intervals, in order to avoid employing undocumented workers. Universities were also required to monitor the attendance of international students. These powers continued to expand under the Coalition government and later under the Conservative majority government. For example, the Immigration Act 2014 piloted the requirement for landlords to check immigration papers, and restricted access to healthcare to some immigrants without permanency (in addition to introducing the charging regime mentioned). The Immigration Act 2016 further extended and normalized these measures by requiring banks and the Driver and Vehicle Licensing Agency (which administers driving licences) to check their clients' immigration status.

The outsourcing of border controls involves the production of new forms of authority and obligation as the legislation gives employees of public sector organizations and businesses the power to routinely check the immigration details of students, colleagues, and members of the public, with heavy fines or other penalties for noncompliance. In so doing, this outsourcing process functions as an example of what Nira Yuval-Davis has called 'everyday bordering' which she defines as 'the everyday construction of borders through ideology, cultural mediation, discourses, political institutions, attitudes and everyday forms of transnationalism' (2013, p. 10). Borders are thus not simply about regulating who can enter or who can leave – they become part of everyday life, and increasingly integrated with the institutions and practices of the welfare state. Borders not only function as a legal mechanism for inclusion or exclusion, they are also cultural and emotional. As Yuval-Davis argues: 'In specific border zones, the geographic state border itself becomes embedded in everyday life and in the meanings attached to the local, as well as national, cultural environment, traditions, social habits and emotions' (2013, p. 15).

As much as they regulate access, borders also articulate who belongs to the political community and who does not, and act as tools for the management of public feelings. For example, during 2015 there were posters in hospitals reading 'The NHS hospital care is not for everyone', and when at a hospital for a routine check-up the author had to confirm on a video touchscreen in the corridor that she had lived in the UK for at least 12 months. Therefore, some people are meant to feel fear or unease around the institutions of the welfare state, as these become increasingly securitized: the unease of being reminded of one's contingent immigration status, or in extreme cases, being afraid to the point of avoiding the hospital or other organizations that could help. Other people are meant to feel reassured that their access to public services is being safeguarded against undeserving outsiders. As Ben Highmore argues in *Cultural Feelings*, this is how feelings become embedded within the routines and habits of everyday life in ways that reflect the 'large structuring effects of political and social events' (2017, p. 10). He uses the example of the changes to airport security after 9/11 (2017, p. 10), but his observation could equally apply to the everyday use of public services. Through embedding borders within everyday practices, the Immigration Acts 2014 and 2016 normalize the idea that immigrants are burdens on the welfare state and their use of public services is a dubious activity. They also naturalize the idea of public services as sites of surveillance and potential abuse and public sector workers as figures of vigilance.

The problem of 'health tourism'

At the time, Theresa May claimed that these measures were introduced to solve the problem of 'health tourism'. A health tourist refers to someone who deliberately comes to the UK to access medical treatment not available in their country (not including, for example, holidaymakers who get sick or have an accident during their visit). What is significant here is that the identification of 'health tourism' as a policy problem is not based on evidence. Estimates show that health tourism only takes up 0.03 per cent of public resources (*Full Fact*, 2016), meaning it is hardly a widespread phenomenon. To return to the earlier discussion of agency, this lack of evidence therefore raises questions about how and why health tourism was identified as such an urgent problem (rather than underfunding of the NHS for example). On the level of rhetoric, it plays to populist resentments, which will be discussed in this chapter.

The use of the term 'tourism' has become increasingly common to characterize the illegitimate use of the welfare state by foreigners ('health tourism', 'benefits tourism', or 'education tourism'). A tourist is imagined to be someone with no commitments or rooted sense of place. Tourists do also generally not have the legal rights associated with a permanent place of residence, as they are just passing through. Because of this, there are few serious consequences in denying a tourist access to benefits, healthcare or schools. As a version of the rootless cosmopolitan, the tourist is not so far away from the 'citizen of nowhere' evoked by May's speech at the 2016 Conservative Party conference. Tourism has associations with leisure and frivolity; although it does not specifically refer to holidaymakers, the term 'tourist' still takes on those associations. To call people tourists therefore plays to the 'producerist' ideology of right-wing populist politics (Müller, 2016), by framing them as unproductive members of society. Although tourists do not represent the corrupt elite which right-wing populists often pit against pure, innocent, hardworking people, they are still associated with entertainment and pleasure, and (it is assumed) belong to a privileged leisure class who takes advantage of the hard work and sacrifices of others. The term 'tourist' therefore does ideological work in stoking public resentment and, within the context of right-wing populism, constructing insiders and outsiders on the basis of nationality and ethnicity (see Chapter Guderjan and Wilding).

Neoliberalization, austerity and securitization

Both the creation of the problem of 'health tourists' and more generally the hostile environment need to be understood as the most recent phase of the neoliberalization of the welfare state, and the resulting marginalization of collective agency and social solidarity. Neoliberalism, although a 'loose and shifting signifier' (Brown, 2015, p. 20), is interpreted here to mean the 'enacting [of] an ensemble of economic policies in accord with its root principle of affirming free markets' (Brown, 2015, p. 28). The effects of neoliberalism include:

> The deregulation of industries and capital flows; radical reduction in welfare state provisions and protections for the vulnerable; privatized and outsourced public goods, ranging from education, parks, postal services, roads, and social welfare to prisons and militaries; replacement of progressive with regressive tax and tariff schemes; the end of wealth redistribution as an economic or social political policy; the conversion of every human need or desire into a profitable enterprise. (Brown, 2015, p. 28)

In considering the neoliberalization of the welfare state, it is important to be cautious about any nostalgic romanticism about what came before. The history of the postwar welfare state was marked by contradictions, particularly around access. For those outside dominant norms of gender, sexuality, nationality, etc. access was limited; feminist, anti-racist, LGBT+ and disabled analyses have drawn attention to a 'false universalism' which was both a product of social inequality and also reproduced it (Lewis, 2003). However, the neoliberalization of public services then significantly undermined this limited conception of universalism by reframing it within the same terms as markets, and citizens as consumers or as self-reliant entrepreneurial individuals. Under the influence of public choice theory, it was assumed that institutions were driven by self-interested and self-seeking motivations (just like markets), rather than by 'altruism, public service goals or professional ethics' (Clarke, 2013, p. 24). Users of public services were also seen primarily as self-interested consumers (Clarke, 2005, pp 199–200, cited in Clarke, 2013, p. 24). To return to the discussion of 'health tourism', there is an easy intuitive link between thinking of citizens as consumers and thinking of some citizens as 'tourists' – as a particular type of consumer. The positioning of the citizen as a consumer therefore plays a role in making the figure of the health tourist thinkable as a particular type of policy problem.

The framing of the citizen as a consumer has also been accompanied by the undermining of any (limited) conception of universalism and its replacement with conditional entitlements, which was explored by Peter Dwyer in *Creeping Conditionality* (2004). According to Dwyer, access to benefits in the UK became increasingly conditional on fulfilling a set of individual responsibilities, with sanctions for non-compliance. This took place in the context of debates about 'active citizenship' (Walters, 1997, cited in Dwyer, 2004) and mostly American discourses about the dangers of welfare dependency (for example Mead, 1986, cited in Dwyer, 2004) justifying the introduction of workfare regimes. At the time the debates focused on welfare rather than healthcare, but since then other types of state benefits have also become more conditional. These discourses around conditionality for the unemployed also have their parallel in policies which limit access to the welfare state for immigrants – which, as discussed, have been based in similar discourses around safeguarding against abuses of the system, and moral panics around the wrong people accessing public services. As Bridget Anderson argues in *Us vs Them* (2014), both the migrant and the 'benefit scrounger' function as categories of citizenship she terms the 'non-citizen' and the 'failed citizen' which are outside norms of respectable citizenship, meaning that they are more likely to be treated as expendable. The category of the 'tourist', although less vindictive than the 'scrounger', is ultimately about othering for the purposes of denying access, particularly within the ideology of 'producerism' which is central to populist politics.

The securitization of the welfare state also needs to be understood in terms of its positioning as an electorally popular measure to address the stretched resources caused by austerity cuts in a way that deflects responsibility from the government. Spending on the NHS rose by only 1.3 per cent since 2010, despite increasing costs and pressures caused by an ageing population and the underfunding of social care. The squeeze on health and social care led to 120,000 deaths in England according to research published in the *British Medical Journal* (Johnson, 2017). Funding cuts have also led to long waiting periods for treatment and failures of emergency services. By promising to safeguard resources for the most deserving British citizen/taxpayers, some of whom are also asked to play a role in safeguarding against abuse – these policy changes reassure concerns about the impact of immigration on public services, and displace questions about the decisions to make cuts in the first place.

Within the context of the neoliberalization of welfare, alternative policy responses based in social solidarity (for example, public investment, or raising taxes for wealthy individuals or corporations), have become inconceivable or at best implausible because social solidarity has become unthinkable. In practice, this means that citizens hear fewer arguments or language promoting social solidarity. The rare times they are articulated, such arguments are readily dismissed as unrealistic, wasteful or out of touch with the current moment (either relegated to the Keynesian postwar era or shelved for a utopian future which will never come). It also means that it is more difficult to think of policies or practices based in solidarity within one's everyday experience, within one's local context, so it is harder to think of examples within lived experience or recent memory and to consider them counterintuitive or far-fetched. Instead, it becomes taken for granted that relationships to other citizens can only be competitive ones, and that people will naturally abuse the system if given the opportunity.

Introducing the principle of conditionality also makes it more socially acceptable to frame access to public services as a privilege rather than a right for some sections of society. Xenophobic and racist rhetoric from media commentators and politicians normalizes the idea that immigrants do not contribute to society and abuse the welfare state, which then justifies harsher measures and rhetoric. This is a vicious cycle which Simon Geuntner et al have characterized as 'welfare chauvinism' (2016, p. 3). Welfare chauvinism is a 'public mood and a policy instrument', involving a 'circular feedback between public attitudes and state action' whereby:

> ... governments not only respond to chauvinist views, but through laws and administrative practices, also they themselves generate chauvinism, legitimizing and

rationalizing popular anxiety about abuse of a publicly-funded system. The constant invention of new categories of non-citizens gives a basis to chauvinistic practices which are then enmeshed in political and public discourses. (Geuntner, 2016, p. 3)

Through creating categories of non-citizenship with restricted access to public services, these approaches continue to pit people against each other in a fearful and resentful competition over scarce resources.

Welfare chauvinism and the securitization of the welfare state also need to be understood within the context of declining agency for national governments to invest in public services. According to neoliberal rationality, the agency of national governments is assumed to be quite limited. In this view, national governments do not have the power to redistribute wealth or to invest meaningfully in public services. It is assumed that decisions to cut public expenditure are outside their control; austerity is accepted as necessary, with spiralling debt or economic collapse the consequences of not cutting spending. National governments are not capable of intervening in processes of privatization and outsourcing as these are assumed to be inevitable and unstoppable; although national governments may technically have the power to intervene, it is not seen as a meaningful or feasible option. As mentioned, social solidarity has also been rendered inconceivable. This means that national governments lack agency due to the constraints of neoliberal thinking. Voters also lack agency because they feel that any proposals or campaigns about redistributing wealth or investing in public services will never be taken seriously by government. According to this logic, the only forms of agency available to national governments within the context of neoliberal rationality involve putting in place ever-stricter border regimes to restrict numbers and make life difficult for foreigners.

'Not an international health service': the welfare state and the Brexit vote

Unsurprisingly, moral panics around health tourism played a significant role in the lead up to the EU referendum, as the NHS and more generally the welfare state was mobilized within nationalist and xenophobic discourses. Both the former Secretary of State for Health, Jeremy Hunt, and Nigel Farage, former leader of UKIP and then of the Brexit Party, one of the main actors of the Leave campaign, have been quoted as saying that the NHS is a national service, not an international health service (*Channel 4 News*, 2013; Riley-Smith, 2015). But what does such a deceptively simple statement actually mean? It is based in a reductive common-sense logic of national welfare state institutions existing for national citizens only (national citizens and taxpayers are imagined to be the same people, eliding the complex reality of the staffing, funding and use of public services). 'National', within this context, refers to a supposedly homogenous Britishness as a counter to globalization. However, Britishness for UKIP and the Conservatives is strongly inflected by Englishness; this has intensified recently, as demonstrated by a recent poll showing that the majority of Conservative Party members would rather see the breakup of the union (losing Scotland and Northern Ireland) than stop Brexit (Smith, 2019). It is also important to remember that other nationalisms have in fact been defined in opposition to this very English Britishness. For example, during the 2014 Scotland independence referendum, one of the cases that was being made for independence in Scotland was that the NHS would be protected from the types of reforms that were being implemented in England under the Conservative-Liberal Democrat coalition government, such as the 2012 Health and Social Care Act.

Similar to the discourse of 'health tourism', which until recently had been largely about non-EU citizens, EU citizens were scapegoated as burdens on the welfare state without any real evidence. The government also defended its right to implement policies without this evidence to justify them. For example, when asked for figures by the European Commission about the scale of 'welfare tourism' by EU citizens, the government's official response was that such questions 'place too much emphasis on quantitative evidence' (Waterfield, 2013). As part of his failed negotiations with the EU shortly before the referendum, former Prime Minister David Cameron proposed an 'emergency brake' that would block European citizens in the UK from accessing in-work benefits, normally paid to low-paid employees, for four years to reduce what he called 'pull factors', whereby EU citizens come to the UK for a supposedly generous benefits system. This was argued despite evidence showing that EU citizens are in fact less likely to claim out-of-work benefits than UK citizens (*Full Fact*, 2015a). Such facts are an inconvenient truth because they do not fit with the logic of right-wing populist politics, which frame immigrants as abusers of the system. According to neoliberal or populist logics, the problem is that there are too many people in the country and that the wrong people are accessing public services, and government must stop them from doing so (assisted by citizens as outsourced immigration officers). By ignoring facts and evidence and affirming populist ideologies, governments can appeal to voters considering shifting their allegiance to the far right.

Similar arguments underpinned claims during the referendum that the EU was also seen to be taking British taxpayer's money which could otherwise be used to fund national public institutions – which were understood to exist only for national citizen-taxpayers. This is what lies behind the intuitive appeal of the 'take back control' slogan of the Vote Leave campaign. 'Taking back control' means restoring the simple logical equivalence of national public services and national citizen-taxpayers. It is assumed that nation states once had the agency to police this relationship but have now lost this power. The Brexit vote was presented as restoring this lost agency. The Vote Leave campaign specifically positioned the NHS as benefitting from Brexit – whereby £350m per week that was being paid to the EU would be redirected to fund the NHS, as in the infamous slogan on their campaign bus. It did not also account for the labour shortages following the Brexit vote as a result of many medical professionals leaving because they felt unwelcome, which would threaten service levels, for example the 96 per cent drop in nurses from the EU registering to work in the UK after the Brexit vote (Siddique, 2017). Labour shortages have now exacerbated the pressures on the NHS and other public services.

Conclusion

What the outlined debates miss is that welfare state institutions have never been purely national organizations, and that the NHS has been an international health service for much of its history. The welfare state is imbricated in the histories and contradictions of Britain's colonial past. This is demonstrated by the legacy of European and Commonwealth immigration in building the postwar welfare state. According to figures from 2015, 24 per cent of doctors employed by the NHS are from outside the UK (*Full Fact*, 2015b). Public services as both staffed and used by those born outside the UK has become a routine, and even banal, aspect of everyday experience. It could be considered an example of the everyday cosmopolitanism as theorized by Paul Gilroy in *After Empire* (2004). As Gilroy pointed out (writing in 2004) such experiences have not really been brought into mainstream political debates because they are perceived to be unpopular. Such experiences sit at odds with both neoliberal rationality and populist, anti-immigration politics. They challenge the normalization of everyday bordering and welfare chauvinism and the received wisdom that there is immediate political capital to be made from being tough on immigrants. The situation has only intensified since the introduction of austerity policies and the recent rise of Eurosceptic movements.

Although there have been testimonials from NHS staff who have decided to leave the country because of uncertainty and xenophobia in the aftermath of the Brexit vote, it remains so unpopular to argue that immigrants are not burdens on the welfare state that politicians are wary to articulate this publicly. Such silence emboldens those who appeal to the simple equivalence between state, nation and citizenship, and prevents any self-questioning of the need for public spending cuts or unresolved issues around the agency of citizens and their governments or citizens resulting from these cuts. It also gives legitimacy to xenophobic populist politics, because fewer counter-arguments are made publicly.

In conclusion, it is now crucial to question how social solidarity could be made thinkable and conceivable again, while recognizing the scale of the challenges involved. In so doing, it is important to acknowledge that other approaches to welfare and immigration which are not based on fear and hostility are possible, even within the relatively parochial context of the UK. For example, one of the central demands of the Scottish independence campaign is for an immigration policy which is more open and welcoming than that of the UK government, and which recognizes the importance of immigration for the Scottish economy and Scottish society, rather than treating immigrants as burdens and threats. The white paper on Scottish independence was openly critical of the 'hostile environment' approach taken by Westminster and called for the autonomy to put in place a different policy. In December 2016 the Scottish government also put forward a paper (which was rejected by the government) setting out a very different form of Brexit than former PM Theresa May's proposal, as it involved staying in the single market and adhering to EU rules on freedom of movement.

This is not to idealize the Scottish independence campaign but to recognize that in addition to the effects of neoliberalism and austerity, the hostile environment is the product of a specifically English nationalism which is based in part in an unwillingness to come to terms with colonial legacies and partly in fears of losing cultural identity (see Chapters Clarke, and Guderjan and Wilding). To recognize this is to acknowledge the hostile environment's geographically and historically contingent nature, rather than assuming it is general and universal. This acknowledgement is at least one step towards it being challenged.

References

Anderson, B. (2014) *Us vs Them: The dangerous politics of immigration control*, Oxford: Oxford University Press.

BBC (2007) 'Reid targets illegal immigrants', *BBC News*, 7 March.

Brown, W. (2015) *Undoing the demos: Neoliberalism's stealth revolution*, New York: Zone Books.

Channel 4 News (2013) '"NHS not an international health service", says Hunt', *Channel 4 News*, 3 July.

Clarke, J. (2013) 'Contexts: Forms of agency and action', in C. Pollitt (ed.) *Context in public policy and management: The missing link?*, Cheltenham: Edward Elgar Publishing.

Dwyer, P. (2004) 'Creeping Conditionality in the UK: From Welfare Rights to Conditional Entitlements?', *Canadian Journal of Sociology*, 29(2): 265–87.

Full Fact (2015a) 'Migration and welfare benefits', *Full Fact*, 4 May.

Full Fact (2015b) 'Some immigration facts… factchecked', *Full Fact*, 25 August.

Full Fact (2016) 'Health tourism: what's the cost'? *Full Fact*, 21 December.

Geuntner et al (2016) 'Bordering practices in the UK welfare system', *Critical Social Policy*, 36(3): 1–21.

Gilroy, P. (2004) *After Empire: Melancholy or convivial culture?*, London: Routledge.

Highmore, B. (2017) *Cultural feelings: Mood, mediation and cultural politics*, Abingdon: Routledge.

Johnson, E. (2017) 'Health and social care spending cuts linked to 120,000 excess deaths in England', *BMJ Open*, 15 November: https://blogs.bmj.com/bmjopen.2017/11/15/health-and-social-care-spending-cuts-linked-to-120000-excess-deaths-in-england/.

Kircup, J. and R. Winnett (2012) 'We're going to give illegal migrants a really hostile reception', *The Telegraph*, 25 May.

Lewis, G. (2003) 'Difference and Social Policy', in N. Ellison and C. Pierson (eds) *Developments in British Social Policy*, Basingstoke: Palgrave.

Müller, J. W. (2016) *What is populism?*, London: Penguin Books.

Riley-Smith, B. (2015) 'UKIP MP refuses to endorse Nigel Farage's AIDS comment', *The Telegraph*, 3 April.

Siddique, H. (2017) '96% drop in EU nurses registering to work in Britain since Brexit vote', *The Guardian*, 12 June.

Smith, M. (2019). 'Most Conservatives would see party destroyed to achieve Brexit'. *YouGov*, 18 June.

Waterfield, B. (2013) 'Britain admits it has no figures on EU 'welfare tourist' numbers', *The Telegraph*, 7 October.

Yuval-Davis, N. (2013) 'A situated intersectional approach to the study of everyday bordering', *EU Borderscapes Working Paper #2*: http://www.euborderscapes.eu/fileadmin/user_upload/Working_Papers/EUBORDERSCAPES_Working_Paper_2_Yuval-Davis.pdf.

10

'Uni-Culti' Myths and Liberal Dreams: Brexit and Austerity from the Perspective of Migrants

Magdalena Nowicka

Introduction

The Brexit vote and its results have become a key theme in European media, and countless experts and journalists have shared their opinions on the reasons behind Brexit and its possible effects. Scholars soon followed with analyses that led to one conclusion: Brexit resulted from a 'toxic mix of immigration and austerity' (Gietel-Basten, 2016). Yet the debates on Brexit focused almost exclusively on the motives of British Leave voters, largely neglecting the voices of migrants, that is, unless they pose the question: will migrants return 'home'? As scholarship linked the Brexit vote to austerity politics, it failed to ask whether migrants' choices and austerity are also connected.

In this chapter, the conjuncture of British austerity politics, the Brexit vote and migrants' perceptions of both are scrutinized. The author draws her insights from a longitudinal study among Polish migrants in London and Birmingham. Out of the 3.8 million EU citizens living in the UK (6 per cent of the country's population), almost 30 per cent were born in Poland. Some 200,000 Poles reside in London, and 17,000 in Birmingham. While analysing migrants' perceptions of austerity politics and the Brexit vote, this chapter also looks at their past experiences. This shows how the Brexit vote exacerbated a longer (and also austerity-fuelled) process of transnational neoliberal disciplining of workers and migrants. Further, it reveals how migrants' perception of their own and others' position in contemporary Britain engage the national welfare-state logic which legitimizes inequalities and discourses of deserving.

Austerity, Brexit and migrants

'Austerity' involves an increasing focus on frugality, self-sufficiency and fiscal prudence in contemporary economic and political life. The austerity agenda that the Conservative–Liberal Democrat coalition government introduced in 2010 built upon longstanding traditions within UK economic policy. Though the immediate justification for the 2010 measures was a presumed need to reduce the national debt, the longer-term goal was to shrink the state, free up the market and set British political economy on a new course. The current cutbacks are of an exceptional scale, speed, composition and social impact (Taylor-Gooby and Stoker, 2011). And the state's resulting withdrawal from providing minimum living standards negatively affects low-income families and their children, women, people with special health needs and migrants. For the latter, language barriers also intersect with gender inequalities and their legal status, further impacting their access to health services, housing and education (Berg, 2018).

Another effect of austerity measures can be found in the growth of the UK Independence Party (UKIP), which increased its support largely at the expense of support for the Conservatives. From 2010 and especially from 2013, until after the 2016 referendum, poorly-educated voters in routine jobs gave considerable support to UKIP (Fetzer 2018), which then transferred to Farage's Brexit Party. The spatial patterns of economic deprivation in the UK overlap the uneven distribution of the new migrants from the EU (Becker et al, 2016). As it happens, places with a high proportion of people with poorer education, older people and those dependent on welfare also attracted more migrants from the newer EU states, who filled labour gaps in retail and manufacturing.

Various post-vote analyses show how the Brexit vote reflects the intersections of populism, nationalism, fragmentation and socioeconomic inequality (Bachmann and Sidaway, 2016) and a mix of emotions and personal risk assessments (Clarke et al, 2017). The Leave campaign skilfully capitalized on the desire for political and cultural singularity (Freeden, 2017), and the Remain campaign also indirectly fuelled anti-immigration sentiments by reducing migrants to a labour force (Hoops et al, 2016). The popular illusion that the Leave campaign propagated was that new migrants were straining infrastructure and public services (Murray, 2016). In setting domestic welfare recipients and migrants against one another (Gietel-Basten, 2016), the Leave campaign directed attention away from the first group's deprivation, aggravated as it was by austerity measures (Morris, 2018), making the Brexit vote a vote against migrants rather than against government policies.

'Uni-Culti': Polish migrants' perceptions of Britain and Brexit

All of these themes appear in the narrations of Polish migrants collected in England since 2010 in three separate studies. The first used in-depth interviews with 25 Polish migrants in London and 19 in the Midlands, all conducted between November 2010 and August 2011. The second project was located in London and Birmingham; in each city, the team conducted three annual interviews with 31 Poles starting in spring 2014. Despite some differences in the interview scripts, both projects prompted accounts of the informants' everyday practices, and their opinions of, and encounters with, people of ethnicities, national backgrounds and religions other than their own. The third study included online focus group interviews (FGIs) with Poles living in London and Birmingham. The first round of online FGIs took place in March 2017, with 12 Poles in London and nine in Birmingham. It targeted their perceptions of life in England after the Brexit vote. The second round took place in November 2018, with nine Poles in London and eight in Birmingham. The participants in online FGIs logged in to a secure chat room; the discussion was moderated and was similar to a traditional face-to-face focus group. Each of the discussions lasted approximately two hours. The data generated is a mixture of self-talk and public discourse (Wilkinson, 2016).

Elsewhere the author has discussed the shift observed in narrations between 2010 and 2018 (Nowicka, 2018). In the early interviews, participants frequently positioned themselves as having successfully built professional careers, and praised the supposedly meritocratic British system. Yet the narrations collected later, in 2015 and 2016, suggest that they became aware of certain ethnic hierarchies that excluded them from desirable middle-class positions. In discussing this, Poles stress both their own productive role within the British economy and their cultural proximity to white British citizens. Following the assimilative logic of national policies towards immigrants (Cederberg, 2014), participants defined migrants as someone from a different culture, with a different skin colour, who is unwilling to become proficient in English and is thus incapable of socializing beyond their own ethnic group.

All the studies' participants experienced the Brexit vote as a shock, yet few referred to the Leave campaign as being directed against migrants from Central and Eastern Europe or Poland specifically. Such narrations became more common only in the 2018 FGIs, at which point some participants reflected the media analyses that unmasked the campaign's anti-immigrant character, and the rise of crimes against 'foreigners' (Corcoran and Smith, 2016). Consistent with the perception of migrants as people who are culturally (racially, religiously) different, many Poles interpreted the Brexit vote as one against the EU's refugee politics, associating this with Chancellor Merkel's decision to accept Syrian war refugees into the core of Europe: '[they voted Leave] because the EU forces them [Britain] to accept more immigrants, meaning Syrians'. Some were rather supportive of the Leave vote, at least from this perspective, but others noticed that the desire to stop immigration is utopian. As one participant from Birmingham put it: 'I don't know how they imagine it, that suddenly this becomes a 'uni-culti' [country]?', alluding to the multiculturalism backlash. Other participants added, 'if they kick out all immigrants, this country will collapse'; 'Brexit is unimportant, the British would not manage without immigrants'; 'the NHS could not function without migrants'; and 'if migrants left, this country would lose its workforce'.

At the same time, Poles distanced themselves from the Leave voters in two ways: first, by stressing Leave voters' intellectual inferiority and simultaneously referring to their own good knowledge of world politics, the functioning of the economy, and the EU. 'A complete lack of education' wrote one participant; 'this nation is not very intelligent', added another; and a third elaborated:

> white working-class people in some regions do not like migrants, as they believe they take their jobs – they voted for Brexit – but this is a class which is not educated (…) people who are left-oriented or simply part of the intelligentsia accept diversity, and for them migrants are equals.

Second, participants stressed that there are no Leave voters in their circles. Any stories about negative reactions towards Poles were told as second-hand accounts or stemming from media reports. Participants claimed that, after the referendum, their encounters with the British were thoroughly positive and empathetic. Many narratives included examples of bosses or colleagues expressing their appreciation of Polish migrants and their contribution to British society, and offering support for the future.

Regarding the outcome of the referendum, participants, puzzlingly, displayed indifference. Not only did they stress that Brexit would not affect their personal or professional situations, but they also stated that they respect it even if it 'feels like a slap in your face', as one of the participants put it in the 2017 FGI. Such emotional reactions in 2017 faded though, and the 2018 interviews included more narrations about stability and a lack of anxiety about their own future in the UK. Participants explained the latter with reference to their contribution to the British economy ('the British could not survive without immigrants') or their personal embeddedness ('I've lived in the UK too long, they cannot do anything to me'). But then they also wrote that: 'if they send us away, we will go'; 'if I have to leave, I will settle elsewhere, and that would be fine too'; and 'I like life here, but I can also live elsewhere in the world, or in Poland'. These statements appear to connect with the relations of migrants, particularly Poles, with the British majority. These are mostly friendly, if superficial, participants stated, but they also note that they feel more like guests than at home in Britain. In this vein, one participant wrote about the Brexit vote: 'their country, their decision [...] I am only a guest here'. Some participants explicitly stressed their respect for the vote, despite their having wished another result: 'Honestly speaking I don't step in because in my view the British have the right to decide about their own country'.

Similar references to national sovereignty appeared in the earlier interviews in 2010 and 2011, in narrations about discrimination against migrants in the British labour market. There, the fact that migrants' education was not recognized was justified with reference to the container concept of nation-states and their assimilationist logic. It results in the systems being incompatible and allows citizens to treat worse those migrants who fail to assimilate. While such explicit narrations are rare in the three sets of interviews, there are multiple hints at the 'national' logic which underpins participants' distanced stance on British citizens' decisions about 'their' country, even if they affect participants negatively. This is not to say that these decisions are considered correct, but participants acknowledge the right of the British to shape their country as they wish, even if they think that the wish for a 'uni-culti' state is nothing but a myth.

The welfare state and austerity measures in the eyes of Poles in England

The 'Brexit' narrations collected in 2017 and 2018 all involve the distinction between 'good' and 'bad' citizens (Nowicka, 2018). The narrations on austerity measures and public spending, if they include migrants, follow the pattern of neoliberal 'culture talk'. The term *culture talk* was used by Stolcke (1995) to denote Europe's rhetoric of excluding non-European immigrants; it is beyond the scope of this paper to discuss how this is linked to neoliberalism (see Romano, 2017). The participants use the Polish term *bezrobotne* or *zasilek dla bezrobotnych* which the author directly translates as 'unemployment allowance'. The term *jobseeker's allowance* did not appear in the discussions, neither in Polish translation nor in English. Examples which illustrate the use of *culture talk* in the interviews include: 'Migrants take jobs which locals avoid, since they know it is easier to be on the dole than bust their own butts', and 'those less educated [British citizens], or without any education, migrants disturb them the most, they shout the loudest that we take their jobs away, despite the fact that they are on the dole, because this is easier'.

In the post referendum discussions, Poles were more strongly and explicitly dis-identifying with the 'bad' people, citizens and foreigners alike, who abuse the welfare state, and who 'got too many rights, NHS, and got lazy'. Participants employ the well-integrated 'model migrant' figure to both validate themselves as respectable citizens (Skeggs, 2002) and counter the stereotype of migrants as a burden on the welfare system that was mobilized around the Brexit vote (Jones and Gunaratnam, 2017). At the same time, participants employ the culture talk of these anti-immigrant campaigns when they associate rubbish on the streets with the presence of non-white migrants (mostly Muslims – see Lisiak, 2018) and with these people's personal deficiencies (no desire for order), rather than with insufficient funding for public services.

Public funding – or its decline – is notably absent from these narrations. Participants complain about public transport worsening but do not link it to the state withdrawing its funding. Many give examples of multiple services that they use (mostly educational courses, student loans, child care, etc.), without showing awareness that these are publicly funded. Similarly, they show little awareness of the austerity measures introduced in 2010, even though all of them arrived in Britain before these reforms; instead, they consider the rigorous budget cuts a general feature of the UK welfare system. Only one participant, whose job is to assist migrants in their settlement process, noted that 'there is less support now than before […], it is now more difficult to get the support, for example a flat, there are fewer offers for free language courses'.

When asked explicitly about their opinion on austerity, most rationalise the measures as necessary for the British economy, particularly with Brexit ahead. Some are critical of welfare transfers in general and say it is a waste of money or a form of populism to court votes. The main argument they give for less state support is that benefits are demotivating, which leads to a growing gap between those who work (hard) and those who 'do nothing'. As one participant in the 2018 London group wrote: 'I feel it is unjust. As far as I know if you have two jobs you automatically pay a higher tax no matter how much you earn but otherwise they pay people who do nothing'.

The FGIs' participants believed state support was justified only for the most vulnerable recipients, but it was hotly debated who is most vulnerable. Some considered being disabled to the point of being incapable of working worthy of support, or living in extreme poverty and in danger of mental illness due to this stress. An animated discussion took place around the homeless, and on whether the state cares enough for them (providing shelters, shared accommodation) so that individual help (such as giving cash on the street) becomes unnecessary. A consensus was reached, that 'rationally administered [welfare benefits] are useful', and it was followed by examples of unjustified payments and cases of misuse or overuse of the system. For example, everybody found NHS services useful and justified, but consider it inefficient and too generous in offering medications free of charge. Similarly, they find unemployment allowances justified if the claimant paid taxes and if it only bridges the 'unlucky' period in their life, but not justified if whole families depend solely on welfare.

Some participants resolutely reject the need for state support, yet count themselves as deserving of it. 'I have a job and don't need the government's help', one said, and another person stressed: 'I don't personally know such people [on benefits], my friends here buy houses and run businesses and send their children to good schools'. But they also admit that they have also used social support: 'My [husband] for just a very short period got the unemployment allowance'; 'years ago I was on unemployment allowance … for just two months or so':

> if you are in a difficult financial situation you can apply for [income] support, we used it many times and now as well because we have a really difficult situation, we are unemployed and we are grateful we can use this help because we have no relatives here to help us, for example with child care.

These narrations are not unique to Polish migrants, also appearing in studies of other ethnic minorities in the UK. And of course, non-migrant claimants of welfare also fear and experience stigmatization (Baumberg, 2016). In the neoliberal order all claimants are 'national abjects' (Tyler, 2013), but migrants are considered even less deserving of public money and attention (Baumberg et al, 2012). The collected narrations thus point to the common understanding in British society that migrants prove how deserving they are by hard work (Davison and Shire, 2015). Poles seem to have already embodied this hierarchy of entitlement that underpins the neoliberal meritocracy. Yet this diagnosis would not be complete without a consideration of how the research participants compared the UK situation to the one they know in Poland.

Neoliberal dreams: adolescence in turbo capitalism

'For me these rules are strange', said one of the discussion participants, 'because I did not encounter them in Poland, for example complimentary medication for children – why should it be free?' Another one responds: 'Hmm ... for me as a Pole it is a strange situation, but I am trying to understand the British, I think they have gotten used to social benefits', to which a third immediately adds 'And we haven't.'

These narrations point towards the specificity of respondents' upbringing in late communist and post-communist Poland, which many scholars called a time of 'turbo capitalism' (Ost, 2005; Hardy, 2009). Poland's economic success, its relatively quick establishment of broad social protection programmes, and neoliberal reforms (the 'shock therapy') of the early 1990s left large groups of people behind. Despite decreasing unemployment and a reduction of absolute poverty, the proportion of people who consider themselves poor has been increasing (Szulc, 2008). Indeed, most social transfers went to people in the middle of the income pyramid, not to the most vulnerable (Keane and Prasad, 2002). In turn, those who profited most from the systemic change were young people in the emerging urban middle classes, yet they also feel the 'liberal competition state' (Münch, 2012) pressure the most. Those on the dole have not only been stigmatized as the losers of systemic transformation, they also struggle to survive, as benefits do not reach them or do not suffice. Poverty became taboo in public discourse (Warzywoda-Kruszyńska, 2009). At the same time, as more foreign companies invested in Poland, the post-communist generation grew up to become accountable, responsible, self-managing and self-regulating subjects (Dunn, 2004). Young people in Poland now aspire to personal material wealth and financial independence, but also to a good education and interesting work (Szafraniec and Boni, 2011), and various authors claim that these aspirations, if they cannot be realized in Poland, are a strong motivator for international migration (overview in Szewczyk, 2015).

As Lisiak and Nowicka (2018) argue, migrants confronted with unfamiliar behaviour and opinions might become critical of their own socialization. And participants in the 2018 FGIs were indeed explicitly negative about the neoliberal pressures in Poland. One noted: 'Simply speaking, in Poland we still feel the need to demonstrate and stress our status with the help of goods. A good car, a huge house, etc. Here I mean this is less the case'. Someone else added: 'due to the years of a shortage of everything in Poland, some attempt to make up for it now, plus there's a Slavic, not just Polish, need to keep up with the Joneses'.

They were equally critical of how employers in Poland require all staff to hold a higher education diploma, and of 'wild capitalism and abuses', as another person wrote. At the same time, they see Poland as lacking a cohesive welfare policy, and describe the new measures as 'just chaos' that 'will lead to a catastrophe' of the economy. 'The UK is more rational', stated one of the participants, referring to British austerity politics.

Participants' socialization in Poland matters in more ways for their perceptions of the welfare state and austerity politics in Britain. First, having grown up among persistent labour-market problems, they tend to perceive a comprehensive welfare state as harmful to the economy (see also van Oorschot et al, 2012). Second, they feel the stigma of claiming benefits doubly, both as migrants in the UK, and as friends or family members under steady observation from relatives in Poland who are eager to judge their migration decisions. Third, they appreciate the availability of benefits in Britain compared to Poland, which gives them more security in times of personal crisis. In turn, they value the positive social consequences of welfare policies. While these positions seem contradictory, we may better understand them if we consider how migrants' past and present experiences in two different welfare systems intersect.

Conclusion

Two and a half years after the Brexit vote, Poles in England show a growing awareness that the vote was 'against them'. Now that their emotions have cooled down, they display a certain indifference to the vote's result, paired with increasingly feeling that they do not belong in Britain. They read the austerity measures that were so important in shaping the vote's result as a feature of the British welfare system, and in fact as a good move on the part of the government to make the economy efficient in the face of Brexit. They consider Prime Minister Theresa May's announcement to withdraw from these politics as merely courting votes. While the participants struggled to achieve consensus over who is entitled to state support, all dis-identified with those needing it, while stressing their own right to claim benefits as good citizens and tax payers.

It might seem paradoxical that migrants – the people most vulnerable to austerity, most likely to be excluded from social transfers, and, in the particular context of Brexit, also affected by anti-immigrant sentiments fuelled by the deepening deprivation of vulnerable non-migrants – are supportive of restrictive welfare politics. Common explanations point to a fear of being stigmatized within the neoliberal context. Culturalist/nationalist approaches suggest that being raised in a country where state support is very limited makes people less likely to fear the negative effects of a welfare system in decline. The most plausible explanation is both the fear of stigma and the socialization thesis. But the narrations also point to something else, which is the 'legitimizing performance of the national welfare state' for social inequality (Beck, 2007). It is visible in the (non)recognition of migrants' degrees and skills in the labour market; the common understanding producing migrants as a labour force valuable to the country's economic performance; or the stigmatization of migrants as 'welfare tourists'. But it is also detectable in how migrants consider multiple forms of excluding minorities to be a quasi-natural right of citizens. Migration to the UK or the follow-up migrations considered by participants after Brexit – is also a form of accepting the sovereignty (and overwhelming power) of nation (welfare) states to determine the course of migrants' lives. The nation-state's logic deprives them of voicing their disagreement of being excluded. Yet to better understand migrants' perspectives, we also need to consider that nation states produce different variants of both welfare regimes and the neoliberal script (Peck, 2004). Migrants positioned between two national systems may combine the two logics. Even if the systems are similar (as largely shaped by a transnational, neoliberal script), they are never identical, so migrants' positions can be conflicting or even paradoxical.

References

Bachmann, V. and J. D. Sidaway (2016) 'Brexit geopolitics', *Geoforum*, 77: 47–50.

Baumberg, B. (2016) 'The stigma of claiming benefits: a quantitative study', *Journal of Social Policy*, 45(02): 181–99.

Baumberg, B., K. Bell, D. Gaffney, R. Deacon, C. Hood, and D. Sage (2012) *Benefits stigma in Britain*, https://wwwturn2us-2938.cdn.hybridcloudspan.com/T2UWebsite/media/Documents/Benefits-Stigma-in-Britain.pdf.

Beck, U. (2007) 'Beyond class and nation: reframing social inequalities in a globalizing world', *The British journal of sociology*, 58(4): 679–705.

Becker, S. O., T. Fetzer and D. Novy (2016) *Who Voted for Brexit?: A Comprehensive District-Level Analysis*, Working Paper Series 305, Centre for Competitive Advantage in the Global Economy: The University of Warwick.

Berg, M. L. (2018) 'Super-diversity, austerity, and the production of precarity: Latin Americans in London', *Critical Social Policy*, OnlineFirst.

Cederberg, M. (2014) 'Public Discourses and Migrant Stories of Integration and Inequality: Language and Power in Biographical Narratives', *Sociology*, 48(1): 133–49.

Clarke, H. D., M. Goodwin and P. Whiteley (2017) 'Why Britain Voted for Brexit: An Individual-Level Analysis of the 2016 Referendum Vote', *Parliamentary Affairs*, 70(3): 439–64.

Corcoran, H. and K. Smith (2016) *Hate Crime, England and Wales, 2015/16*, Statistical Bulletin 11/16.

Davison, S. and G. Shire (2015) 'Race, migration and neoliberalism', *Soundings*, 59(59): 81–95.

Dunn, E. C. (2004) *Privatizing Poland: Baby food, big business, and the remaking of labor*, Ithaca, NY: Cornell University Press.

Fetzer, T. (2018) *Did Austerity Cause Brexit?: cesifo Working Papers*, vol 7159, München.

Freeden, M. (2017) 'After the Brexit referendum: revisiting populism as an ideology', *Journal of Political Ideologies*, 22(1): 1–11.

Gietel-Basten, S. (2016) 'Why Brexit?: The Toxic Mix of Immigration and Austerity', *Population and Development Review*, 42(4): 673–80.

Hardy, J. (2009) *Poland's new capitalism*, London: Pluto.

Hoops, J. F., R. J. Thomas and J. A. Drzewiecka (2016) 'Polish 'Pawns' between nationalism and neoliberalism in British newspaper coverage of post-European Union enlargement polish immigration', *Journalism: Theory, Practice & Criticism*, 17(6): 727–43.

Jones, H. and Y. Gunaratnam (2017) *Go home?: The politics of immigration controversies*, Manchester: Manchester University Press.

Keane, M. P. and E. S. Prasad (2002) 'Inequality, Transfers, and Growth: New Evidence from the Economic Transition in Poland', *Review of Economics and Statistics*, 84(2): 324–41.

Lisiak, A. (2018) 'A sense of disorder: orientation and migration in the 'new' West', in K. Bystrom, A. Harris and A. Webber (eds) *South and north: Contemporary urban orientations,* London: Routledge Taylor & Francis Group.

Lisiak, A. and M. Nowicka (2018) 'Tacit differences, ethnicity and neoliberalism: Polish migrant mothers in German cities', *Gender, Place & Culture*, 25(6): 899–915.

Morris, L. D. (2018) "Moralising' Welfare and migration in Austerity Britain: a backdrop to Brexit', *European Societies*, 64(6): 1–25.

Münch, R. (2012) *Inclusion and exclusion in the liberal competition state*, Abingdon, Routledge.

Murray, C. (2016) *Becoming one of us: Reforming the UK's citizenship system for a competitive, post-Brexit world*, https://www.ippr.org/files/publications/pdf/becoming-one-of-us_August2016.pdf.

Nowicka, M. (2018) 'Cultural Precarity: Migrants' Positionalities in the Light of Current Anti-immigrant Populism in Europe', *Journal of Intercultural Studies*, 39(5): 527–42.

Ost, D. (2005) *The Defeat of solidarity: Anger and politics in postcommunist Europe*, Ithaca: Cornell University Press.

Peck, J. (2004) 'Geography and public policy: constructions of neoliberalism', *Progress in Human Geography*, 28(3): 392–405.

Romano, S. (2017) *Moralising Poverty: The 'Undeserving' Poor in the Public Gaze*, Florence: Taylor and Francis.

Skeggs, B. (2002) *Formations of class and gender: Becoming respectable*, London: SAGE.

Stolcke, V. (1995) 'Talking Culture: New Boundaries, New Rhetorics of Exclusion in Europe', *Current Anthropology*, 36(1): 1–24.

Szafraniec, K. and M. Boni (2011) *Młodzi 2011*, Warszawa: Kancelaria Prezesa Rady Ministrów.

Szewczyk, A. (2015) "European Generation of Migration': Change and agency in the post-2004 Polish graduates' migratory experience', *Geoforum*, 60: 153–62.

Szulc, A. (2008) 'Checking the consistency of poverty in Poland: 1997–2003 evidence', *Post-Communist Economies*, 20(1): 33–55.

Taylor-Gooby, P. and G. Stoker (2011) 'The Coalition Programme: A New Vision for Britain or Politics as Usual?', *The Political Quarterly*, 82(1): 4–15.

Tyler, I. (2013) *Revolting Subjects: Social Abjection and Resistance in Neoliberal Britain*, London: Zed Books.

van Oorschot, W., T. Reeskens and B. Meuleman (2012) 'Popular perceptions of welfare state consequences: A multilevel, cross-national analysis of 25 European countries', *Journal of European Social Policy*, 22(2): 181–97.

Warzywoda-Kruszyńska, W. (2009) 'Bieda w Polsce przed wstąpieniem i po wstąpieniu do Unii Europejskiej: (Poverty in Poland prior and after the EU accession)', in UKIE (ed.) *5 lat członkostwa Polski w Unii Europejskiej w perspektywie społecznej: (5 years of Polish membership in the EU in social perspective)*, Warszawa, pp 106–20.

Wilkinson, S. (2016) 'Analysing Focus Group Data', in D. Silverman (ed.) *Qualitative research*, Los Angeles, London, New Delhi, Singapore, Washington DC, Melbourne: SAGE, pp 83–99.

PART III

Austerity and Brexit in a Divided Union

11

From Brexit to the Break-Up of … England? Thinking in and Beyond the Nation

Allan Cochrane

Introduction

Political debate around the nature of the 2016 Brexit referendum campaign – the promises made and the strategies employed – and about the implications of the vote have remained fierce in the period since it was held. The fault line between Remainers and Leavers is one that reflects different conceptions of the UK and its future. This chapter identifies some of the geographical differentiation that was apparent in the vote, in order to reflect on the underlying social, economic and political relations reflected in it.

Discussion around the break-up of Britain is usually approached through the tensions associated with nationalism and national identity in Northern Ireland, Scotland and Wales – England remains the residual territory or nation around which whatever remains of the UK might be expected to cohere. Some of those tensions are apparent in the voting patterns of the referendum, even if the messages are by no means clear cut. But here the focus is more specifically on 'England' and the tensions that define it as a potential politic-economic space, or set of connected spaces.

Looking at the patterns

The overall UK vote to leave the EU masked significant variation not only between the component parts of the UK as a state made up of four distinctive territorial government units (England, Northern Ireland, Scotland and Wales) but also within those nations and territories that make up the UK. The Electoral Commission reported the votes at a regional level in England and at the level of the nations and devolved administrations in Scotland, Wales and Northern Ireland. This is an unusual scale at which to report results in England, since the regions have no governmental status, but it does help to highlight the broad pattern of the vote across the country. It also confirms, if confirmation were needed, that it is necessary to recognize the extent to which the other nations of the UK are quite distinct political entities. In other words, there is no longer – if there ever was – a unified UK-wide set of more or less shared political understandings.

In the referendum, there was a substantial vote for Leave in England – over 53 per cent of those who voted recorded a Leave vote. Some have suggested that the vote in England can even be understood as a reflection of the rise of a form of English nationalism, perhaps reflected in the rise of UKIP as a powerful political force, at least in the years up to 2016. But even in England, this vote masked significant geographical variation. In London nearly 60 per cent voted Remain and in the South East of England 51.8 per cent (close to the UK average) voted Leave. Every other English region recorded solid Leave majorities, as is apparent in Table 11.1. By contrast Scotland (62 per cent) and Northern Ireland (55.7 per cent) produced Remain majorities, while in Wales the Leave vote was lower than in England, at 52.5 per cent. Anthony Barnett (2017, p. 101) argues that what he calls 'England-without-London swung the outcome. It voted by a majority of over 2½ million for Leave, the other four parts of the Kingdom combined voted by just under 1½ million for Remain'. However, there is a danger that presenting the figures in this way implies a greater level of shared political identity at regional level in England than there actually is. For example, the position of large cities and urban areas is obscured in these figures.

The balance between the votes is much closer across the country, than is implied by simply operating at a regional level. There is not only a fairly solid band of Remain support around London, but it extends along a line to Bristol and Cardiff, as well as having a strong expression around some cities in the North of England. There are some areas in which the Remain vote was close to 70 per cent; and similarly in

Table 11.1 Votes in the 2016 referendum

Region/nation	Numbers Remain	Numbers Leave	Percentage Leave
East of England	1,448,616	1,880,367	56.5
East Midlands	1,033,036	1,475,479	58.8
London	2,263,519	1,475,232	40.1
North East	562,595	778,103	58.0
North West	1,699,020	1,966,925	53.7
South East	2,391,718	2,567,965	51.8
South West	1,503,019	1,669,711	52.6
West Midlands	1,207,175	1,755,687	59.2
Yorkshire and Humberside	1,158,298	1,580,937	57.7
Northern Ireland	440,707	349,442	44.3
Scotland	1,661,191	1,018,322	38.0
Wales	772,347	854,572	52.5

Source: Electoral Commission, 2017

other areas the Leave vote was close to 70 per cent. But elsewhere the differentiation is less sharply defined. Even in the Midlands and the North of England the Leave vote is not universally strong.

The detail is valuable because of the extent to which it enables a more nuanced understanding of the geography behind the Brexit vote. As well as London, it confirms that a majority in several other big (and some not so big) cities in England voted to remain: Liverpool, Manchester, Bristol, Newcastle, Leeds, Cambridge, Oxford, York, Exeter, Brighton. It also confirms that even as most of the suburban home counties of the South East (Oxfordshire, Surrey and Sussex) voted Remain, other parts of that supposedly prosperous region (including much of Kent and Hampshire) voted to leave. Even in London, several of the boroughs on the outer east of the city (including Barking and Dagenham) voted Leave.

This is a divided country, but the question being explored here is whether the divisions have anything more to tell us about the UK – or whether they reflect the working out of underlying economic and social processes, questions of agency, and, if so, what those are. It is important to recognize that snapshots of voting data like these freeze a particular moment in place and time. But they do not necessarily tell us much about the economic, social and political relations that underpin it, and which have come together to construct it and bring it into being. What is captured and apparently fixed, is the product of more complex and continuing processes of change and settlement, and it is on those that this chapter is focused.

One way of approaching these issues is to look at the characteristics of different agents and how they voted in the different areas. Work by political scientists such as Clarke et al (2017) who have stressed the extent to which Leave voters can be characterized as the 'left behind', or Jennings and Stoker (2016) who distinguish between (liberal) people who live in cosmopolitan areas and (illiberal) people who live in what they characterize as backwaters. Commentators emphasize the extent to which those with lower levels of educational qualification were more likely to vote Leave and highlight the gap between older and younger voters. While these distinctions have some explanatory force, it is hard to escape the rather dismissive implications of the terms being used – the 'left behind', poorly educated, old people living in backwaters being implicitly (and sometimes explicitly) contrasted with the more dynamic, highly educated young people living in cosmopolitan areas.

This chapter takes a rather different approach, not dismissing a particular set of agents as populists (or left behind) but looking at what the vote tells about the way in which uneven development has left its mark in economic, social, and cultural as well as political divisions across England. As a first step, therefore, rather than looking for the answers in some of the Leave areas, the chapter starts from the London experience – looking out from London to understand how the UK is constructed from within its globalized heartland, before turning to consider the tensions and uncertainties associated with the position of England within the UK as an increasingly unstable multinational settlement in the wake of Brexit.

Looking out through the lens of London

This section focuses on the particular case of London, not in its own right but as a way into untying some of the complicated knots that surround debates about national identity, in England, Northern Ireland, Scotland and Wales, as well as the UK (or Britain) in the wake of the Brexit vote. Problematizing the London experience, rather than simply taking it for granted as the driver of the UK's growth and the epitome of a new economic model based around services and finance, provides a fruitful way in to those debates because of the extent to which it highlights the dynamic underpinnings of uneven development. Uneven development may find expression in patterns of geographical inequality, as some areas face deindustrialization, even as others (like London) seem to grow inexorably. But it is important not to assume that there is any inevitability about this, or that those living in declining regions are somehow to blame, because they have low skills or because they are not prepared to move elsewhere to seek work. Instead what matters is to identify the relations of power – the sets of social, political and economic relations – that help to generate forms of inequality and particular structures of difference.

Rather than taking London for granted and assuming the centrality of its position, it is necessary to reflect more fully on its relationship with the regions of England and the nations of the UK. The aim, here, is to understand some key aspects of the dynamics that shape London, but also to reflect on some of the ways in which they shape uneven development and inequality across the UK. By looking through the lens of London, it becomes possible to explain some of the divisions reflected in the pattern of votes cast in the referendum, and to highlight some of the tensions associated with the UK as a nation state – and England as a distinct political and economic space within it

In many respects the UK has a highly centralized social, political and economic geography, with London (or the wider London city region) at its core. This is generally taken for granted as a fact of life, although modest attempts to rebalance are made from time to time. The referendum vote and the consequences of Brexit highlight some of the tensions between London not only across the UK, but also specifically within England.

The tensions associated with those places identified as global city regions are continuing ones: are they part of the nation states in which they find themselves or better understood through their connections within wider networks? These questions are more intense when a city – like London – has been the metropolitan centre of an imperial project, remains a capital city and is at the centre of an extensive urban (mega) region. Since the referendum, some have begun to argue that London needs to be understood as a political territory in its own right, positioned within a global network, even as others have complained about its role in stunting development possibilities elsewhere in the UK.

David Lammy, Member of Parliament for Tottenham, explicitly argued (in an article for the *Evening Standard* in 2017) that London should be recognized as a city state, an internationally operating entity in its own right. Lammy sets out to equate London's position with that of Scotland. He cannot, of course, point to a continuing national story for London along the same lines as in Scotland, but he does point to a historical record of past city states and suggests that the position of London in a changed global context opens up new possibilities.

He mobilizes the language of devolution and stresses how different London is from the rest of the UK – with a 60 per cent Remain vote and an economic base that runs counter to the visions he identifies with Brexit, that is 'smalltown conservatism, resurgent nationalism and anti-immigrant sentiment'. In this context, of course, the nationalism to which he is referring is that of England (or the UK), rather than those of Scotland, Wales or Ireland.

Lammy identifies particular priorities for the emergent city state that would provide it with more internal and external opportunities: increased tax raising powers and separate visa arrangements to enable labour migration to London, even as controls are imposed elsewhere. He stresses what he sees as the need for huge investment to meet London's housing crisis and the need for policies to challenge the sharp divide between (sometimes very) rich and poor in the city. From Lammy's perspective London is already a de facto city state even if the institutional arrangements are lagging behind and he argues that it will become increasingly necessary to recognize this. For good measure, even as he identifies London's special status, he suggests that the tax raised in London provides a crucial underpinning for social spending elsewhere in the UK – in other words, he argues that money is being extracted from London that should be spent there instead.

In some discussions of London's position, it feels as if it is somehow floating free in a globalized world, only touching down reluctantly because of the crude expectations and requirements of material existence. Yet, the sets of relations through which the city region is defined are stubbornly connected through a range of spatial practices, which find a clear expression in the uneven development of the UK. There is a sharp tension between those who see London as driver of the national economy and those who see it as an actor in generating wider regional inequality. So, for example, Ian Gordon and others (2003) strongly argue that London is a net contributor to the rest of the country through its taxes and the public expenditure for which they pay. Peter Hall (2009) goes further to argue that one solution to regional inequality might simply be for the London city region to expand its footprint to incorporate other cities, including Birmingham. Not surprisingly, this is a position that has been endorsed by a series of London mayors, from Ken Livingstone, through Boris Johnson to Sadiq Khan.

From another perspective, however, the matter has been understood quite differently. London's position within the UK's economic geography reflects a deeply unequal set of social and economic relations – there is a bigger gap between the wealth and economic prosperity of London and the more disadvantaged regions and territories of the UK than there is in most advanced economies. As Phil McCann (2016) puts it: 'the economic geography of the UK nowadays increasingly reflects the patterns typically observed in developing or former-transition economies rather than in other advanced economies'. Ash Amin, Doreen Massey and Nigel Thrift (2003) argue that the centralization of power in London means that a 'significant element of national policy making effectively functions as an unacknowledged regional policy for the South Eastern part of England' (2003, p. 17). As a result, they argue that national economic policy is overly influenced by the state of the regional economy in London and South East, with steps being taken to restrain the economy when the region is 'overheating', even when the rest of the country still has significant capacity for growth.

Despite a rhetorical shift in the language of national policy in England towards other possible growth regions, such as the Northern Powerhouse or the Midlands Engine, and towards forms of devolved government in the UK's nations, the logics of development continue to reinforce the centrality of the Greater South East in public policy practice (Martin et al, 2016). The recent history of megaprojects certainly points in this direction. For example, the success of London's bid for the 2012 Olympic Games was a reflection of London's position as a world city – previous attempts by UK cities were said to have failed because of their lower position in urban hierarchies. The bidding process was a national initiative, with London at its core, and the bid was underpinned by the promise to transform (regenerate or remake) a significant area of East London. The infrastructural investment that followed has been reinforced since then, in the form of Crossrail as well as parkland and support for the building of new residential areas and new forms of commercial development. Major infrastructural development associated with Crossrail (cutting across London from east to west) and a new high-speed railway line (HS2) providing faster connections between London and the North West of England also provides the basis for major state sponsored and private sector led development around two new rail terminals in a previously rundown part of the city. National priorities and national investments seem to have a continuing role in reinforcing London's position within England's uneven economic geography. As Ian Gordon puts it, one consequence of London's ability to draw upon the generosity of the UK nation state in the form of 'bail-outs, implicit subsidy and quantitative easing […] have been translated specifically into employment/spending power within London and overseas rather than elsewhere within the UK' (2016, p. 336).

In this context, Doreen Massey (2007) suggests that the political emphasis on London's global role is a political strategy, as much as an economic reality, because of the way in which it reinforces particular ways of thinking, which she identifies as neoliberal. The 'geographical concentration' of the very wealthy in London and the South East, 'into a self-referential echo chamber reinforces their distance from the rest of us' (2007, p. 66), and serves to reinforce a policy agenda which includes a commitment to deregulation, an emphasis on the 'untouchability' of the financial sector, and a drive to privatization of various sorts (including 'competitive individualism and personal self-reliance') (pp 38–40). For her, the role of elite agents associated with London's financial services sector is fundamental in shaping the policy agenda pursued by successive governments. The 'global' is mobilized precisely to reinforce the city's national dominance to the extent that the 'Reinvigoration of London [...] represents the rise of a new elite, and the culture in which it is embedded' (Massey 2007, p. 49).

Disunited England, divided London?

The referendum vote highlighted aspects of the disconnection between the London city region and the rest of England. As discussed, all of England's regions, outside London, recorded a vote to leave the EU, although a majority in most of the larger (more cosmopolitan) cities voted for the UK to remain a member. Of course, the English 'regions' should not be seen as homogenous entities and there was significant variation between them, just as there was within and between Northern Ireland, Wales and Scotland. But what matters here is to recognize that the pattern of voting reflected patterns of uneven development within England. In England, in a sense the vote was a form of resistance, a rejection of the existing set of arrangements, even if the nature of the alternative was not clear. In many of the older industrial (and deindustrializing or post-industrial) regions, the EU and its precursors had been active participants in the process of restructuring and consolidation that shaped their changing regional economies, and the payments made through various regional development schemes did not compensate for those shifts. Indeed, the allocation of such money could be seen as little more than a confirmation of the problems faced, rather than a serious contribution to confronting them. To put it at its most modest, people living in these regions had little reason to feel positively about the EU. The referendum threw up a strange alliance between those in the Conservative heartlands for whom traditional forms of social and political authority were being undermined in the context of 'post-imperial melancholy' (Gilroy, 2004) or 'self-pity' (O'Toole, 2018) and those in the deindustrialized regions for whom post-imperial decay was associated with economic decline while the promise of 'Europe' was always tarnished by the same experience.

In this context, the evidence that such regions are the ones most dependent on trade with Europe, or indeed most reliant on grants from Europe becomes irrelevant. This has been captured in popular and journalistic language in the notion of the 'left-behind'. The argument has been that those who have been 'left-behind' by globalization and the patterns of growth associated with it, were those who voted to leave. Once, however, it is recognized that uneven development is a process which actively repositions places and people through forms of economic restructuring – in other words a process in which there is a continuing relationship between the geographies of 'growth' and 'decline' – then a rather different set of conclusions can be drawn. From one perspective it is possible to interpret the vote as an expression of agency by those who were previously excluded, but, even if that may be a step too far, it can certainly be understood as a reaction to the process by which forms of spatial and social inequality are generated and maintained.

London is less reliant on the EU than some other regions of England, precisely because it is connected into much more extensive global networks, but voting to leave the EU was also a way of voting against the effects of uneven development driven through an economic and political system focused on London and the needs of its elites. Incidentally, this also raises some fundamental questions for those who see the English vote as representing the rise of a new English nationalism – it may do, but it also highlights the extent to which 'England' itself is fundamentally divided, rather than united around some clear-cut national agenda.

And London itself is also deeply divided. London's role as financial centre has shaped its relationship with the rest of the UK, but London is more than that. Uneven development is a more complex process. A series of inequalities and exclusions go alongside the defence of privilege in the city and its region. As a result, there may also be a danger of understating – or perhaps better, failing sufficiently to recognize – the ambiguity of London's position. In emphasizing the role of the elite two other aspects of change may be underplayed. The first is simply to recognize that even the industrial sectors dominated by the elite, particularly by business services, higher education, the media, publishing and tech industries, require a workforce that is not reducible to that elite. London draws in young people from across the UK and beyond to work in the new post-industrial industries that dominate it, even as they face dramatically increased living costs as they seek to do so. They may not be poor, but nor are they (yet) part of the elite.

Second, non-elite transnational aspects of the London experience may be downplayed in this narrative. London's success relies on the more mundane contributions of migrant labour and production, in which poverty exists alongside wealth, immiseration alongside gentrification (Judah, 2016). Not only do many of those living there identify with London more than with any national formation but the white British population as defined by the Census became a minority: those identifying as white British declined from 60 per cent to 45 per cent between 1991 and 2011 (ONS, 2012). The linkages and connections to elsewhere that are implied by such a population highlight what it means to imagine a global city region from below as well as above. London is one of the places within which living with difference is taken for granted, rather than being an exceptional experience. Stuart Hall's insight that London is made up of an intricate lattice of differences, is one that opens up a range of possibilities (Hall, 2006). It certainly has the potential to generate dramatic divisions (expressed, for example, in the 2011 riots) but it is also a space within which, whatever the tensions, people learn to live with difference, in the context of 'superdiversity' or what has been called everyday multiculture (Neal et al, 2018).

While the outcome of the Brexit vote was undoubtedly a reaction to some of the issues generated by the processes of uneven development identified by Massey and others, it is also important to recognize the extent to which the vote in London and the South East was also a reflection of the emergence of forms of transnational and differently cosmopolitan politics – in which those who live in London often stress a London identity above a national one. These are not necessarily members of a global elite – the divisions within London and the wider city region make it impossible to identify them in this way. But that not only raises questions about the nature of the 'England' to which an English nationalism may hope to appeal, but also to open up the possibility of generating a political identity and agency, within and beyond the nation, linked into wider transnational networks but also deeply rooted in place. This is reflected in David Lammy's evocation of London as a potential city state, but there is a danger of exaggerating London's exceptionalism, since the interests of many of its residents may also provide the basis for political alliances stretching out into England's other regions.

London is the UK's world city and in that role it has helped to maintain and reinforce patterns of inequality across that wider geography. The interests of its elites have tended to dominate political and economic decision-making, and that has been reflected in the patterns of infrastructural investment as well as the language of politics. But London is more than its elites and that too has begun to develop rather different sets of political and economic initiative – uneven development is complex and ambiguous. The Remain vote in London was not just a vote of the elites (many of whom live in the wider South East), it was a vote of the young, the multicultural and the dispossessed as well as the privileged.

From European Union to Disunited Kingdom?

The weight of London and the South East of England at the heart of the UK's political settlement is not a new phenomenon, but its particular contemporary form certainly is, because of the way it is linked into wider global circuits of finance and service industries. The repositioning of London is a response to living in a post-imperial world – no longer at the centre of an empire, even a declining and fading one, but one node (one world city) among others. But, as Tom Nairn (1975) recognized long ago, this also means that some of the other assumptions about London as capital city of an imperial state no longer hold as they once did. Cities such as Glasgow and Belfast may once have been deeply embedded in the imperial project, supplying ships and heavy engineering (as well as people) but they no longer are.

England was understood to be the foundation on which Britain, Great Britain and the UK were built – hence, there are no specific government institutions for England. There is no separate English parliament, although since 2015 where it is deemed that particular bills only affect England (or England and Wales) they can only be passed into legislation if a majority of MPs elected for English constituencies (or English and Welsh MPs where appropriate) support them. In a sense, England's constitutional position reflects the extent to which England has been positioned as the norm against which other national formations are assumed to define themselves. It is not uncommon for England and Britain to be used interchangeably in popular speech in England and by many of those commenting from outside the UK. So, for example, the UK's current Queen is always identified as Queen Elizabeth II, although the first Queen Elizabeth was only Queen of England.

The votes in the Brexit referendum reflected some significant differences between the ways in which national identity is understood in the various nations and territories that make up the UK. It has been argued that the Leave vote and support for the UKIP leading up to the vote was, at least in part, an expression of English nationalism. However, this is a 'nationalism' with a rather uncertain presence, and uneasy expression. The England to which it appeals is wrapped up in nostalgia for a past that never was and fits uneasily with the reality of a national formation that is already deeply divided, between London and a set of deindustrializing or deindustrialized regions, between big cities and small towns, between areas at ease with multicultural expression and migrant populations and those (often neighbouring) that are not.

The vote highlighted some real divisions, rooted in material experience and not just irrational rage. To that extent, it was a reflection of the working out of uneven development across England. This is not a straightforward story of the break-up of Britain, both because the divisions do not neatly play across the territorial constitution of the UK, and because the national identities in play are more complex and ambiguous than any such conclusion would require. In one sense, the UK is more divided than the breakup story might suggest – 'England' is by no means a unified territory or nation, and the tensions that cut across any attempt to define its national identity are deep. The vote in England clearly reflected those divisions, whether from the perspective of London (and the cities) or those of the 'regions'.

References

Amin, A., D. Massey and N. Thrift (2003) *Decentering the Nation: A Radical Approach to Regional Inequality*, London: Catalyst.

Barnett, A. (2017) *The Lure of Greatness: England's Brexit and America's Trump*, London: Unbound.

Clarke, H. D., M. Goodwin and P. Whitley (2017) *Brexit: Why Britain Voted to Leave the European Union*, Cambridge: Cambridge University Press.

Gilroy, P. (2004) *After Empire: Melancholia or Convivial Culture?*, London: Routledge.

Gordon, I. (2016) 'Quantitative easing of an international financial centre: how London came so well out of the post-2007 crisis', *Cambridge Journal of Regions, Economy and Society*, 9(2): 335–53.

Gordon, I., T. Travers and C. Whitehead (2003) *London's Place in the UK Economy 2003*, London: Corporation of London.

Hall, P., R. Imrie, L. Lees and M. Raco (2009) 'Planning London: a conversation with Peter Hall', in R. Imrie, L. Lees and M. Raco (eds) *Regenerating London: Governance, Sustainability and Community in a Global City*, Abingdon: Routledge.

Hall, S. (2006) 'Cosmopolitan promises, multicultural realities', in R. Scholar (ed.) *Divided Cities: The Oxford Amnesty Lectures 2003*, Oxford: Oxford University Press, pp 20–51.

Jennings, W. and G. Stoker (2016) 'The bifurcation of politics: two Englands', *The Political Quarterly*, 87(3): 372–82.

Judah, B. (2016) *This is London. Life and Death in the World City*, London: Picador.

Lammy, D. (2017) 'London must look to be a city-state if hard Brexit goes ahead', *Evening Standard*, 20 March.

Martin, R., A. Pike, P. Tyler and B. Gardiner (2016) 'Spatially rebalancing the UK economy: towards a new policy model?', *Regional Studies*, 50(2): 342–57.

Massey, D. (2007) *World City*, Cambridge: Polity.

McCann, P. (2016) *The UK Regional-National Economic Problem: Geography, Globalisation and Governance*, Abingdon: Routledge.

Nairn, T. (1975) 'The Modern Janus', *New Left Review*, 1(94): 3–29.

Neal, S., K. Bennett, A. Cochrane and G. Mohan (2018) *Lived Experiences of Multiculture: The New Social and Spatial Relations of Diversity*, London: Routledge.

O'Toole, F. (2018) *Heroic Failure. Brexit and the Politics of Pain*, London: Head of Zeus.

ONS (2012) *Ethnicity and National Identity in England and Wales: 2011*, Newport: Office for National Statistics: https://www.ons.gov.uk/peoplepopulationandcommunity/culturalidentity/ethnicity/articles/ethnicityandnationalidentityinenglandandwales/2012-12-11.

The Electoral Commission (2017) *EU Referendum Results*: https://www.electoralcommission.org.uk/find-information-by-subject/elections-and-referendums/past-elections-and-referendums/eu-referendum/electorate-and-count-information.

12

Understanding Brexit in Wales: Austerity, Elites and National Identity

Hugh Mackay

At first glance, the figures show that support for Brexit in Wales was similar to that in England. As in England, there was a correlation in Wales between voting preference in the referendum with age, level of education, a concern about immigration driving wages down and generating pressure on public services, political alienation and authoritarian attitudes (Seidler, 2018; Awan-Scully 2017). An important issue for Leave voters was a sense that those with power were looking after themselves rather than after 'us', the 'ordinary people'. Voting Leave was thus a political act against the establishment, against those who run the country.

Despite these important commonalities across the nations of the UK, one can identify distinctive dimensions of support for Brexit in Wales. These are the focus of this chapter. Compared with England, Wales is poorer and the devolved government is more social-democratic. It also has an elite with different characteristics from the English elite and a powerful sense of Welsh national identity. This chapter takes as its starting point the similarity in voting in Wales and England, but suggests that this might be for different reasons. It argues that the Leave vote in Wales was lower than might be expected given the demographics of Wales because of (a) the nature of the elite in Wales and (b) national identity in Wales.

This chapter explores some implications of the distinct nature of the elite in Wales for Leave voters, for many of whom voting Leave was voting against the elite. By and large, the Welsh elite is not an economic elite but a cultural, political and professional one. While Wales shares much of its history with England, its history is also divergent – in terms of its incorporation with England in the 1536 Act of Union, its language, its limited economic power, its poverty and its Labour traditions. Together these mean that, in Wales, members of the elite are much less separated from ordinary people, that social hierarchies are less harsh or obvious (Clayton, 2013).

The other issue addressed in this chapter is the connection between national identity and voting Leave. The chapter explains that in England, those with the strongest sense of English national identity voted most heavily for Leave, whereas those who identified as British more than English tended to vote Remain. In Scotland, the situation was the reverse, with Britishness being associated most strongly with voting Leave, and Scottish identification with voting Remain. In Wales, by contrast, Welsh identification does not map onto voting one way or the other, with strong Remain votes in parts of rural Wales and strong Leave votes in the Valleys, the two areas where Welsh identification is the strongest. If one examines areas where the Welsh language, which is commonly associated with strong Welsh national identification, is strongest, however, then there *is* an association with voting Remain. So not only are strong Welsh-speaking areas not coterminous with areas where Welsh national identification is high (as is commonly assumed) but also it is the Welsh language, not Welsh national identification, that was associated with voting patterns in the referendum – with Welsh-speaking areas voting Remain.

The chapter argues that, while the outcome of the vote was similar in Wales to England, and Leave voters experienced similar constraints on their agency, the reasons for the voting behaviour can be seen as different in some ways.

Who voted Leave in Wales?

The outcome of the referendum on 23 June 2016 in the nations of the UK was as follows (see also Table 12.1):

The strongest support for Remain was in Scotland; then Northern Ireland; followed by Wales; with England just slightly lower. In England, London was the only region to vote Remain, and the vote for Leave was higher in every region of England bar London than was the vote for Leave in Wales (or Northern Ireland or Scotland). The outcome for the UK, because England has about 85 per cent of the population of the UK, was the overall slender majority for Leave.

Table 12.1 Outcome of the 2016 referendum in the nations of the UK

	Leave %	Remain %	Turnout %
England	53.4	46.6	73.0
Wales	52.5	47.5	71.7
Scotland	38.0	62.0	67.2
Northern Ireland	44.2	55.8	62.7
UK	51.9	48.1	72.2

Source: Electoral Commission, 2016

In all of the south Wales former coal mining valleys, the majority voted Leave. This is an area which shares many of the characteristics of the deindustrialized parts of England that voted Leave. Only five Welsh local authority areas (of 22) voted Remain. These were a combination of more cosmopolitan and affluent places (Cardiff, Monmouthshire and the Vale of Glamorgan) and the rural Welsh heartland, *y Fro Gymraeg*, where Welsh nationalism and the Welsh language are strong (Ceredigion and Gwynedd). The latter is the electoral base of Plaid Cymru, the staunchly pro-European nationalist party, which received 20 per cent of the vote in Wales in the 2016 Assembly election; they are areas that voted strongly for devolution in 1997.

Voting Leave occurred most strongly where there was support for UKIP in the National Assembly for Wales election in 2016. In that election, up to 22 per cent of the vote in the industrial valleys of south Wales, places which had voted solidly Labour for about a century, went to UKIP. Overall, UKIP in that election gained 13 per cent of the vote in Wales and took seven seats in the National Assembly – in part because of its system of partial proportional representation.

The areas of Wales that voted most strongly for Leave were among the poorest (which also meant that they were the areas receiving considerable EU structural funds). Blaenau Gwent had the largest Leave vote (62 per cent) and is the local authority with the second highest rate of child poverty in Wales. Despite massive EU structural funding, the economic situation of its residents had not improved. The value of EU structural funds in these communities was dismissed because material conditions had remained so poor (Ifan et al, 2016).

In the vast and growing literature on Brexit, there is general agreement as to the causes of Leave voting and the characteristics of Leave voters. Critical factors for Leave voters included austerity policies, the reduction in the scope and scale of the welfare state, and a sense of experiencing reduced agency (Fetzer, 2018; see Chapters Grasso and Montgomery, Guderjan and Wilding, Mckenzie, and Morelli). Drawing on Lord Ashcroft Polls (2016), Goodwin and Heath (2016) and Becker et al (2016), the following summarizes the evidence on the characteristics of those who voted Leave.

Support for Leave was 10 percentage points higher among those earning less than £20,000 per year than it was among those with an income of £60,000+ per year. As Wales is a poorer place, relative to the other nations of the UK, one would expect support for Brexit to be *higher* in Wales than in England (which it was not). 24 per cent of people in Wales live in relative income poverty, after housing costs, compared with 22 per cent in England, 19 per cent in Scotland and 20 per cent in Northern Ireland. ('Relative income poverty' means living in a household where total income from all sources is less than 60 per cent of the median UK household income.) Similarly, an individual in Wales has a 13 per cent chance of living in persistent poverty, compared with 12 per cent in England, 11 per cent in Northern Ireland and 8 per cent in Scotland. ('Persistent poverty', a Department for Work and Pensions category, is when, after housing costs, an individual is living in relative income poverty for three out of four consecutive years.)

In addition to poverty, unemployment, low skilled or manual occupations and lower levels of education are characteristic of those who voted Leave: 59 per cent of those out of work voted Leave, whereas 45 per cent of those in full employment did so; 71 per cent of those in low-skilled and manual occupations voted Leave compared with 41 per cent of those in professional occupations; 75 per cent of voters with GCSEs or less voted Leave, whilst 68 per cent of those with a degree voted Remain.

As shown in the Table 12.2, the young were much more likely than the elderly to vote Remain, with a levelling off at the upper end of the age range.

Table 12.2 Percentage of Leave voters (by age) in the 2016 referendum

Age	Percentage voting Leave
18–24	27
25–34	38
35–44	48
45–54	56
55–64	57
65+	60

Source: Lord Ashcroft Polls, 2016

Leave voters also show a distinctive set of qualitative or attitudinal characteristics. Those who feel 'left behind' by rapid economic change and cut adrift from the mainstream consensus were the most likely to support Brexit. They had concerns about immigration (in the sense of a rise in the level of immigration not the proportion of immigrants in the area); jobs being taken and wages being depressed; a desire to 'take back control', or exercise sovereignty; and right-wing perspectives in general (Seidler, 2018; Taylor, 2017).

Given the characteristics of Welsh society and its economy, with a relatively elderly and low-skilled population, one might expect that in Wales there would be stronger support for Leave than in England. However, support for Leave was slightly lower in Wales than in England. Possibly, the relative lack of support for Leave is due to specifically Welsh factors, which are explored in the remainder of this chapter.

Wales's political elite and egalitarian culture

Nation building in Wales can be traced back for centuries but took a major step at the end of the 20th century with the establishment of the National Assembly for Wales in 1999. Until recently, the main focus of nation builders was on cultural institutions, and much of the nationalist strand of politics has been cultural. Because of this the elite in Wales has been largely a cultural one (Day et al, 2006). There is little in the way of a prominent economic elite in Wales, because the economy is largely owned and controlled from outside Wales and because, by and large, captains of industry and the corporations which run the economy of Wales are seen as outsiders by the Welsh population. This is very different from the situation in England and Scotland. Over the past two decades the political elite has coalesced and come to the fore, as the devolution project has been realized and has developed. The political and cultural elite in Wales almost entirely supported Remain, seeing the well-being of Wales as best assured by membership of the single market, the customs union and EU membership generally. Given the growing support for devolution in Wales, one might expect the political elite in Wales to have had some influence on voting in the referendum.

The Welsh government has consistently been led by Labour, and there were no Leave voices among their Assembly Members (AMs) during the referendum campaign. The single Liberal Democrat AM and the independent AM, a defector from Plaid Cymru, who propped up the Labour Party in government, have both strongly supported Remain. The Welsh Conservatives were also largely pro Remain – though the leader at the time of the referendum (Andrew R. T. Davies) provides a notable exception, and was ousted as leader in 2018 in part because of his vociferous pro-Leave stance. Plaid Cymru AMs have all been staunchly pro-European. Internationalism is core to the ideology of Plaid Cymru, with 'Independence in Europe', the notion of bypassing the British state, being one of its mantras. The notion of 'Wales in Europe' has had strong support in Labour as well as Plaid Cymru circles. The exception to this support by political leaders in Wales for Remain is UKIP, which since the 2016 election has had seven AMs, due in part to the proportional representation mechanism in the voting system to the Assembly.

Turning to the Westminster level, in Wales there are 40 Members of Parliament (MPs) of whom, at the time of writing, 28 were Labour, eight Conservative and four Plaid Cymru. At the time of the referendum, all supported Remain, bar one Labour MP and four Conservative MPs. None of these five were prominent pro Brexit voices in the referendum campaign or subsequently.

As well as being strongly pro Remain, the dominant discourse is that the elite in Wales is less distanced from ordinary people. To understand the relatively egalitarian culture of Wales the notion of the *gwerin* is helpful. It is an important term for the 'ordinary or common people' but encompasses, too, notions of being respectable and cultured (Lord, 2013). In the national psyche, Wales is seen as a cultured nation, and those who have experienced upward social mobility tend to be proud of their relatively humble origins (Clayton, 2013). This is almost the reverse of snobbery about a relatively elevated class position.

A corollary of this is a distinct and perhaps dominant view of the elite, embodied in the term *crachach*, a pejorative word to refer to those who pretend that they are a cut above the others; but also to the powerful, the elite. At different times and in different contexts, it has been used to refer to leaders of the established church, to Tories, to those from public schools and to those with bourgeois or upper-class English traits; and it has been applied to those with power in Wales, including Welsh speakers and leaders of the Labour Party (O'Leary, 2017).

Compared with MPs, AMs are much more embedded in Welsh society: their children use the same schools and they use the same health care and transport systems as their constituents. There is a much stronger public-sector ethos in Wales than in England, with more universal and less competitive and privatized forms of state provision. Plus, of course, there is geography: Wales is a small place, and Cardiff too – so the political elite experiences everyday life much more as do their constituents than is the case with MPs who spend the week in London. Elites in Wales are less divorced from ordinary people – with fewer public schools, the Welsh language, a shared passion for the national rugby team and bound together by a shared 'other'. There is a relative strength to the interconnectedness of social relationships in Wales – because of its small scale and its well-defined boundaries (Williams, 2018).

In Wales, social cohesion is helped by people seeing the economic elite, and especially the 1 per cent and the City of London, as living in England or further afield and as not being 'Welsh'. The major industries and businesses in Wales, historically and today, are not owned or controlled by people in Wales. This increases social solidarity across classes within Wales.

Debates and policy on welfare and social justice take a much more social-democratic form in Wales – where, unlike England, there are no academy schools or school league tables, and medical prescriptions are free. The rhetoric is about collaboration and partnership, rather than competition and the market, with voices on the right relatively marginal compared with the situation at Westminster (Morgan, 2003). As a result, Welsh politics remain social democratic, with what has been referred to as 'clear red water' separating Welsh Labour from the then New Labour project; and a First Minister who is a supporter of Jeremy Corbyn.

As well, many of the dominant institutions, especially the National Assembly and associated statutory bodies, but also the institutions of civil society, are relatively new, and hence surrounded by hope and expectation, rather than mired in traditions of inefficiency, corruption and self-interest. The evidence is that Cardiff Bay politicians and political institutions are held in higher esteem than their Westminster equivalents (Scully and Wyn Jones, 2015). This, however, was insufficient for them to sway the electorate at the EU referendum. One could argue that the nature of the elite in Wales is the reason why, given its demographics, the vote for Leave was not higher in Wales. On the other hand, one could consider why there was a similar vote for Leave when the Welsh elite is so different from the elite in England. There are three possible explanations for this.

First, the referendum seems to have been perceived by the political elite and by voters as a Westminster rather than a devolved matter, hence involving the UK or London-based elite, rather than the Welsh elite. As with so many elections, voters were responding to UK-wide political factors. They see the London elite as the elite – the 1 per cent, the Westminster government, the economic elite and/or the UK establishment. The Welsh elite is more of a subaltern elite, and perhaps is seen as such within Wales. If this is the case, it has implications for all sorts of areas of politics and policy, and raises questions about the maturity and significance of the Welsh political system.

Second, it could be that support for Welsh Labour is waning (see Edwards, 2010 for a thorough account of the growth and decline of support for Labour in Wales). In many areas support for Labour shifted to UKIP in the 2016 Assembly election and the vote was for Leave in the Brexit referendum, though support reverted to Labour in the general election of 2017.

A third possible explanation is the relative silence of the elite in Wales in the run-up to the Brexit referendum. Even though the political leadership in Wales, as in Westminster but more so, is predominantly Remain, in the campaign its profile was remarkably low. Until the final week of the campaign, there was very little activity by Welsh politicians in the referendum campaign. Welsh politicians, by and large, left it to their counterparts at Westminster to take up the cause (where Labour activists were reluctant to support Cameron or to work actively to resolve an internal Conservative Party affair, and Corbyn expressed minimal support on the part of Labour). So Remain voices were not prominent in Wales; but nor was there much in the way of vocal Leave voices in Wales, let alone any equivalent of Nigel Farage, Boris Johnson or Jacob Rees-Mogg.

Welsh identity and language

Clearly, senses of Englishness have come to the fore in recent years, and connect with attitudes to the EU. There is a body of evidence showing that, for at least 20 years, people in England have generally felt both British and English, with a slight but gently declining preference for 'British' (Curtice, 2013). When forcing people to choose only one of these two national identities, the data shows that, since devolution in 1999, the number choosing 'English' has increased, and the number seeing themselves as 'British' has declined. The significance of these identifications can be explored using 'the Moreno question', which classifies voters' national identifications in terms of (in the case of the English and British): (a) English not British; (b) More English than British; (c) Equally English and British; (d) More British than English; or (e) British not English.

Using this approach, in the period 1997–2009, there was a significant increase of those in England identifying as 'English not British' and a decline of those seeing themselves as 'equally English and British'. Nonetheless, only a minority (17 per cent in 2009) assert that they are 'English not British'. In Scotland, by contrast, the figures for Scottish identity are much higher: about 75 per cent choose 'Scottish not British' when forced to choose between Scottish and British in the period 1992–2011, with a growth in 1992–97, followed by a levelling off until 2011.

In Wales, if forced to choose just one national identity, only just over half choose 'Welsh'. When asked the Moreno question, about 40 per cent say they are 'Welsh not British' or 'more Welsh than British' – compared with about 60 per cent who say the equivalent in Scotland. So, overall, national identification is strongest in Scotland and lowest in England, with Wales in between (Curtice, 2013).

How does this relate to attitudes to the EU? Pre-referendum data suggest little relationship between Welsh and Scottish identity and views on Europe – whereas strong feelings of Englishness were associated with a Leave vote in England (Ormston, 2015). This is the opposite of the situation in 1975, when England was the nation which voted most strongly to join the European Economic Community. This turnaround can be traced to 2006, when the British Household Panel Survey first identified the trend for England to diverge from Scotland and Wales by becoming negative about the EU (Henderson et al, 2016). By 2014, the Future of England Survey shows very clearly that in Wales and Scotland, national identity does not appear to structure attitudes on EU membership; whereas the more English an identity, the more likely was a respondent to be negative about, or to want to leave, the EU. In the referendum, people who felt strongly or exclusively English remained more sceptical of the EU than those who felt more British; whereas in Scotland, those who identified as British were more negative about the EU than those who identified as Scottish. Those who see themselves as more British than English also include those who want to avoid associating themselves with English nationalism and its football violence and extremism.

In England Remain voters were nearly twice as likely as Leave voters to see themselves as 'more British than English' or 'British not English'; while Leave voters were more than twice as likely as Remain voters to describe themselves as 'more English than British' or 'English not British'. To put it another way, over two thirds of those who considered themselves 'more English than British' voted to leave; while nearly two thirds of those who considered themselves 'more British than English' voted to remain (Lord Ashcroft Polls, 2016).

This link between English national identity and Euroscepticism came into play in the referendum, connecting with the 'resentful nationalism' of UKIP (Mann and Fenton, 2017). English nationalism has become a focus or rallying point for those who feel 'left behind', or feel that they have less agency, and who have become disillusioned or angry with the elite. It has come to be associated with economic marginalization and with concerns about immigration (see Chapters Morelli, Cochrane, and Mckenzie). The arrival of the Welsh Assembly and the Scottish Parliament have exacerbated a crisis of national identity and feelings of a democratic deficit in England (Henderson et al, 2016), exemplified by the limited nature of devolution in England and the absence of an English Assembly or Parliament.

Welsh national identity, however, correlates with neither Remain nor Leave voting (see Table 12.3). There is a shift at this juncture from data on individuals' attitudes and their voting behaviour, to the characteristics of local authority voting areas. This is because in Wales, there is a lack of data to explore this issue directly, so one has to consider local data on Welsh identity and speaking Welsh. Although Richard Wyn Jones has argued that Britishness is associated with anti-European sentiment in Wales as in Scotland (and unlike in England) this does not seem to be the case (Wyn Jones, 2018). If we examine the percentage in an area 'who consider themselves Welsh', the areas with the highest figures are Blaenau Gwent (81 per cent), Merthyr Tydfil (80 per cent), Neath Port Talbot (80 per cent), Caerphilly (80 per cent), Rhondda Cynon Taff (80 per cent), Bridgend (74 per cent) and Torfaen (74 per cent) – which are roughly the south Wales valley areas where the Leave vote was highest (StatsWales, 2019a). These are areas where immigration from England and elsewhere is lowest (StatsWales, 2019c).

At the other end of the voting spectrum, the five localities in Wales which voted Remain have much lower percentages who consider themselves Welsh. The five areas include three affluent or cosmopolitan areas (Cardiff (60 per cent), Monmouthshire (53 per cent) and the Vale of Glamorgan (63 per cent)), and two areas in *Y Fro Gymraeg*,

Table 12.3 Welsh and British identification as reflected in the 2016 referendum

	Overall %	Leave voters %	Remain voters %
Welsh not British	11	11	12
More Welsh than British	20	18	21
Equally Welsh and British	29	31	28
More British than Welsh	8	8	7
British not Welsh	25	25	24

Source: Lord Ashcroft Polls, 2016

the Welsh-speaking heartland (Gwynedd (68 per cent) and Ceredigion (54 per cent)) (StatsWales, 2019a). These generally are areas of high immigration, most of which is from England (StatsWales, 2019c).

Whilst identification as Welsh does not correlate with voting Remain, speaking Welsh (which is often seen as synonymous with national identification) does so. The percentage of people able to speak Welsh is highest in Gwynedd (65 per cent), and Ceredigion is third in the table (47 per cent) (StatsWales, 2019b). In other words, there *is* a relationship between areas with a high proportion of Welsh speakers and voting Remain. Returning to the Valleys – the deindustrialized, Leave-voting region, with the highest Welsh identity – we find the *lowest* level of Welsh language speakers: 8 per cent in Blaenau Gwent, 10 per cent in Torfaen and 9 per cent in Merthyr Tydfil. Here the relationship between speaking Welsh and having a Welsh identity is inverse.

Voting in the referendum not correlating with identification as Welsh is confirmed by a post-referendum poll of 629 respondents in Wales in June 2016. This shows an even split between those who identify as 'more Welsh than British' or 'Welsh only', those who identify as 'equally Welsh and British' and those who identify as 'British not Welsh' – with about a third in each of these three groups, and with a roughly similar spread for Remain as well as Leave voters (Lord Ashcroft Polls, 2016). In conclusion, Welsh identification did not structure voting in the referendum in Wales, despite the very strong sense of Welsh identity. Welsh language speaking areas, however, showed a high level of support for Remain.

Conclusion

The referendum result in Wales resembled that of England but was slightly less pro Leave. The nature of Wales' demographics and its economy might lead one to expect Wales to be *more* pro Leave than it was. This chapter has examined this in terms of two factors: first, a different sort of elite and a more social-democratic culture; and second, Welsh national identity and the Welsh language.

The chapter has argued that in Wales the elite is different from the Westminster, London or British elite. In London one finds the economic elite and those in the Westminster bubble – cosmopolitan beneficiaries of globalization. By contrast, the elite in Wales is a cultural and political but not an economic elite, and the politics is more social-democratic and less market-focused. In this situation, one might expect less sense of a lack of agency, and less negativity about the elite. The outcome is that Wales is less divided as a society – which may explain the lower support for Brexit, compared with England and with what one might expect given the socio-economic characteristics of Wales.

The other argument that has been explored is the salience of Welsh national identity for the vote. Here the evidence suggests that there is no relationship between national identification and voting in the referendum – which is different from the situation in both England and Scotland (albeit with the opposite voting consequences in these two nations). It counters arguments that Wales, by dint of its historical relationship with England, is more Euro-positive in culture or politics than the UK as a whole. Local data on Welsh identity and speaking Welsh shows that identification as Welsh is strongest where the Leave vote was highest; and that where Remain was highest, Welsh identification was lower than in these core Leave areas. If we examine the Welsh language, however, we find an association between areas where Welsh speaking is high and a strong Remain vote. Such support for Europe on the part of Welsh speakers refutes arguments that voting Leave is a sign of rural parochialism – and also shows how the language is not coterminous with national identity.

While it is not obvious why Wales voted as it did, its elites and politics, and the Welsh language, but not Welsh identification, offer explanations of the voting pattern. These factors help us to explain why, considering the characteristics of Wales, the Leave vote was not higher than it was.

References

Awan-Scully, R. (2017) 'New Research shows deep divisions persisting on Brexit', *Blog post*, 26 October: https://blogs.cardiff.ac.uk/brexit/2017/10/26/new-research-shows-deep-divisions-persisting-on-brexit/.

Becker, S. O., T. Fetzer and D. Novy (2016) *Who Voted for Brexit? A Comprehensive District-Level Analysis*, Working Paper 305, Warwick: Centre for Competitive Advantage in the Global Economy, University of Warwick.

Clayton, A. (2013) *Good Eggs, Fixers and Movers: the Cultural Elite in Wales*, PhD thesis, Cardiff University.

Curtice, J. (2013) *National Identity and Constitutional Change*, Foresight Project on Future Identities, London: Government Office for Science.

Day, G., D. Dunkerley and A. Thompson (2006) *Civil Society in Wales. Policy, Politics and* People, Cardiff: University of Wales Press.

Edwards, A. (2010) 'Labour traditions', in H. Mackay (ed.) *Understanding Contemporary* Wales, Cardiff: University of Wales Press, pp 197–230.

Electoral Commission (2016) 'Results and turnout at the EU referendum', https://www.electoralcommission.org.uk/who-we-are-and-what-we-do/elections-and-referendums/past-elections-and-referendums/eu-referendum/results-and-turnout-eu-referendum.

Fetzer, T. (2018) *Did Austerity Cause Brexit?*, Working Paper 381, Warwick: Centre for Competitive Advantage in the Global Economy, University of Warwick.

Goodwin, M. J. and O. Heath (2016) *Brexit vote explained: poverty, low skills and lack of opportunities*, York: Joseph Rowntree Foundation.

Henderson, A., C. Jeffery, R. L. Ira, R. Scully, D. Wincott and R. Wyn Jones (2016) 'England, Englishness and Brexit', *Political Quarterly*, 87(2): 187–99.

Ifan, G., E. G. Poole and R. Wyn Jones (2016) *Wales and the EU Referendum: Estimating Wales' Net Contribution to the European Union*, Cardiff: Wales Governance Centre, Cardiff University.

Lord Ashcroft Polls (2016): https://lordashcroftpolls.com/wp-content/uploads/2016/06/How-the-UK-voted-Full-tables-1.pdf, p. 293.

Lord, P. (2013), 'Welsh Keywords: Gwerin', *Planet*, 211: 26–34.

Mann, R. and S. Fenton (2017), *Nation, Class and Resentment. The Politics of National Identity in England, Scotland and Wales*, London: Palgrave Macmillan.

Morgan, R. (2003) 'Clear Red Water', *Agenda*, Cardiff: Institute of Welsh Affairs, Spring, pp 13–14.

O'Leary, P. (2017) 'Welsh Keywords: Crachach', *Planet*, 227: 24–32.

Ormston, R. (2015) *Disunited Kingdom? Attitudes to the EU across the UK*, London: NatCen Social Research.

Scully, R. and R. Wyn Jones (2015) 'The public legitimacy of the National Assembly for Wales', *Journal of Legislative Studies*, 21(4): 515–33.

Seidler, V. (2018) *Making Sense of Brexit*, Bristol: Policy Press.

StatsWales (2019a) 'National identity by area and identity', *Annual population survey*, Cardiff: ONS, Welsh Government.

StatsWales (2019b) 'Welsh speakers by local authority', *2011 Census*, Cardiff: ONS, Welsh Government.

StatsWales (2019c) 'Migration flows in Wales and with UK countries, by origin and destination', Cardiff: ONS, Welsh Government.

Taylor, G. (2017) *Understanding Brexit. Why Britain voted to leave the EU*, Bingley: Emerald Publishing.

Williams, D. G. (2018) 'Welsh Keywords: Dinasyddiaeth', *Planet*, 231: 28–36.

Wyn Jones, R. (2018) 'Holyhead will be one of the biggest losers from Brexit', *Irish Times*, 4 January.

13

Scotland, Brexit and the Broken Promise of Democracy

Klaus Stolz

Introduction

Britain's Brexit vote in June 2016 can quite plausibly be interpreted as a reaction to a broken (or at least unfulfilled) 'promise of democracy' (Dallmayr, 2010) – a promise that includes economic, social, cultural and political participation and allows for individual as well as collective forms of agency in addition to decision-making by distant governments and corporate business elites. In England and Wales, populist Leave campaigners successfully portrayed the European Union as the very opposite of the democratic promise and an obstacle to social, cultural and political agency from below. While political disillusionment is certainly no less prevalent north of the border, in Scotland the response to this unfulfilled or broken promise has taken a rather different form. In the Brexit referendum a huge majority of Scots (62 per cent) rejected the simplistic notion that leaving the European Union would actually allow ordinary people to take back control over their daily lives.

This chapter explores how we can explain the different attitudes towards European integration in Scotland. Scotland was much more Eurosceptical than England in the 1975 referendum on entry to the European Community (58 per cent approval in Scotland versus 69 per cent in England), so any essentialist reading of a pro-European national character can be rejected from the outset. Instead, the first historical conjuncture since then that might help to reveal Scotland's deviation can be seen as the era of Thatcherism. Section two argues that Thatcherism created the perception of 'a democratic deficit' in

Scotland, long before debates around the democratic legitimacy of the EU had emerged. Section three looks at the then-fledgling Scottish self-government, and shows that many of Scotland's attempts to overcome this deficit were closely linked to the European integration process. Europe has thus been seen predominantly as part of the solution rather than the problem. How this fundamental difference played out during the Brexit referendum campaign is discussed in section four. Section five finally deals with the effects the Brexit decision and the subsequent negotiations may have on Scotland's constitutional status. The conclusion summarizes and contextualizes these findings focusing on Scotland's quest for democracy and agency throughout its distinct Brexit experience.

Scottish agency, that is Scotland's capacity for collective action, can be seen as conditioned by a constantly changing yet 'distinctive combination of institutional infrastructure, identity, and interests' (Moore and Booth, 1989, p. 151). Institutionally it is constrained first and foremost by the unitary character of the British state. Before devolution, there had been no authoritative form of interest aggregation at the Scottish level at all and thus no unified Scottish actor. Scottish input into meaningful decision-making had been restricted either to formal representation at Westminster, largely via the Labour Party, or to informal policy networks, usually organized around a Scottish Office department (cf. Midwinter et al, 1991, p. 202).

This changed fundamentally in 1999 with the establishment of a Scottish parliament endowed with a wide range of legislative competences on domestic issues. Not only did the institutions of Scottish self-government allow a much wider range of groups and individuals to exercise agency in the domestic Scottish arena, it also entailed the creation of a unified Scottish actor, the Scottish Executive, with the potential to exercise Scottish agency in the UK arena and beyond. However, as the Brexit process shows, this capacity remains seriously hampered by the unaltered unitary character of the British state that has no formal role for the devolved executives.

Apart from formal institutional structures, agency also depends on social interaction and negotiations (McAnulla, 2002, p. 286). Pre-devolution, agency in Scotland was expressed most notably in the 'capacity of Scottish civil society to resolve its internal social and political tensions for itself' (Paterson, 1994, p. 181); in a 'managed autonomy' the limits of the Scottish civil society were constantly renegotiated with the central state. In the absence of formal institutional powers, Scottish agency in the UK arena depended – and still depends – to a large extent on common interests and on the capacity to find common ground with non-Scottish actors in the pursuit of common projects. One such large-scale project was the postwar establishment of a British welfare state; including regional policy measures for Scotland. It is thus unsurprising that Margaret Thatcher's fundamental attack on this common project together with her attack on Scotland's managed autonomy triggered major discontent in Scotland.

Thatcherism in Scotland

Margaret Thatcher's radical neoliberal dismissal of the Keynesian postwar consensus was contentious throughout the UK, but also had a clear and explicit territorial dimension to it. While Thatcherism provoked hostile reactions in Wales and Northern England, in Scotland it has been the origin of political divergence from the rest of the UK that eventually led to the Scottish independence referendum in 2014.

In terms of public policy, Thatcher's government could have hardly been more at odds with Scottish attitudes and preferences. Deindustrialization led to factory and pit closures causing social and economic hardship in the Scottish industrial heartlands. The privatization of public services and austerity policies at the time contracted the Scottish public sector, which had traditionally been much more important to the Scottish economy than elsewhere in the UK. Cuts of welfare budgets and the introduction of the highly controversial 'poll tax' one year earlier than in the rest of the UK were of particular concern to the poorest segments of Scottish society.

Yet, Thatcher's neoliberal agenda not only had detrimental material effects on Scotland, it also stood in direct opposition to its fundamental values and norms, including its self-perception as a distinct nation within the UK. Thatcher's deep individualism and her rejection of the notion of 'society' conflicted fundamentally with a much more social-democratic and community-oriented attitude in Scotland. Her centralization of state power at Whitehall and her strict enforcement of the unitary principle at the expense of traditional interpretations of Britain as a union state can be seen as a direct revocation of the historic compromise between the British state and Scottish society. Culling discretionary powers of state administration, draining local government of its financial resources and attacking trade unions and other civic bodies was widely deplored across the UK. In Scotland, however, this was perceived above all as 'an attack on Scotland itself' (McCrone, 1992, p. 172) and on its established system of 'managed autonomy' (Paterson, 1994).

Margaret Thatcher's premiership also highlighted the representational deficits of the majoritarian British political system. While Thatcher's Conservatives won three consecutive general elections in the UK, they had been continuously and quite drastically rejected at the Scottish ballot box from day one. Decreasing their share of votes down to 24 per cent and their number of Scottish seats to ten in 1987, many Scots openly questioned the Conservative government's mandate to rule over Scotland. The rejection of the UK government in one of its constituent nations together with the failure of the first-past-the-post electoral system to produce regular government alternation (a mechanism that lies at the heart of majoritarian democracy) produced a serious crisis of political legitimacy for the British state in Scotland. The traditional Westminster system was increasingly seen as anachronistic and undemocratic, denying Scotland political voice and agency.

During this period, the Scottish voice was loudest in the cultural sphere expressing grievances and misgivings, as the historian Christopher Harvie put it: '… the 1980s saw a nationalist stance become general among the Scottish intelligentsia […]. The orthodoxy is now that the revival in painting, film and the novel, in poetry and drama – staged and televised – kept a "national movement" in being' (1991, p. 30). This politicization also extended to the music scene, where folk and rock bands not only combined traditional expressions of Scottishness (for example accent, content, music) with wider cultural trends, but also openly put forth progressive political messages. By using their 'Cultural Weapons' (Harvie, 1992) artists, writers, actors and musicians engaged in what Dallmayr might call 'transformative democratic agency' (2010, p. 20). This transformation more than anything else provided large parts of the Scottish population with an inclusive national identity that allowed them to demand national self-government without feeling tainted by parochialism (cf. Paterson, 1991, p. 114).

The role of Europe in the Scottish constitutional debate

This cultural renaissance and the anti-Westminster stance that became common in civic Scotland helped the self-government movement to recover from the abortive devolution referendum and the election of Thatcher in 1979. However, in stark contrast to the 1970s, the revival of the nationalist movement in Scotland had a strong pro-European strand to it. As Lindsay Paterson observes:

> The old Scottish preference for an assimilationist nationalism now seems to be focused on Europe. In the new Scottish culture of the 1980s and 1990s, to be European has been equated to being progressive and democratic, in almost the same way as being British was in the eighteenth and nineteenth centuries; and to be British has been tantamount to being anachronistic. (1994, p. 176)

The Europeanization of the Scottish constitutional debate found its expression in two different visions. Moderates and gradualists among the nationalist movement were striving for Scottish self-government within a British state (devolution), while the Scottish National Party (SNP) set its eyes on full independence.

Devolution: Scotland as a European region

Devolutionists included a wide range of grass-root organizations, traditional civic institutions (for example the Church of Scotland) and the Scottish sections of the Liberal Democrats and the Labour Party, which eventually formed the Scottish Constitutional Convention in 1989. Especially for the Scottish Labour Party, their conversion to the cause had much to do with the experience of Thatcherism in Scotland. Since the UK's entry to the European Community (EC), these organizations had established increasingly close-knit relations to the European Commission and other European bodies. As many of their positions closely resonated with the Commission under the French socialist Jacques Delors, groups such as Labour-run local authorities and the Scottish trade unions began to see the EC as a potential ally in their opposition to a neoliberal, centralizing British government, culminating in the notion of a 'Westminster by-pass' (cf. Keating and Jones, 1995).

The positive image of the EC was further reinforced by its support for regionalization through the introduction of the subsidiarity principle, the expansion of the European Regional and Cohesion Policy and the establishment of a Committee of the Regions in the Maastricht Treaty of 1992. Europe and in particular the idea of a 'Europe of the Regions' was seen more and more as instrumental to Scottish aspirations. Harvie (1994, p. 219) summarized this perception as follows: 'Scots increasingly see their future in a settlement in which European authority imposes a devolution of power'. Regionalization was seen as the realization of an explicitly European institutional design but also as a functional necessity. As Paterson, Brown and McCrone expressed it at the time: '[…] it is this European dimension, moreover, that continues to make

Scottish self-government highly likely in the medium term: powers will probably continue to move from the old states, upwards to Brussels and, by reaction, also downwards. Eventually the UK will have to join this process, however reluctantly' (1992, p. 638). Of course, it was not the EU itself but the Westminster Labour government that finally implemented devolution, establishing a Scottish parliament in 1999. Apart from inspiring Scottish expectations, the EU had little to do with the devolution settlement, which in its pragmatic, piecemeal and asymmetric form clearly reflects a rather British approach to constitutional politics. Furthermore, while the Scottish parliament has emerged to be one of the most powerful legislative bodies in Europe in terms of its competencies for 'self-rule', Scotland's position in EU policy-making had not improved to any great extent. Despite the rhetoric of a Europe of the Regions, the EU is still largely run by its member states and Scotland's involvement in European affairs depends largely on the domestic inter-governmental relations between Westminster and the devolved administrations, which are notoriously informal and Westminster-dominated.

Independence in Europe

The second vision of Scottish self-government in Europe came about when the SNP revoked its opposition to the EC at its party conference in 1988 embracing a new slogan: 'Independence in Europe'. This change of policy was partly a knee-jerk reaction to the Eurosceptic Conservative government in London, but also reflected the positive role of small European nations such as Ireland, Belgium, and Denmark, which seemed to be thriving as a part of the European integration project. The turn towards Europe was not based on any detailed analysis of the costs and benefits of EC membership, but the idea of independent statehood within the EC/EU rather helped the party to move from the isolationist corner it had fought itself into. Acknowledging the EC as an external support framework for a future Scottish state presented secession as a much less radical and much less dangerous prospect. Economic fears and images of control posts at the English border could be refuted as membership in the common market and the customs union would make separation from the rest of the UK less absolute and thus less relevant. Some critics noted that 'Scotland in Europe' was mainly 'projected as an easy escape route from the problems of seeking a constitutional settlement with England' (Lindsay, 1991, p. 84).

It took a quarter of a century, until the 2014 Scottish independence referendum, before this vision came anywhere near its realization. The party political constellation during this referendum was to some extent similar to the situation during the Thatcher era: the Conservatives led a Westminster government with hardly any support in Scotland (in 2010 the Conservative share of the vote in Scotland had fallen to 17 per cent and only one MP). This government responded to the financial and fiscal crisis with even harsher austerity measures than had Thatcher in the 1980s, increasing already intolerable levels of social and economic polarization. Contrary to the 1980s, though, the Labour Party was not the major beneficiary in Scotland. Bereft of its traditional structural base (that is the industrial working class) and tainted by Blairism and a rather mediocre performance at the head of the Scottish Executive, Scottish Labour increasingly lost support to the SNP. Many Scots turned to the latter, because it was seen as better equipped to defend Scottish interests against the neoliberal onslaught by the UK government. When in 2011 the SNP gained the absolute majority in the Scottish parliament, the independence question got serious, even though there had not been a significant surge in popular demand for it.

The following referendum campaign saw an unprecedented political mobilization in Scotland, reflected in the highest turnout (85 per cent) for any UK election since the introduction of universal suffrage. Even more important was the immense participation in public debates, rallies and festivals and on new social media platforms. This mobilization spread far beyond political parties and traditional civic bodies and included the most deprived and disenfranchised people of Scotland, among whom distrust in British democracy ran even deeper than during the Thatcher years. Neither party political changes in government nor the introduction of devolution had been able to protect them from unleashed market forces. The independence referendum, however, offered a realistic exit-option and thus – unlike British general elections – a real chance to make a difference, that is to exercise agency.

During the campaign, Europe rarely took centre stage. Whenever it did, though, it was controversial. While the SNP suggested that Scotland would either automatically remain part of the EU after its secession or it would be granted immediate and frictionless accession via the route of 'internal enlargement', British government and EU officials expressed quite a different view. According to them, breaking away from the UK would be tantamount to leaving the EU. An independent Scotland would thus have been at the end of a long queue of accession states with a complex application process and no guarantees as to its final admission. In order to stay inside the EU, the unionist 'Better Together' campaign argued, Scotland would have to remain part of the UK. Uncertainty about Scotland's EU membership may not have been their most important argument, but it may have helped to tip the balance towards No.

The Brexit referendum: a tale of two campaigns

The Brexit campaign, like the Scottish independence campaign, can be read as a response to austerity and political disenfranchisement (see Chapter Guderjan and Wilding). Populist leaders such as Nigel Farage and Boris Johnson successfully turned the material and social insecurity of large parts of British society (the older, the less well-off, the less educated) and their deep-seated distrust of political elites into a campaign against immigration and against an establishment of career politicians, business and financial elites, journalists and academics far removed from their everyday lives. The EU was portrayed as the major obstacle to national immigration control, while the 'Brussel bureaucrats' served as the epitome of detached elite rule. Exit from the EU was supposed to return sovereignty to the UK parliament and thus bring back control to British citizens. From this perspective, the referendum itself appears as a seminal exertion of agency by the British people that would, in turn, transform the long-term structural conditions for a more general agency in the UK.

In Scotland, this rhetoric did not resonate – at least not to the same degree as in England and Wales. Counterintuitively, though, Scotland's anti-Brexit vote is not due to considerably lower levels of Euroscepticism. In fact, British and Scottish social attitudes surveys have consistently shown only minor deviations in this regard. Criticism of European integration was always to be found in rural areas and in fishing communities especially on the east coast, where grievances about the EU regulations on agriculture and fishing have been growing over the years to produce a vocal minority of strong Brexiteers. During the Euro-crisis, when the rich northern member states (especially Germany) were seen to impose drastic austerity measures on the poor south (for example Greece), the traditional left-wing criticism of the EU as a neoliberal project also gained ground in Scotland. In the nationalist camp, Eurosceptic voices included the fundamentalist wing (for example Alex Neill, Jim Sillars and others), those who were concerned about the EU's apparent democratic deficit, and those who felt appalled by the reluctance of EU officials and European politicians to support Scottish independence during the referendum.

The reason behind Scotland's clear rejection of Brexit can thus not be found in individual attitudes towards the EU but in the particular nature of the Scottish public discourses and the positioning of major actor(s). In contrast to England, the Scottish Brexit debate took place in the context of an already existing debate about the nation's constitutional status. In a nation that voluntarily handed over parts of its sovereignty in the Union of 1707, the idea of absolute sovereignty resting in Westminster found little resonance. On the contrary, since the 1970s this constitutional debate has increasingly placed Scotland in a multi-level system of government. Any vision of Scottish self-government – devolution, independence, and even the ideas of those who rejected independence in 2014 – has since been closely, and positively, linked to Europe. It is thus hardly surprising that the Leave campaign in Scotland was less well supported than elsewhere in the UK.

By far the most important actor in the pro-EU campaign was the SNP, which univocally supported Remain. The abortive independence referendum of 2014 had further strengthened the SNPs position in Scotland. Less than one year after the lost referendum, the SNP won the majority of seats in the 2015 general election in an unprecedented landslide (winning 50 per cent of the Scottish vote and 56 of 59 Scottish seats) and it quadrupled its membership to become the third largest political party in the whole of the UK. By the time of the Brexit referendum campaign, the SNP had thus become the dominant party in Scotland. The absence of any serious Scottish organization campaigning against Europe together with its strong pro-European message provided the basis for Scotland's resolute rejection of Brexit (62 per cent Remain).

The SNP's rejection of Brexit had an impact beyond Scotland. Dominating Scottish politics, the SNP had also raised its profile as Scotland's voice in the UK. Initially this voice had been heard during the 2015 general election campaign, when the new SNP leader Nicola Sturgeon championed a strong anti-austerity sentiment in Britain, capitalizing on the rather conservative fiscal policy consensus among Conservatives, their Lib-Dem coalition partner and the Labour opposition. In a similar vein, the SNP (together with the diminished Liberal Democrats) took centre stage in the British Brexit debate as the party that took the most unambiguous pro-EU stance. Despite strong Scottish majorities, the SNP (and Scotland) lost on both counts, revealing once again the unitary character of the UK and the almost complete exclusion of the constituent nations as meaningful actors in vital state-wide political decisions.

Delivering Brexit: challenges and opportunities

At first glance Brexit may look like a window of opportunity for the SNP and Scotland's independence movement to achieve its ultimate goal. The Brexit referendum result had turned the unionists proposition during the Scottish Independence referendum on its head: staying in the British union was far from guaranteeing continued EU membership. Instead, Scotland was now to be dragged out of the EU by an English (and Welsh) majority against its own will. Hence, quite predictably, the first response of the SNP government was to claim a mandate for a new independence referendum. After all, nobody can deny that Brexit constitutes a 'significant and material change in the circumstances that prevailed in 2014' (SNP, 2016, p. 23) and thus fully conforms to the criteria the SNP defined for a second referendum in its 2016 election manifesto.

At the same time, though, Brexit also represents a major threat to the economic, social and political well-being of Scotland. The European single market is the major export market for Scotland; almost half its exports go to the EU. Any constraints on frictionless access to this market would thus damage the Scottish economy and the Scottish people. Similarly, like Wales and Northern Ireland, Scotland benefited considerably from the common agricultural policy and EU regional and structural funds. Whether future UK governments would maintain funding at similar levels as the EU has provided remains to be seen. Finally, demographic trends make Scotland much more dependent on immigration than the rest of the UK. The end of the EU's freedom of movement would thus produce a significant shortage of labour, in particular in the agricultural sector.

The Scottish government has consistently argued for the UK to remain part of the single market after Brexit. As a fallback position it has also outlined various special arrangements that would allow Scotland to remain inside the market (Scottish Government, 2016). However, the UK government has followed a distinctly unilateral approach in its Brexit negotiations, paying little attention to Scottish interests and the preferences of the Scottish and the other devolved governments. Unlike in Northern Ireland with the DUP supporting the Conservative minority government, special arrangements for Scotland were rejected from the outset.

Exit from the European Union will therefore have considerable repercussions for the British devolution settlement. According to the EU Withdrawal Act 2018, non-reserved matters (devolved matters), such as agriculture, fisheries and the environment, will be repatriated – at least in the first instance – to Westminster and not to the devolved parliaments. This was deemed necessary for the UK in order to create its own internal market with a unified regulatory framework. Legislation passed by the Scottish parliament that would have repatriated devolved powers to Scotland (crucial sections of the Continuity Bill) was struck out by the Supreme Court. This episode reveals two major insights. First, devolution dynamics do not automatically lead to an expansion of devolved powers. As the EU Withdrawal Act 2018 clearly shows, taking back powers from the devolved parliaments is not only legally possible, but also politically feasible in certain circumstances. Second, even after the Sewel convention, that is the principle whereby 'the parliament of the United Kingdom will not normally legislate with regard to devolved matters without the consent of the Scottish parliament', has been put on a statutory footing in the Scotland Act 2016 (2016, p. 8), Westminster may still legislate on devolved matters without the consent – or even against the explicit will – of devolved parliaments.

Both of these points have added to Scotland's substantial Brexit grievances and demonstrate the limits to the agency of the Scottish political actors under the condition of a unitary state architecture. Within the nationalist movement there is little doubt that sooner or later Brexit will trigger a second independence referendum. What is less clear, though, is the timing and its result. Following a decision by the Scottish parliament, the SNP already requested the authority from the UK government to hold a second independence referendum, only to be told by Prime Minister Theresa May that this had to wait until the Brexit negotiations were completed. Some activists have since been pushing the SNP leadership to schedule the poll at the earliest possible point in time, capitalizing on its own governmental position and the disastrous public image of Westminster politicians during the Brexit negotiations. More cautious sections of the party, however, have suggested waiting until opinion polls show a clear majority for independence. This might mean waiting at least as long as it takes for the expected negative Brexit impact to hit home. Opinion polls since the Brexit referendum have so far revealed very little change to the original referendum result of September 2014. Scotland still seems almost evenly divided between separatists and unionists. This might look like a remarkably high base line to some – especially given that opinion polls before the last referendum campaign had consistently put support for independence at just 30 per cent – yet it remains a far cry from guaranteeing victory in a referendum; a referendum that would, in all probability, be the last one on this issue for a generation.

A narrow focus on opinion poll figures conceals the real impact of Brexit on the Scottish constitutional question. The Brexit referendum result has not only revealed a deeply disunited kingdom, but also amplified this division. Perceptions of the political impotence of Scotland, reflected in an almost complete lack of agency in the Brexit negotiations, together with nightmare scenarios of a low-tax/low-wage British casino capitalism as propagated by Brexiteers in England have further distanced Scotland from the British *body politic*. At the same time, however, Brexit is changing fundamentally the question any new plebiscite would have to answer. With the UK leaving the EU, Scottish secession would not be cushioned by common membership of a supranational organization. Rather, Scottish independence in Europe would turn the Scottish–English border into an external border of the EU, magnifying the economic and fiscal problems that had already tipped the balance in favour of the British union in the last independence referendum. Overall, Brexit may intensify English–Scottish divisions, while it also throws a lifeline to the union. As Europe can no longer be projected as an 'easy escape route', Scotland has to rethink its options for strengthening democratic self-government by re-evaluating its relationship with the UK and the EU at a time when these two unions seem to be drifting apart. This is a complex process that has only just begun.

Conclusion

If one reads the Brexit debate as a (misguided) battle against the broken promises of democracy, Scotland's experience seems to diverge from that of the rest of the UK. Here, the perception of political disenfranchisement set in earlier and found quite different forms of expression: the neoliberal and austerity-driven infringements on individual economic, social and political participation during the Thatcher years coincided with a disempowerment of collective institutions, notably labour and community bodies, raising demands for Scotland to become more democratic by way of devolution or secession. In this context, and despite the neoliberal tendencies and democratic shortcomings of the EU, Scottish self-government came to be positively linked with European integration and has since been almost exclusively envisaged within a European framework. The continuing social polarization and the new wave of austerity that followed the financial crisis thus did not provoke a strong popular resentment against the EU, but a deepening disillusionment with British democracy that found expression in the Scottish independence referendum.

If anything, the Brexit referendum result and the almost complete exclusion of Scottish preferences and Scottish actors from the subsequent Brexit negotiations have further undermined Scotland's trust in the British union. However, Britain's exit from the EU also means that Scottish independence in Europe constitutes a much starker choice for Scotland than before. Whatever Scotland decides in a potential second independence referendum, as a small European nation, the quest for Scottish democracy will remain fundamentally dependent on both its relationship to the (rest of the) UK and to the European Union, as both political structures will persist in shaping the exertion of Scottish agency.

References

Dallmayr, F. (2010) *The Promise of Democracy. Political Agency and Transformation*, Albany: State University of New York Press.

Harvie, C. (1991) 'Nationalism, Journalism, and Cultural Politics', in T. Gallagher (ed.) *Nationalism in the Nineties*, Edinburgh: Polygon, pp. 29–45.

Harvie, C. (1992) *Cultural Weapons. Scotland and Survival in a New Europe,* Edinburgh: Polygon.

Harvie, C. (1994) *Scotland and Nationalism. Scottish Society and Politics 1707–1994*, London/New York: Routledge.

Keating, M. and B. Jones (1995) 'Nations, Regions and Europe: the UK Experience' in B. Jones and M. Keating (eds) *The European Union and the Regions*, Oxford: Oxford University Press, pp. 65–114.

Lindsay, I. (1991) 'The SNP and the Lure of Europe', in T. Gallagher (ed.) *Nationalism in the Nineties*, Edinburgh: Polygon, pp. 84–101.

McAnulla, S. (2002) 'Structure and Agency', in D. Marsh and G. Stoker (eds) *Theory and Methods in Political Science* (2nd edn), Basingstoke: Palgrave Macmillan, pp. 271–91.

McCrone, D. (1992) *Understanding Scotland. The Sociology of a Stateless Nation*, London/New York: Routledge.

Midwinter, A., M. Keating and J. Mitchell (1991) *Politics and Public Policy in Scotland*, Basingstoke: Macmillan.

Moore, C. and S. Booth (1989) *Managing Competition: Meso-corporatism, Pluralism and the Negotiated Order in Scotland*, Oxford: Clarendon Press.

Paterson, L. (1991) 'Ane End of Ane Auld Sang: Sovereignty and the Re-Negotiation of the Union', in A. Brown and C. McCrone (eds) *Scottish Government Yearbook 1991*, pp. 104–22.

Paterson, L. (1994) *The Autonomy of Modern Scotland*, Edinburgh: Edinburgh University Press.

Paterson, L., A. Brown and D. McCrone (1992) 'Constitutional Crisis. The Causes and Consequences of the 1992 Scottish General Election Result', *Parliamentary Affairs*, 45: 627–39.

Scotland Act 2016 (2016) Chapter 11, Part 1(2), http://www.legislation.gov.uk/ukpga/2016/11/pdfs/ukpga_20160011_en.pdf.

Scottish Government (2016) *Scotland's Place in Europe*, Edinburgh.

Scottish National Party (2016) *Re-Elect. SNP Election Manifesto 2016*, Edinburgh.

14

Brexit, Devolution and Northern Ireland's Political Parties: Differential Solutions, Special Status or Special Arrangements?

Derek Birrell and Paul Carmichael

Introduction

To understand agency in the situation in Northern Ireland requires an appreciation of the underlying constitutional fault line underpinning politics and government in the Province. Northern Ireland's disputed status and divided society, based on a constitutional cum ethno-national cleavage with diametrically opposed views as to its long term geo-political position and best interests, provides a distorting lens or prism through which agency is refracted. One community sees Northern Ireland as continuing as an integral part of the UK ('Unionist' or 'Loyalist'); the other desires a rupture of that Union and reunification with the rest of the island to form an all-island 'United' Ireland ('Nationalist' or 'Republican'). With the collapse of its devolved institutions in January 2017, the Province's direct and formal political input into the negotiating process around Brexit has been much reduced, notwithstanding the 'backdoor' influence enjoyed by one of the leading political parties, the Democratic Unionist Party (DUP), as a result of its 'confidence and supply' arrangement (involving a formal written agreement) with the minority Conservative government at Westminster, following the general election in spring 2017. Agency 'can be constrained by unequal power relations and/or the absence of enabling affordances and thus is not regarded as dependent on an individual's will or capacity alone but as a contextually enabled and constrained capacity' (Miller, 2016, p. 350). Thus, in terms of Hay's 'questions of political power [and] the question of who holds the whip hand' (1995, p. 206), for the time being, it has been the DUP which has enjoyed an unexpected leverage over Westminster arithmetic and UK government policy. Concurrently, for the DUP's erstwhile coalition partners in the Northern Ireland Executive, with that avenue of influence not available (and from its perspective unsought anyway), Sinn Féin has pursued its own agenda with robust lobbying instead in the Republic of Ireland, seeking to outflank the Dublin government on the Brexit issue, with a view to building up its domestic political capital as the next Irish general election approaches.

This chapter examines Brexit and devolution, insofar as these relate to the devolved government in Northern Ireland, but also to those in Scotland and Wales to afford comparative perspective. It outlines the responses of the three devolved administrations and explores Brexit with reference to the special and distinctive issues which arise in Northern Ireland. The chapter comments on the positions of the two leading political parties in Northern Ireland and the interplay of regional, national and EU politics. It considers the possibility of special arrangements or status for Northern Ireland, and notes that the Irish border was one of the three issues – along with a financial settlement and citizens' rights – that dominated the first phase of UK–EU negotiations on withdrawal terms (Curtis et al, 2017). The chapter highlights the role of the devolved government and main political parties, chiefly the DUP, as actors and the type of agency they have exercised. Their agency has been enabled or constrained by various factors, sometimes simultaneously enabled and constrained. The DUP's agency has been enhanced by its confidence and supply arrangement at Westminster. By contrast, constrained by its self-imposed absence from Westminster, Sinn Féin's otherwise reduced agency is partially enabled through its closer proximity to the Irish government's position.

Response to the referendum

While the referendum result for the UK demonstrated a small but clear margin for Leave, the results in the four nations of the UK differed considerably (see Table 14.1). Specifically, while England and Wales both voted Leave, Scotland and Northern Ireland voted Remain.

Table 14.1 UK 2016 referendum result on the question of remaining in or leaving the European Union

Country	Leave %	Remain %
Scotland	38.0	62.0
Northern Ireland	44.2	55.8
Wales	52.5	47.5
England	53.4	46.6
Overall UK	51.9	48.1

Source: BBC, 2019

Under the prevailing constitutional norms, however, the only material result was the overall UK outcome – Leave.

One of the interesting questions that has arisen is why continued EU membership attracted far more support in Scotland and Northern Ireland than in Wales or England (even though Wales has received more in EU funding per capita than other parts of the UK; similarly, English regions that are net recipients of EU funding polled most strongly against continued EU membership).

Since 1999, when Labour implemented its plans for devolution to Scotland and Wales, the salience of the UK operating as a form of multi-level government has increased dramatically. In accordance with the EU Acquis Communautaire, EU matters are constitutionally not devolved. Rather, they remain the formal responsibility of the member state, that is the UK. Frequently, too, the EU may not have competence in a policy area, especially many that are devolved, for example aspects of social policy, health, education, housing, children's services, and aspects of welfare benefits. To allow some form of representation from the constituent nations in national decisions on EU matters, a formal concordat sets out the relationship of devolved governments with the UK government, as mediated by the Joint Ministerial Committee (JMC). In relation to the EU and Brexit, this includes participation in the JMC on EU Negotiations. There are three territorial offices in Brussels, one for each of Scotland, Wales and Northern Ireland, each providing additional scope for influencing EU policy making and allocation of funding.

Uppermost among the concerns of the devolved governments was the likely loss of EU funding under its various structural funds. All three nations have been substantial beneficiaries of the European Regional Development Fund (ERDF) and European Social Fund (ESF) for infrastructure, education and training, plus farm support payments under the Common Agricultural Policy (CAP). In Northern Ireland, there is an additional revenue stream via the unique

EU Peace and Reconciliation funding that has been worth over £1.3bn cumulatively since the first tranche in 1994, along with special programmes promoting cross-border cooperation (INTERREG). Additionally, for the higher education sector, research funding under successive Framework Programmes and student exchange funding under Erasmus, represent an appreciable source of income. The devolved governments also expressed concern around the loss of labour market mobility and related workforce issues, affecting especially health and social care provisions, agri-food sector and tourism (Birrell and Gray, 2017). There were concerns over their economic interests and social protection including safeguarding employment rights and regarding the voluntary sector, an adverse effect on local government and their EU networks and the loss of status internationally. All told, this would mean a significant loss of agency for a wide range of agents in the devolved territories, but especially those in Northern Ireland.

Sidelining Scotland and Wales

Following the referendum result, the responses of the three UK devolved administrations differed. In Scotland, the strongly pro-Remain Scottish government advocated a differentiated solution. In *Scotland's Place in Europe* (Scottish Government, 2016), the government argued for Scotland to remain in the European single market, effectively allowing for Scotland to vary from what might eventuate for the rest of the UK (or, at least, England and Wales). Specifically, the Scottish government wished to maintain freedom of movement. If such exceptionalism was not afforded, and Scotland was taken out of the EU against the wishes of its electorate, preparations would be made for a second independence referendum on secession from the UK (see Chapter Stolz). In Wales, while accepting that most Welsh voters had backed Leave, the Welsh government said it would seek to protect the interests of the Welsh people through retaining access to the single market. It sought to participate fully in the UK preparations for the negotiations with the EU and stated firmly that, in a future referendum, it would campaign for Remain.

Set against their broad aspirations, there has been a sidelining of the devolved administrations. Although the devolved governments were originally consulted before negotiations began with the EU on UK withdrawal through the Joint Ministerial Committee (European Negotiations) (JMC(EN)) representing all four governments, subsequently, the JMC(EN) has been used in a limited way as a mechanism for engagement. The devolved governments were not consulted on the withdrawal legislation while the UK government formally excluded the Secretaries of State for Scotland, Wales and Northern Ireland from the 'Exiting the EU' Cabinet Committee. Despite the criticism of the UK government's 'hard Brexit' approach, legal decisions confirmed it was not necessary for the UK government to involve the devolved governments, notwithstanding any political imperatives suggesting otherwise.

Regarding the repatriation of EU powers, Scotland and Wales rejected the UK government's proposal for the UK parliament to acquire the repatriated powers in devolved matters (including agriculture, fisheries, environmental protection), before deciding what to devolve in due course. Indeed, Scotland called for additional new devolved powers over employment and immigration. In a joint statement, the First Ministers of Scotland and Wales (July 2017) described the UK action as a power grab for matters already devolved, claiming it would undermine the overall UK devolved constitutional settlement. The Scottish Parliament and Welsh Assembly threatened not to pass legislative consent motions on the Withdrawal Bill. Though this has no legal capacity to delay matters, it posed a political challenge to the basis of the Sewel Convention, whereby the UK government refrains from legislating in devolved policy areas unless with the prior agreement of the devolved government(s) concerned. While a settlement was negotiated with the Welsh government, the Scottish government remained opposed to the UK government strategy. Subsequently, the dispute over the repatriation of powers was considered by the UK Supreme Court which ruled that the Scottish government could not block action by the UK government.

In Scotland, the devolved government response was one of concern over Scotland's exclusion from 'full engagement and meaningful influence'. Frustrated by their exclusion, Scottish leaders sought an impact by holding more than 100 engagements with EU leaders and politicians including the French President. Yet, the Scottish First Minister announced in June 2017 that her government would not seek to introduce legislation for an independence referendum immediately. The SNP was chastened by the outcome of the snap UK general election earlier that year, when a surge by the Scottish Conservative and Unionist parties left the SNP dramatically reduced in its parliamentary strength at Westminster, including losing its leader there, albeit remaining the largest Scottish party. Under these conditions, the opportunity costs of a new independence referendum would be too high to exercise this type of agency.

The Welsh government produced *Brexit and Devolution* (Welsh Government, 2017) which argued that the UK government and devolved administrations should work together in a deeper and more structured way. It advocated an increase in inter-connected competencies. The Cardiff administration was at pains to say that Brexit risked undermining devolution and that there was a need to safeguard economic well-being in Wales, particularly given the scale of EU funding. Support was expressed for continuing to adhere to the EU's regulatory framework. Hunt and Minto (2017) provide interesting insights on why Wales and Scotland adopted different strategies to influence the negotiations, linked to their perceived political leverage and opportunity costs.

Political response in Northern Ireland

Northern Ireland has the UK's only shared land border with another EU member state (the Republic of Ireland, ROI). The land border is over 300 miles long with over 200 road crossings. Today, the border is largely invisible but has heightened political significance due to the conflict in Northern Ireland, and sensitivities about its appearance remain. If the UK were to leave the EU, the border would no longer be an internal but an external EU border. Northern Ireland's unique circumstances and problems demand bespoke measures and solutions, though there is a reluctance to accept the term 'special status'. Since 1923, the Common Travel Area (CTA) has encompassed the British and Irish Isles as well as the Channel Islands, and Isle of Man. Historically, Northern Ireland has always been a 'place apart', with a form of 'parity with particularity' with respect to aspects of policy and politics in the rest of the UK (Rose, 1971). After 1968, the onset of the 'Troubles' (to 1996) and subsequent peace process elicited support from the EU, with successive Peace and Reconciliation Funding programmes (known as 'PEACE') and Special European Union Programmes Body (SEUPB) funding of over £2bn since the 1980s.

There are certain legal privileges for Irish citizens in the UK, and vice versa, on voting, social security, employment and other rights. There is also the right of all citizens in Northern Ireland to hold Irish passports and hence be EU citizens. The CTA confers mutual rights and recognition that long predate EU membership (HM Government, 2018a). A fundamental question arose as to whether the CTA remains compatible with the EU Treaties and rules of the single market and customs union if one of the member states secedes from the EU. As both member states joined concurrently, the issue has never arisen – until now. While continuation of the CTA appears assured, for now, it is not clear what rights in law this confers other than travel.

There is a desire for the continuation of the frictionless border and the movement of people, goods and services across Ireland, supported by the Northern Ireland government, Irish government, British government and EU leaders and negotiators. Some 30,000 people commute across the border regularly to work (Centre for Cross Border Studies, 2016). Protection of the agri-food industry is a particularly acute concern given the intensity of cross border operations and the importance of this sector to the overall economic well-being of the island, north and south (Directorate General for Internal Policy, 2017).

Uniquely, since the Good Friday (Belfast) Agreement of 1998, Northern Ireland has statutory power-sharing arrangements between its main political parties. The political parties in Northern Ireland are distinctive within the UK and must confront difficulties posed by Brexit. Underpinning those difficulties are fundamental policy cleavages between the two largest political parties within the currently suspended Northern Ireland Assembly and Executive: the DUP, which is in favour of Leave, and Sinn Féin, which favoured Remain. That the DUP is in a pivotal position in Westminster and is sustaining the UK government in office has had implications for efforts to restore the devolved government which have so far failed. Inevitably, this fissure also carries implications for Brexit negotiations, as the lack of consensus in Northern Ireland on Brexit means there is no agreement by government departments or Assembly committees publishing reports, and little response to fears in civil society about the consequences of the Brexit.

Following the 2017 general election, with 36 per cent of the popular vote, the DUP returned 10 MPs to Westminster, Sinn Féin had seven MPs (with 29.4 per cent of the popular vote) and other parties gaining just 1 MP (albeit their combined share being the remaining 34.6 per cent of the votes). The results were a product of the first-past-the-post electoral system used in UK general elections. With no party nationally having secured an overall majority, a confidence and supply agreement allowed the Conservative Party to govern with DUP support for passing the EU Withdrawal Bill, given in exchange for more funding for Northern Ireland. The DUP secured over £1bn beyond that to which it is ordinarily entitled under the prevailing mechanism for distributing funding (the Barnett Formula), plus other political concessions. Though skilful negotiators, the party is wary of facilitating the assumption of power nationally by the UK Labour Party, under the leadership of Jeremy Corbyn, which has been resurgent in the polls and flushed with its relative electoral success in the last general election. Thus, the DUP's critics have asked whether its electoral pact with the governing party in London is viewed as worth more than the restoration of devolution at home, notwithstanding the party's protestations to the contrary.

The DUP is pledged to there being no hard border but is adamant that no special status should be established for Northern Ireland (with or without the Republic of Ireland) nor any internal borders with the rest of the UK. A border poll (on Irish unity) is viewed as being destabilizing and unnecessary since there is no demonstrable evidence that such a plebiscite would command majority support for a change in the constitutional status of the Province. Instead, the focus is on restoring the devolved arrangements. For the DUP, there can be no question of joint sovereignty (with Dublin) or another form of influence or control by the Irish government over the internal affairs of Northern Ireland. Its 'red line' has been that of no deviation of Northern Ireland from the rest of the UK on EU matters.

For Sinn Féin, the maintenance of no hard border within Ireland is paramount. Consistent in calling for special status for 'the north' (the party refuses to use the legal name of Northern Ireland), Sinn Féin has been vocal in pressing for the preservation of funding levels for farming and other structural funds after Brexit via successor arrangements with comparable resources. The party has advocated a border poll as a priority, contending that a 'Tory hard Brexit' runs contrary to the will of the people of the north, threatening the integrity of the Good Friday (Belfast) Agreement and subsequent agreements through a destabilization of both the institutions as well as the background conditions in which they must operate. Notwithstanding their potentially pivotal role in the House of Commons, Sinn Féin has refused an opportunity to exercise its potentially powerful agency through insisting that there would be no change in the party's abstentionist approach regarding assuming its seven seats at Westminster as a means of influencing the parliamentary arithmetic by voting with the combined parties of the opposition, to defeat the Conservative minority government. Critics and observers have also asked whether the party's wider ambitions to gain power in the Republic of Ireland render the devolution arrangements in Northern Ireland expendable.

The effects of the party-political differences are clear. The continued and prolonged absence of the devolved government has created a political vacuum in the Province both over domestic public policy, in terms of its interface with Westminster, and over Brexit. With no consensus between the DUP and Sinn Féin (in terms of their respective election manifestos and subsequent stances), there has been no detailed report from any of the political parties, nor the Assembly committees of government departments. No clear, agreed, Northern Ireland position on Brexit exists, nor any forum for debate (Murphy, 2016). There have been no discussions on repatriation of powers, nor has the Executive had any involvement with the UK or EU. With no devolved Assembly or Executive in operation – due to an impasse over, *inter alia*, a botched renewable heating initiative, an Irish Language Act, continued prohibition of same sex marriage legislation (thanks to the DUP's repeated use of the 'Petition of Concern' mechanism within the Northern Ireland Assembly) and a general distrust between the major parties and their respective leaderships – the prospects for any rapprochement or meeting of minds (at least prior to UK secession from the EU) remain bleak. The Westminster Parliament's decision to abrogate the devolved settlement by legislating directly to introduce same sex marriage legislation and also abortion reform in October 2019, following the failure of the Northern Ireland parties to agree to restore devolution, served to further erode trust between the DUP and the Conservative Party.

EU membership for the UK and Ireland has provided an essential context for the conception and implementation of the Good Friday (Belfast) Agreement. Through the North South Ministerial Council, the Irish government agreed to work with the Northern Ireland Executive to ensure that Northern Ireland's interests are protected, and that north–south co-operation is recognized in future negotiations. Agreement was given to a letter from the leaders of the two governing parties in the Northern Ireland Executive that there should be no impediment to cross border movement of people and goods and they would work closely to secure the best deal. However, when the Joint Ministerial Committee (European Negotiations) began to meet to bring together the UK, Scottish and Welsh governments to discuss the repatriation of powers, Northern Ireland was represented by a senior civil servant. Inevitably, absence of political voices for Northern Ireland in these discussions compromises the exercise of agency with, potentially at least, a deleterious impact on the social and economic conditions for people in the Province, although this is offset by (and skewed towards) the DUP's stance and continued influence via its confidence and supply arrangements with the governing Conservative Party.

The border and special arrangements for Northern Ireland

At the outset of Brexit negotiations, all parties were agreed on the avoidance of a 'hard border' in Ireland, so it was surmised – optimistically – that a workable solution was straightforward. From being a relatively minor concern, the Irish Border became the principal impediment to progress towards an overall deal. Much of the discussion regarding Northern Ireland has revolved around whether or the extent to which the Province warrants differential treatment to that of the rest of the UK, or whether the Republic of Ireland itself merits special arrangements or special status within the EU. Do the circumstances in and of Northern Ireland (and indeed, the Republic of Ireland) warrant 'special status' for one or both?

The UK and Irish governments have produced position papers on this matter. The UK position was to uphold the Good Friday (Belfast) Agreement; maintain the Common Travel Area; avoid a hard border for the movement of goods; and to seek to preserve North–South and East–West co-operation (HM Government, 2017). Nationalists and Republicans in Northern Ireland, along with the government of the Republic of Ireland, have called for a special status for Northern Ireland. The language of special status is anathema to Northern Ireland's Unionists and the UK government. Making 'special arrangements' or special provisions may be more acceptable and nuanced vocabulary though even then, any trace or hint that it might drive a wedge between Northern Ireland and the rest of the UK is fiercely resisted. Precisely what constitutes special, unique, niche, bespoke, creative, innovative, idiosyncratic, customized, flexible, and variable is, of course, open to interpretation while being scrutinized forensically to ensure 'red lines' are not breached. Likewise, what circumstances, treatment, arrangements, provisions, adjustments and allowances are devised or proposed for Northern Ireland are also examined in minute detail by the various parties. For any deal to be forthcoming, maximum linguistic dexterity is required to assuage the fears of the opposing camps in Northern Ireland and to remain consistent with the red lines of London, Dublin and Brussels.

Throughout, the key actors – the EU's lead negotiator, the EU Council and the UK and Irish governments – have been at pains to stress that no hard border should be reimposed in Ireland. It has been argued that some form of special status or arrangements should be presented as a response to the peace process, the circumstances of Northern Ireland, and the UK's commitments under the Good Friday (Belfast)

Agreement (Doyle and Connolly, 2017). Ensuing protracted wrangling over 'backstop' arrangements (that is, an insurance mechanism for trade and customs provisions that would prevent a hard border if the EU and the UK cannot agree on their future relationship) proved to be the last major obstacle to the conclusion of the Withdrawal Treaty between the UK and the EU. The Irish border has consistently dogged the entire Brexit process. Brussels has insisted that London enters a legally binding commitment to keep Northern Ireland in the EU's customs territory as means of safeguarding the latter's integrity. The UK has contended that no British government could consent to what would amount to an internal border, moreover one that places part of the UK subject to the supremacy of EU law. Such is the binary nature of customs and international trade as to render the impasse intractable since a country can belong to only one customs union and single market at any given time. Likewise, regulatory divergence within a state would jeopardize the integrity of the national single market. The Withdrawal Agreement and Political Declaration of November 2018, represented the UK and EU's attempt to reconcile these conflicting imperatives though, from the perspective of Northern Ireland's Unionists, it amounted to an unacceptable infringement of the constitutional integrity of the UK and even an existential threat to Northern Ireland's position within it. For its part, in response, the DUP has behaved as a 'veto player', exerting maximum pressure as an actor and on whose opposition rests the form, timing and even the very implementation of Brexit.

The EU approach has been a legal and technocratic one whereas the UK sees any agreement as a product of politics and bargaining. In its bid to break the impasse, the Withdrawal Treaty and Political Declaration (HM Government, 2018b) seemingly 'solved' the Irish land border issue. It proposed continuation of a customs union – of sorts – involving free trade in goods, regulatory alignment in goods (common rulebook), and procedures for ensuring that goods that pass through the UK destined for the EU pay the right import duties and observe the correct regulations. These complex arrangements would have meant that no consignments of goods need be stopped at any UK border, including those of Northern Ireland. The subsequent revised agreement concluded with the EU by Boris Johnson's government saw the removal of the backstop only to reintroduce regulatory cum customs checks between Northern Ireland and Great Britain, creating the very border in the Irish Sea which he had pledged never to countenance. In the time-honoured tradition of EU negotiations, the countdown involved a measure of brinkmanship punctuated with public spats, the making of amends, the promise of last-minute concessions and breakthroughs, with accusations of betrayal from the DUP by its erstwhile partners – the parallels to the tortuous process that created the Good Friday Agreement are striking. It was this sudden and dramatic change of approach by the UK Government which shattered DUP confidence and culminated in the announcement of a General Election for 12 December 2019.

Conclusion

In this chapter, we have explored how the idiosyncracies of Northern Ireland were magnified and distorted by the outcome of the 2017 UK general election. Given that result, the complex intersection of multi-level governance has been given added piquancy – efforts to restore devolved government have floundered concurrent with (and inextricably linked to) Northern Ireland being thrust into the heart of national politics (via the DUP-Conservative agreement) and the debate about the UK's secession from the EU. In different circumstances, with a single party government in Westminster, the leverage of Northern Ireland, and its parties, would have been much reduced, their agency minimized if not minimal. Hence, whether it is considered extraordinarily good fortune or sheer bad luck, that election outcome enabled one of the key Northern Ireland actors in particular, the DUP, to exert a disproportionate influence over the pace, direction and ultimate outcome of the Brexit process. Most of Northern Ireland's political parties have found themselves reduced to spectator status, their agency curbed. By contrast, by virtue of its direct route into national power-broking, the DUP has exploited its position at the fulcrum of the British parliamentary process to maximum advantage. It has precipitated a political crisis that raises fundamental issues about the nature of the devolved constitutional settlement, parliamentary processes, even the UK's continuing integrity as a cohesive political entity, as well as destabilizing the otherwise largely normalized and much improved UK–Irish relationship.

However, despite its current extensive (arguably 'super') agency, the DUP's influence with the Conservatives, especially Brexiteers, and on the overall Brexit process has proved transient. Depending on the outcome of the General Election 2019, its influence on UK politics longer term remains uncertain. Questions remain about the validity of the DUP's arguments and fundamental 'red line' given the alacrity with which it promulgates other deviations from the 'UK norm'. Moreover, if 'agency ... can be defined as the ability or capacity of an actor to act consciously and, in so doing, to attempt to realize his or her intentions' (Hay, 2002, p. 94), then the DUP may well have overplayed its hand, potentially inviting unintended consequences, including the very antithesis of its raison d'etre as a political party. For its critics, within Northern Ireland and beyond, there is an irony in the DUP's stance. Its approach could be counter-productive since, in cleaving so rigidly to its over-riding 'red line' (namely, that there can be no deviation by Northern Ireland from the rest of the UK on Brexit if not other matters), it has polarized opinion locally by reawakening dormant atavistic divisions thought by some to have been dissolved by the Good Friday accord. In so doing, and mindful of shifting long-term demographics and electoral opinion in Northern Ireland, it is contended that the party could undermine support for the very union it so resolutely seeks to maintain. Were that to happen, it would surely represent a case of agency catastrophically mishandled.

References

Anderson, J. (2017) 'Ireland's Border After Brexit', *Society Now*, Summer: 14–15 (Swindon: ESRC).

BBC (2019) EU Referendum Results, https://www.bbc.co.uk/news/politics/eu_referendum/results

Birrell, W. D. and A. M. Gray (2017) 'Devolution: The Social, Political and Policy Implications of Brexit for Scotland, Wales and Northern Ireland', *Journal of Social Policy*, 46 (4): 765–82.

Cairney, P. (2012) *Understanding Public Policy: Theories and Issues*, Basingstoke: Palgrave Macmillan.

Centre for Cross-Border Studies (2016) 'Brexit and UK–Irish Relations', *A Briefing Paper*, October, Armagh: The Centre for Cross-Border Studies: www.crossborder.ie.

Curtis, J., P. Bowers, T. McGuinness and D. Webb (2017) 'Brexit Negotiations: The Irish Border Question', *Commons Briefing papers CBP-8042*, London: House of Commons.

Directorate General for Internal Policies (2017) *UK Withdrawal (Brexit) and the Good Friday Agreement*, Brussels: European Parliament: http://www.europarl.europa.eu/RegData/etudes/STUD/2017/596826/IPOL_STU(2017)596826_EN.pdf.

Doyle, J. and E. Connolly (2017) *Brexit and the Future of Northern Ireland*, Working Paper, Dublin: Dublin City University.

EU (2018) *Brexit: Protocol on Ireland and Northern Ireland*: https://ec.europa.eu/ireland/news/brexit-protocol-on-ireland-and-northern-ireland_en.

Hay, C. (1995) 'Structure and Agency' in G. Stoker and D. Marsh (eds) *Theory and Methods in Political Science*, Basingstoke: Palgrave Macmillan.

Hay, C. (2002) *Political Analysis: a critical introduction*, London: Palgrave Macmillan.

HM Government (2017) *Northern Ireland and Ireland*, Position Paper, London: HM Government: https://assets.publishing.service.gov.uk/government/uploads/system/uploads/attachment_data/file/638135/6.3703_DEXEU_Northern_Ireland_and_Ireland_INTERACTIVE.pdf.

HM Government (2018a) *The Future Relationship Between the United Kingdom and the European Union*, London: HM Government (Cm 9593, 12 July): https://assets.publishing.service.gov.uk/government/uploads/system/uploads/attachment_data/file/725288/The_future_relationship_between_the_United_Kingdom_and_the_European_Union.pdf.

HM Government (2018b) *Withdrawal Agreement and Political Declaration*, London: HM Government: https://www.gov.uk/government/publications/withdrawal-agreement-and-political-declaration.

House of Commons Library (2017) *Brexit Negotiations: the Irish Border question*, Briefing Paper number 8042, 17 July: https://researchbriefings.parliament.uk/ResearchBriefing/Summary/CBP-8042#fullreport.

Hunt, J and R. Minto (2017) 'Between intergovernmental relations and paradiplomacy: Wales and the Brexit of the regions', *The British Journal of Politics and International Relations*, 19(4): 647–62.

Irish Government (2017) *Ireland and the negotiations on the UK's withdrawal from the European Union: The Government's Approach*, May, Dublin: Government of Ireland: https://merrionstreet.ie/MerrionStreet/en/EU-UK/Key_Irish_Documents/Government_Position_Paper_on_Brexit.pdf.

Komorova, M. (2017) 'Now you see it, now you don't. Brexit and the In/Visible UK-Ireland Land Border', *Journal of Cross-Border Studies in Ireland*, 12: 11–22.

Le Grand, J. (2006) *Motivation, Agency and Public Policy: Of Knights & Knaves, Pawns & Queens*, Oxford: Oxford University Press.

Magennis, E., A. Parker and L. Henry (2017) 'Brexit and the Border Corridor on the Island of Ireland: Risks, Opportunities and Issues to Consider', *Journal of Cross-Border Studies in Ireland*, 12: 24–62.

Marsh, D. (2010) 'Meta-Theoretical Issues', in D. Marsh and G. Stoker (eds) *Theory and Methods in Political Science*, Basingstoke: Macmillan.

Miller, E. (2016) 'The ideology of learner agency and the neoliberal self', *International Journal of Applied Linguistics*, 26(3): 34865.

Murphy, M. (2016) 'Northern Ireland and the EU Referendum: the Outcome, Options and Opportunities', *Journal of Cross-Border Studies in Ireland*, 11: 18–31.

Northern Ireland Affairs Committee (2018) *The Land Border Between Northern Ireland and Ireland*, London: House of Commons, HC329: https://www.parliament.uk/business/committees/committees-a-z/commons-select/northern-ireland-affairs-committee/inquiries/parliament-2017/future-of-the-irish-land-border-17-19/publications/.

Rose, R. (1971) *Governing without Consensus: An Irish Perspective*, London: Faber.

Scottish Government (2016) *Scotland's Place in Europe*, Edinburgh: Scottish Government: https://beta.gov.scot/publications/scotlands-place-europe/.

Seanad Special Select Committee (2017) *Withdrawal of the United Kingdom from the European Union: Brexit, Implications and Potential Solutions*, June, Dublin: Houses of the Oireachtus (Senate of the Irish Parliament).

Tonge, J. (2017) 'Northern Ireland: the DUP Hits the Jackpot', *Political Insight*, 8(2): 18–19.

Welsh Government (2017) *Brexit and Devolution: Securing Wales' Future*, Cardiff: Welsh Government: https://beta.gov.wales/sites/default/files/2017-06/170615-brexit%20and%20devolution%20%28en%29.pdf.

15

More Than the Border? Looking at Brexit through Irish Eyes

Kevin Bean

Introduction

An exchange between BBC Radio 4 journalist, John Humphrys and Ireland's Europe minister Helen McEntee in early 2019 in which he suggested that '… the Republic of Ireland, leave the EU and throw in their lot with this country [Britain]' seemed to sum up the destructive impact of Brexit on Anglo–Irish relations (O'Carroll, 2019). In the entirely predictable media spat between politicians and media commentators that erupted on both sides of the Irish Sea, it seemed as if long forgotten memories and historical animosities between Dublin and London had been stirred back into life. After decades of close cooperation during the Northern Irish peace process, hopes for a more harmonious relationship between Ireland and Britain were drowned out in yet another war of words over Brexit. The proximate cause of the current breakdown in Anglo–Irish relations relates to a dispute around the future status and nature of the border between the Republic of Ireland (ROI) and the UK.

The border question emerged as the most vexed issue in the Brexit negotiations when Ireland, with support from the other member states of the EU, refused to countenance a hard economic border on the island of Ireland, suggesting that the UK government must bear sole responsibility for designing a border to satisfy the demands of the Brexiteers. Consequently, in order to secure a withdrawal agreement, the UK either had to accept a de facto customs and regulatory border between Northern Ireland and Great Britain or agree to remain inside the single market and the customs union. The 'backstop solution' was designed as a compromise between the British government's promise to deliver Brexit and the promise of no 'hard border' on the island of Ireland. However, in taking the UK out of the EU while keeping it aligned to the EU's regulatory framework, customs union and the single market, the backstop had become a major, and potentially fatal, obstacle to winning Parliamentary backing for the withdrawal agreement. Thus, an issue which had hardly featured in the 2016 referendum campaign suddenly became the dominating topic in British politics. However, although both Dublin and London spent two years arguing about the border they seemed not to be talking in the same language.

Much of the debate in Britain has focused on the seemingly narrow technical aspects of customs and immigration controls along the notoriously porous 350 km border. From an Irish perspective, the problem appeared much more alarming (Connolly, 2017). Where London sought solutions in surveillance technology and trusted trader certificates, Dublin saw Brexit as an existential threat to future peace and prosperity on the island of Ireland. Irish political leaders and media commentators regarded Britain's emphasis on 'technological solutions' as a deliberate attempt to avoid much more profound questions about 'the totality of relationships within these islands' and the future of the peace process in Northern Ireland. As one Irish critic noted about the deeply symbolic issue of a hard border, 'the backstop isn't just about trade. Is that so hard to understand, Britain?' (McDonald, 2019).

Britain's withdrawal from the EU has fundamentally re-shaped long-established political and economic relationships between the ROI and the UK. Throughout the Brexit negotiations, the Irish state has made it very clear that its relationship with Britain is expendable. By refusing to throw in its lot with Britain and its determined positioning as one of the 27 member states of the EU, Ireland has signalled a radically altered understanding of its place in the world.

From this starting point, this chapter adopts a largely historical perspective to consider key aspects of the change in Anglo–Irish relations in the light of Brexit. Initially, it outlines the development of the ROI's relationship with the EU, in particular the impact membership has had on the Irish state's national project and its relationship with the UK. It continues by looking at the possible impact of Brexit on Ireland, focussing on the debate amongst Irish policy makers and commentators about the implications of Britain's withdrawal from the EU for the peace process. It argues that looking at Brexit through an Irish lens allows a different perspective and a deeper understanding of what it means for Ireland and the UK. The chapter argues that historically the UK has limited the political and economic agency of Ireland, while for Irish policy makers the EU has facilitated it, suggesting that the more recent links between Ireland and the EU will prove stronger than the older ties binding it to Britain.

The ties that bind

The debate on Brexit in the ROI is framed by the unique set of historical, political, economic and cultural relationships that bind Ireland and Britain together. Although reimagined in recent years through narratives of historical reconciliation and future partnerships, the contradictory character of these troubled relationships frequently combines close mutual co-operation with underlying political tensions. Perhaps the most important historical dynamic to emerge has been the national project of Irish independence. From the late 18th century Ireland's endeavour to establish sovereignty and unfettered control over its economic destiny was understood both by Irish nationalists and British governments to be contrary to British interests. Politically, economically and culturally Ireland defined itself in opposition to Britain (O'Toole, 2018). Achieving self-determination meant breaking the political and economic chains that tied Ireland to Britain, and developing a sense of agency unconstrained by Ireland's dependence on the UK.

The new state that emerged after 1922 failed to achieve these political and economic aims. Politically, the national project was incomplete because Ireland was partitioned – six counties remained within the UK – whilst the new Irish Free State, consisting of 26 of Ireland's counties, was granted dominion status within the British Empire (Coakley and Gallagher, 2018). While Ireland declared itself a republic and left the British Commonwealth in 1948, in practice it merely achieved a truncated form of national independence. For successive Dublin governments, the pursuit of the national project was focused on consolidating their own distinctive 'southern' state and developing their own economy and society. Although the 1937 Constitution had declared that sovereignty resided in the people of Ireland and that 'the national territory consists of the whole island of Ireland', ending partition had become a largely rhetorical political slogan. This partitionist mentality was reinforced by a pragmatic acceptance of the relative balance of political and economic power between Dublin and London, the geopolitical realities of Ireland's close proximity to its powerful British neighbour, and recognition of the depth of Northern Irish unionist hostility to reunification.

The limited political success of the Irish national project was matched by a similar pattern of economic failure. Despite attempts in the 1930s and 1940s to develop an independent manufacturing base and its own internal market, by the 1950s the ROI still remained essentially underdeveloped, an exporter of livestock, agricultural products and people to Britain, with the UK supplying consumer and manufactured goods in return. Irrespective of the ROI's formal political independence, this web of dependence was further reinforced by banking and other financial ties, limiting the agency of the Irish government.

As part of the Sterling Area, Ireland's economy remained effectively dominated by the UK. For many Irish people, one of the most bitterly resented consequences of this historical imbalance between the two economies was the high rate of emigration from Ireland to Britain in the 1950s and 1960s. Under the terms of the Ireland Act 1949, the ROI was not defined as a 'foreign country' in British law: the Common Travel Area allowed free movement between the two jurisdictions and effectively granted Irish citizens full residence and citizenship rights in the UK.

However, and again paradoxically, it was another aspect of the failure of the national project – the outbreak of serious political conflict and violence in Northern Ireland after 1968 – which drew Ireland and Britain into their final and closest embrace. Both states shared a common interest in containing the violence and finding a political solution. Dublin feared that an incipient civil war would spread south and engulf its own state, whilst Britain believed that Dublin could be a valuable partner in stabilizing the conflict. Whilst tensions over the detail of Northern Irish policy remained, the two governments had essentially established the main parameters of a common approach by 1973. Whether in the form of cross-border institutions in support of a power-sharing executive and assembly in Northern Ireland (Sunningdale, 1973) or formal intergovernmental cooperation (the Anglo–Irish Agreement, 1985), the Irish government became an indispensable political actor in any attempts at settling the political conflict in Northern Ireland. The political partnerships of Albert Reynolds and John Major, and Bertie Ahern and Tony Blair were crucial actors for the successful management and choreography of the peace process and the development of the Good Friday Agreement in the 1990s. The strategy of coordinated Anglo–Irish diplomacy continued in the years after 1998. Throughout the recurring crises in the peace process both governments worked closely together to manage their respective nationalist and unionist 'partners' to ensure that the power-sharing institutions of the new dispensation could eventually function. The mood music of Anglo–Irish relations remained overwhelmingly harmonious throughout the first decades of the 21st century, reflecting a joint commitment to the peace process and, perhaps even more importantly, a strong common interest in sustaining the long-established habits of Anglo–Irish diplomatic and policy co-ordination in the EU (Harris, 2001).

The ties that liberate

From the 1960s, there had been a broad consensus among the ROI's political class and commentariat on the positive benefits of membership in the common market. For many Irish politicians and business leaders who identified the common market with modernity and economic progress, membership held open the promise of developing a more independent economy and thus lessening Ireland's subordination to Britain. The European Economic Community (EEC) would be an opportunity to finally escape from behind the shadow of the UK and assert the political subjectivity of the Irish state. The wider political implications of membership were not lost on Irish politicians and policy makers, who plainly understood that in acceding to the EEC, the ROI would *increase* its impact on a larger international stage. This was largely perceived positively in terms of pooling sovereignty rather than giving it up in the movement towards an ever-close union. As one diplomat noted in 1972, EEC membership might entail 'some diminution of our present sovereignty', but this should be balanced against 'the long-term political aim of reduced dependence on the British market'. Furthermore, membership of the EEC would give Ireland a stronger global voice and, 'a world-wide political influence which could not be ours in isolation' (Department of Foreign Affairs, 2014).

These and related arguments proved persuasive in the 1972 referendum campaign, which saw an overwhelming 83 per cent vote in favour of membership on a turnout of 71 per cent. Both the content and tone of the referendum debate shaped the narrative of the Irish political class for the next forty years. It became part of Ireland's common sense to regard 'Europe' as a key factor in driving economic development and the wider transformation of Irish society in the 1980s and 1990s. The increasing Europeanization of the Irish economy was explicitly understood in terms of a decisive economic break with Britain, especially in such symbolic aspects as ending the Irish pound's parity with Sterling in 1979 and joining the European Monetary Union in 1999. The political and psychological impact that EU membership had on the Irish state's sense of itself and its ability to shape its own future cannot be overstated.

European structural and cohesion funding came to be seen as an essential component for developing the infrastructure of communications and public services that would underpin internally generated economic growth and foreign investment. The Common Agricultural Policy improved farm incomes and raised living standards in the countryside. Likewise, it was widely argued that membership of the single market not only aided Irish exporters but encouraged multinationals from outside the EU to set up shop in one of Europe's fastest growing economies. This pattern of economic transformation culminated in the Celtic Tiger period of the late 1990s–early 2000s, which saw Irish GDP and growth rates outstripping those of other EU states, placing Ireland amongst the fastest growing and richest economies in the world. The reversal of historical patterns of emigration was also celebrated as a significant marker of the transformation that Ireland was undergoing: from the 1990s, Ireland became a net receiver of immigrants, as Irish people returning home joined migrants from other EU countries attracted by a booming economy and rising living standards. For many Irish politicians and celebrity members of the entrepreneurial elite these economic successes fed a new rhetoric of triumphalism, often combined with a rather unattractive self-satisfaction. In particular, a note of *schadenfreude* was detected by some Irish commentators in comparisons between the *wirtschaftswunder* of the Irish economy and the less impressive performance of their British neighbours (*The Economist*, 2011; Foster, 2008).

Advanced unceasingly by the political and business elite, the modernizing narrative that linked contemporary Ireland's success to its status in the EU's project was widely accepted throughout Irish society. The EU was almost uniformly identified with self-conscious narratives of progressive change even among former critics of the 'rich man's club'. As in all member states, EU legislation and rulings by the European Court of Justice had a direct impact on public policy, domestic legislation and government in Ireland. For social activists, NGOs, and trade unions, European agendas acquired a normative status in areas such as gender equality, women's rights, employment law and abortion, whilst the various institutions and mechanisms of the Union could act as pressure points and levers to initiate social change in Ireland. For many campaigners, victories that could not be gained at home might be won and enforced by 'Europe.' Whether it was these hopes of social progress, the 'boosterism' of the Celtic Tiger or the pragmatic calculations of farmers and workers, the EU was providing a political, economic and regulatory framework which was perceived as enabling agency. This is indicated by opinion polls and other surveys such as

Eurobarometer which consistently found the Irish to hold some of the most favourable attitudes towards the EU amongst European voters, especially in comparison to Britain (Coakley and Gallagher, 2018).

'Ireland is a European nation now...'[1]

There was a widespread political consensus in the ROI that Brexit would have a serious impact on all aspects of society on both sides of the border. The Irish economy in particular would be especially affected by a hard border. Bilateral trade between the ROI and the UK was estimated in 2016 to be worth €60bn, directly supporting 400,000 jobs on the two islands, with perhaps the same figure again indirectly linked through supply chains and related activities. Ireland's important agribusiness sector in particular remains highly dependent on the UK. More than 50 per cent of Irish exports went to the EU (excluding Britain) in 2017 and the share of Irish exports going to the UK declined from 50 per cent in 1973 to 17 per cent in 2016, but goods and services exported to the UK still amounted to almost a fifth of the Republic's GDP in 2014. According to the Irish Department of Finance, the UK is the source of almost 30 per cent of Irish imported merchandise, and Ireland is the fifth largest and Northern Ireland is the largest market for UK goods.

Despite some references to the impact of Brexit on cross-border trade and communities along the Irish border, the main economic concerns expressed by Irish policy makers during the referendum campaign focused on East–West trade between the Republic and Great Britain. In terms of cross-border trade, 30 per cent of Northern Ireland's exports go to the ROI, with just 1 per cent of the Republic's exports going to the North. Given that some 85 per cent of the Republic's total EU freight trade goes via British ports, maintaining this 'land bridge' as an unimpeded route remained a key policy objective for Dublin (House of Lords, 2018).

These prosaic realities did not remain the central concern for the Irish government during the post referendum negotiations between the EU and the UK. Rather it was the highly charged issues of upholding the Good Friday Agreement and preventing a hard border that became the main publicly stated aims of Irish policy. Significantly, in a triumph for Irish diplomacy and a major strategic defeat for the British, they also became key 'red lines' for the EU as a whole during the long drawn out Brexit endgame. Irrespective of the nature of Brexit, it was inevitable that the only land frontier between the UK and the EU would become an important issue in the withdrawal negotiations. What was unexpected, however, was the Irish government's success in seamlessly joining the issue of the customs border to the more elevated concerns of peace-building and the Good Friday Agreement. The crowning achievement was to align the EU's negotiating priorities to their own diplomatic ambitions. It is possible to see this focus on the border and the threats that Brexit supposedly posed to the Good Friday Agreement as simply political weapons deployed during complex and protracted negotiations. However, this overlooks the important role the EU has played in the peace process since the early 1990s.

The most visible aspect of this role has been financial support since 1989 through contributions to the International Fund for Ireland and a series of EU regional development initiatives and Peace and Reconciliation Funding programmes (PEACE). The PEACE programme, which began in 1995 and is scheduled to continue until 2020, consists of a series of cross-border initiatives between the ROI and the UK which 'encourage cohesion between communities involved in conflict in Northern Ireland and the border counties of Ireland' through strengthening economic and social stability. Significantly, the EU regards these programmes as examples of good practice in peace-building that can be shared throughout Europe and beyond. Apart from the direct effects on particular communities and regeneration projects, these programmes had a profound political impact: the EU's involvement in Northern Ireland helped to define a very powerful discursive framework where the policies of peace building and regional development merge (Buchanan, 2014).

Above all, because of shared Irish and British membership, the legal, political and institutional framework of the EU and the single market significantly shaped the Good Friday Agreement itself. The agreement was predicated on the presumption of continuing EU membership, with the Union's *acquis* ensuring that 'both jurisdictions ... were embedded in a deep and evolving 'totality' of legal/regulatory relationships', such as those facilitating the ending of the trade border (D'Arcy and Ruane, 2018). These frameworks defined the institutional and policy common sense and the way of doing things, both within Northern Ireland and the putative all-island economy that emerged after 1992 (Murphy, 2018). Furthermore, the Good Friday Agreement's important commitment on citizenship and identity, ensuring that any individual born in Northern Ireland could identify and be accepted as Irish or British or both, was likewise underpinned by shared Irish and British membership and acceptance of the wider legal, economic and institutional framework of the EU.

Whilst the agreement is often thought of as an internal settlement *within* Northern Ireland, it also carries weight as an international treaty between the Irish and British governments. Following a referendum which endorsed the changes introduced by the treaty, the Irish government withdrew its territorial claim to the whole island of Ireland and instead made future reunification contingent on the consent of a majority in both jurisdictions. This was a de jure recognition of what had long been a de facto acknowledgement of the constitutional status of Northern Ireland as part of the UK. However, the more important change that the agreement brought about was a redefinition of the Irish nation and the Irish state's national project. Because the Irish constitution now recognized the 'entitlement and birth right of every person born on the island of Ireland…to be part of the Irish nation', the nation was no longer understood in *political* terms as a territorial jurisdiction in which citizens exercised sovereignty. Instead 'Ireland' was now defined through the radically different and ambiguous language of *cultural* diversity and pluralist identities.

The ability to self-define as Irish or British creates a tension between the legal category of 'state citizenship' and the much more tenuous designation of 'cultural nationality' (O'Caoindealbhain, 2006). For the Irish political class, the merging of identity and citizenship in the Good Friday Agreement reflected the redefinition of their own national project as a type of post-nationalism now located in a broadly popular, if somewhat amorphous 'European' identity. Although this process of redefinition can be traced back to the partition of Ireland and the creation of a distinctive 'southern' state and identity after 1922, it had been accelerated and given a new, specifically 'European' form after 1973 (Hayward, 2009). Thus, it was the existential threat that Brexit posed to this project rather than mere economic calculation that determined the Irish government's strategy to counter British withdrawal after 2016. In this way, standing by the Good Friday Agreement became the central goal for the Irish government during the Brexit negotiations.

'Supported by … gallant allies in Europe'?

This phrase, taken from the Proclamation of the Irish Republic issued during the 1916 Easter Rising, referred to the assistance given to Irish republicans by the German government. Such allusions to the support given by European allies during Ireland's independence struggle were not simply rhetorical flourishes. It was significant that Irish political debates on Brexit were contextualized in terms of historical agency and the fulfilment of an Irish national project. In these readings, 'history' was not a deterministic straitjacket, but the very foundation of the political subjectivity of the contemporary Irish state (Charlemagne, 2016). By marrying these older tropes of Irish nationalism with the contemporary discourses of post-nationalism, it was now possible for the Irish political class to realise and legitimate its national project through the wider European project.

Thus, writing in 1991 on the 75th anniversary of the Rising, from which the modern Irish state traces its origins, the celebrated Irish commentator Fintan O'Toole suggested that Ireland's membership of the EU was the culmination of a national project to regain political agency that had begun in 1916:

> 1991 is not just the seventy fifth anniversary of the Rising. It is also the year before 1992 [the introduction of the European single market and the signing of the Maastricht Treaty, deepening political and economic relationships within the EU] ...They may not have known it but what the men and women of 1916 fought for was an Irish seat at the European table. The Rising began with a European conflict and may well end, at long last, with a European integration. (O'Toole, 1991)

As one of Ireland's leading public intellectuals, O'Toole encapsulated the dominant discourse identifying the Irish state's project with the future of the EU. During the Brexit negotiations his was a widely heard voice, self-confident and assured in tone. O'Toole's analysis of Brexit as a profound mistake, the product of self-pity, 'sado-populism' and the silent rise of English nationalism, was not only broadly shared by the Irish political class, but was well received in Britain amongst liberal Remainers as well. There was a certain hubris in these assessments tinged with a note of sadness about what was seen as 'England's paranoid fantasy'. For many commentators the imperial nostalgia of English Brexiters contrasted badly with the post-nationalism of a contemporary Ireland which had come to terms with its past (O'Toole, 2018).

Irish politics, for so long a battleground for competing visions of the national project – the Gaelic and Catholic nation, the post-colonial nation or the liberal democratic state – now seemed to have reached its own end of history in the EU. For the contemporary political class, whatever form Ireland takes, the future is clearly European as it finally turns its back on Britain and takes its rightful place amongst the nations. Still, behind these new certainties doubts remain. For example, there was an unmistakable paradox during the withdrawal negotiations in a modernizing Taoiseach driving a post-nationalist project using the rhetoric of traditional Irish nationalism. It was an irony that frequently was lost on English Tories who, drawing on their own historically informed prejudices, frequently took the rhetoric as good coin. At times the exchanges across the Irish Sea seemed to echo the tensions of the early 1970s, a time when the Irish state was frequently reminded by the UK of its place in the world (Connolly, 2017). For Irish commentators such arrogance was only to be expected from a Britain besotted with imperialism and nationalism. But why did Taoiseach Leo Varadkar, the epitome of the new Ireland – gay, modern, young, and European, and the leader of the historically most anti-republican Fine Gael party to boot – frequently wrap himself in the Green Flag in his dealings with Britain?

The answer lies in a question common to Leo Varadkar, Theresa May, Angela Merkel, Emmanuel Macron, Donald Tusk and many European political leaders: how to re-engage with an increasingly disaffected and alienated electorate. The Brexit vote in Britain, the *gilets jaunes* in France and the growth of the AfD in Germany along with the rise of populist parties and governments disrupting 'normal' politics and reflecting deep anger with the status quo, all point to serious challenges ahead for both the individual member states and the wider 'European consensus' (Mueller, 2016) (see Chapter Guderjan and Wilding). This current political moment is one in which the institutions and meanings of Western democracy have been hollowed out, leaving politicians 'ruling the void' (Mair, 2013).

Even the self-confident Irish political class is not immune to these developments. Its post-national, European project is one attempt to rebuild the Irish state's legitimacy in the wake of the implosion of the Celtic Tiger, the post-2008 banking crisis, the intervention by the European Commission, the European Central Bank and the International Monetary Fund in 2010, and the resulting collapse of confidence in established political and social authority. Leo Varadkar's playing with old-style nationalism during the Brexit negotiations is one facet of this, but much more important to 'official' Ireland as it struggles to rebuild its authority in its new relationship with Europe.

Conclusion

By irrevocably loosening the ties that bound it to the UK, Brexit has given Ireland the chance to complete its new *post-national* project through this wider European framework. For all of Ireland's modern history, its sovereignty and political agency have been circumscribed by the UK – both states knew their place in the world and acted accordingly. In contrast to the Brexiteers in Britain, the Irish political class sees the EU as a means of expanding its political agency and increasing its influence internationally. Thus as Britain retreats in on itself, Ireland will instead continue its historical reorientation away from the UK, and, by replacing these old ties with new partnerships, finally realise itself as a political subject within the EU.

Note

[1] Stephens, 2018.

References

Buchanan, S. (2014) *Transforming conflict through social and economic development: practice and policy lessons from Northern Ireland and the Border Counties*, Manchester: Manchester University Press.

Charlemagne (2016) 'A terrible problem is born,' *The Economist*, 23 March.

Coakley, J. and M. Gallagher (2018) *Politics in the Republic of Ireland*, Abingdon: Routledge.

Connolly, T. (2017) *Brexit and Ireland: The Dangers, the Opportunities and the Inside Story*, London: Penguin.

D'Arcy, M. and F. Ruane (2018) *The Belfast/Good Friday Agreement, the Island of Ireland Economy and Brexit*, London and Dublin: The British Academy and the Royal Irish Academy.

Department of Foreign Affairs (2014) *History of Ireland's Integration into the European Union*, Dublin: DFA.

Foster, R. (2008) *Luck and the Irish: A Brief History of Change from 1970*, Oxford: Oxford University Press.

Harris, C. (2001) 'Anglo-Irish Elite Co-operation and the Peace Process: the Impact of the EEC/EU', *Irish Studies in International Affairs*, 12: 203–14.

Hayward, K. (2009) *Irish Nationalism and European Integration: The Official Redefinition of the Island of Ireland*, Manchester: Manchester University Press.

House of Lords (2018) *House of Lords European Union Committee Report, Brexit; UK–Ireland Relations*, 12 December.

Mair, P. (2013) *Ruling the Void: The Hollowing of Western Democracy*, London: Verso.

McDonald, D. (2019) 'The backstop isn't just about trade. Is that so hard to understand, Britain?', *The Guardian*, 31 January.

Mueller, J. W. (2016) *What is Populism?*, London: Penguin.

Murphy, M. (2018) *Europe and Northern Ireland's Future: Negotiating Brexit's Unique Case*, Newcastle: Agenda.

O' Carroll, L. (2019) 'Ireland dismisses suggestion it should quit EU and join UK', *The Guardian*, 26 January.

O'Caoindealbhain, B. (2006) *Citizenship and Borders: Irish Nationality Law and Northern Ireland*, Dublin and Belfast: Centre for International Borders Research, Queen's University, Belfast and Institute for British–Irish Studies, University College Dublin.

O'Toole, F. (1991) 'They fought for a seat at the European table', *The Irish Times*, 30 March.

O'Toole, F. (2018) *Heroic Failure: Brexit and the Politics of Pain*, London: Apollo.

Stephens, P. (2018) 'Ireland is a European nation now; despite our shared history we cannot help over the border', *The Telegraph*, 12 September.

The Economist (2011) 'After the Race-Ireland's crash', 17 February.

Conclusion

Marius Guderjan, Hugh Mackay and Gesa Stedman

Introduction

This book has explored dimensions of contestation in British society, politics, economics and culture. It has treated Brexit not as an isolated phenomenon but as a reflection of broader social processes, some of them distinctly British, others comparable with issues and events in other parts of the world. Organizing the book around the themes of agency and austerity has allowed us to make sense of this political conjuncture.

This conclusion reflects on the developments since the EU referendum was announced. It revisits the relationship between Brexit, austerity and agency and identifies the common themes addressed in the individual chapters while linking them together as well as drawing connections between them. The chapter addresses the question of how to overcome Britain's current social, political, economic and cultural challenges by restoring agency. The multidisciplinary insights of the case studies in this volume enhance our understanding of the conditions, agents and actors, and types of action that inform an agency-centred analysis.

Three phases of Brexit

Brexit was a reaction against globalization and a strong corrective to the integration of Europe which has been a political trajectory since World War II. It also reflected the specific history and culture of the UK, particularly its post-colonial standing. That it surfaced in Britain and took the form it did, reflected some core dimensions of British society. At the same time, however, the result of the EU referendum was due to its ad hoc and opportunistic nature. Unlike the Scottish independence referendum, which took about seven years of preparation by officials and at least two years of well-informed debate, David Cameron announced the date of the referendum only four months in advance in the hope of settling the EU debate quickly within his party. Far from settled, Brexit has been a messy process, leaving citizens and politicians, outside and inside the UK, frustrated and uncertain.

Four years after the announcement of the referendum one can distinguish three distinct phases of Brexit. First, the run-up to the referendum, which was characterized by the oddly skewed campaign by the Leave camp, the lack of active support for Remain on the part of the Labour leadership, and a rather lackadaisical approach by some voters who had never thought that the issue, which had for many years interested only the Tory Party, would one day affect Britain as a whole. The second phase, post-referendum, was characterized by an increase in hate crime, an intensification of national concerns over international ones, and the return of unilateralism instead of multilateralism as a political and cultural discourse and practice. The third phase followed the triggering of article 50 of the Treaty of the European Union and is still ongoing at the time of producing this book. It is characterized by a lack of consistency and clarity, and an unprecedented lack of agreement within the government and between MPs.

Without a doubt Brexit has posed a huge challenge to Britain and has created political turmoil which has rarely been seen in Westminster. The political agenda throughout the UK has been dominated by the stalemate and crisis of parliamentary democracy in the House of Commons and government. The political process is characterized by a lack of honesty and hypocrisy as has rarely before been seen. Leading politicians and campaigners who are promoting a hard Brexit, use widespread deceit, misinformation and disdain for facts and expert opinion. Despite it having been rejected by MPs and the government on many occasions, a no-deal Brexit had become the best outcome for them, and Irish unity and Scottish independence have been seen as a cost well worth bearing. Considerable damage has been done to whatever beliefs voters might have had regarding their politicians' capacity to act with integrity and to focus on the national interest; Britain's reputation has been damaged, as well as its economy; the population is fiercely divided over Brexit; and the Union may break up.

Quite apart from the long-term legal issues involved in disentangling the UK from European legal frameworks and contracts, and the government resources that have been tied up in this, it is obvious that the UK has turned inwards during all three phases of Brexit, even to the extent that its diplomatic presence, input or voice has become marginal whenever international affairs have required attention. Strikingly, in all three phases of Brexit, two types of time have been in play. On the one hand, under Theresa May's rule, the time of political negotiations has been characterized by long drawn-out legal fine-tuning of contracts, motions and memoranda. On the other hand, since Boris Johnson became Prime Minister in July 2019, in order to 'get Brexit done', agreements with the EU have been reached in a remarkably short time at the cost of a thorough assessment of their consequences for the UK. This reflects the Brexiteers' expectation that 'taking back control' would become a reality almost overnight, giving rise to the fictions of restored imperial glory, global trade relations and national sovereignty. This turn inwards has been fed relentlessly by a nostalgic, neo-imperial discourse and a resurgence of tropes of the deserving and undeserving poor, and of those migrants who deserve citizenship (the Windrush generation facing sudden deportation after decades of life in the UK) and those who do not. Residual structures of feeling, in the term used by Raymond Williams (1977), overlap here with dominant ones regarding the inclusion and exclusion of parts of (British) society, who deserves to be in and who should be kept out. Migration from Europe is on the wane with negative long-term consequences for the economy. Meanwhile, many Britons have taken the citizenship of Ireland, France, Spain, Germany and other EU countries so that they will be able to continue to travel and work freely within the EU.

Austerity politics, although claimed by the government to have ended, have contributed to the re-emergence of such conflicting residual structures of feeling in all parts of society. Austerity's long hand is present in all three phases of Brexit, as a contributing factor during phase one, as a continued impact in phase two, and as a threat during phase three. It was not the financial crisis that created austerity politics, but it provided an opportunity for the government of the time to introduce a policy agenda that has challenged the role of the state, social coherence, people's trust in elites, liberal values and even the UK's territorial integrity. It has changed the way in which political agency is and can be exercised in the UK today, albeit in different ways according to class, gender, ethnicity and geography.

Brexit, austerity and agency revisited

The chapters in this book represent the individual expertise of scholars from various disciplines who were asked to engage with agency as a perspective to understand the links between austerity politics and Brexit. While some common themes became obvious at the early stages of this research collaboration and inspired the overall focus of this volume, others emerged only during the writing process.

Considering the conditions and contexts that were identified as enabling or constraining agency within the first phase of Brexit prior to the referendum, the chapters by Clarke, Cochrane, Montgomery and Grasso, Guderjan and Wilding, Mackay, Mckenzie, and Morelli have taken the severe socio-economic and geographic inequalities and levels of deprivation across the UK as a starting point for their analysis. In line with a critique of neoliberal thinking, Forkert, Montgomery and Grasso, Griffiths, Mckenzie, and von Rosenberg have highlighted that austerity was an opportunity to transform and contract the state, in terms of its welfare and cultural policies. In this way it was a political choice rather than a fiscal necessity in response to the economic crisis. By calling up an allegedly shared history of 'everyone being in it together', in the reference to postwar austerity, the nature of this political project was discursively obscured. The power of discourse, however, is constrained by material reality. Stark reality has made itself felt with a vengeance in many areas of the UK, where people are unable to compensate for the reduction of welfare provision following the 2010 Conservative-led coalition government's austerity measures, in particular in those areas already hardest hit by de-industrialization during the 1980s.

Simon Griffiths' analysis of the 'contracting state' has demonstrated how, after 2010, privatization and the retrenchment of public services, health, education and welfare has severely undermined the agency of those who depend on these services. Replacing state control with that of markets has changed the relationship between state and citizens, who have become consumers of education, health and other services, free to choose between the public and private providers, and between different providers within each of these categories. This understanding of agency assumes that over-reliance on the state would limit the agency of people who are expected to support themselves. Apart from the fact that private service providers are concerned with financial profits rather than public interest, and therefore are less incentivized to facilitate the agency of their clients, not all citizens are equally fit to handle the 'newly gained freedom' to choose the best doctor or school. At the same time, financial sanctions were introduced or increased for benefit claimants who are assumed to be unwilling rather than unable to work. As Griffiths has stated: 'For many welfare claimants, or former welfare claimants now struggling without state support, the promises made of a more efficient, effective benefit system, offering them greater agency and control, have failed to materialize.' Instead, people have lost resources to support their living costs and have been forced into poverty.

Austerity has affected not only public service delivery but a wide range of sources of people's agency. Ingrid von Rosenberg has shown that public expenditure cuts in the culture sector, including museums, libraries, theatres, and arts and music teaching, are not a 'luxury concern' but 'disadvantage the poorer sections even more with crippling effects on future generations'. By handing over the responsibility and costs to promote and deliver cultural activities to volunteers, philanthropic donors and commercial interests, Cameron's idea of the Big Society did not empower individuals but reduced their quality of life (chances). Steven Truxal comes to a similar conclusion in his account of reductions in legal aid, representation and counsel, which has disempowered agents who lack financial means and deprived them of their rights as citizens.

Carlo Morelli has provided a differentiated examination of Brexit's impact on various business sectors (manufacturing, financial services, and agriculture) and the social consequences of current economic transformations. He has suggested that, while the financial sector in particular has played an important role in the withdrawal negotiations, the future of welfare policy is highly uncertain as those in need had little agency during the second and third phases of Brexit. The chapters by Kirsten Forkert and by John Clarke have complemented this view by addressing how neoliberal or corporate welfare reforms and the creation of a 'hostile environment' – measures that have introduced competition, consumer choice and the departure from universal access to social benefits and services – have individualized welfare responsibility and eroded commitments to social solidarity and the means to exert collective agency. The effects of austerity and neoliberal thinking on the working classes in St. Ann's in Nottingham and in the East End of London have been studied in Lisa Mckenzie's ethnography. She has explained the stigmatizing effects on agents living precariously 'at the bottom of society' and has used the term 'breaking' to describe the asymmetrical and unfair impact on different agents. They have lacked the necessary capabilities and means to take collective action as they have lacked the networks and identities (the social capital) to which people in employment enjoy access, for example trade unions. The frustration and anger at being ignored by the political class and being 'left out' of the prosperity promised by global capitalism led them to vote Leave, 'not because they thought their lives would be better if Britain was not in the EU [but] because they just couldn't stand it being the same'.

Allan Cochrane has explained that it was the young, cosmopolitan and multicultural, as well as a transnationally operating economic elite, in London, in other major English cities and some other rural areas which voted in favour of Remain. People in post-industrial areas, who felt economically and culturally neglected, rejected and resisted both these uneven developments and elitism and cultural change. Nostalgia and the intention to restore national sovereignty were expressed through a form of ethnic nationalism that has not resonated as strongly in Wales, Scotland and Northern Ireland. Marius Guderjan and Adrian Wilding have explained how UKIP, parts of the Leave campaign and subsequently even Theresa May used simplified, emotional and deceitful rhetoric to present themselves as champions of the 'real people' who were fighting against the 'metropolitan-cosmopolitan elite'. It is important to distinguish here between inclusive left-wing populism focusing on socio-economic issues and the exclusionary right-wing nature of UKIP et al. The latter cultivated an illiberal, authoritarian ideology feeding nationalist and xenophobic views into the British population.

The post-referendum phase has fostered discrimination against immigrants and ethnic minorities (and many who support Remain). As John Clarke has pointed out, the competition over public resources and the erosion of social solidarity allowed national populist voices to evoke a nativist 'fantasy' of a 'sovereign people' that could 'take back control' from the EU and from immigrants. Kirsten Forkert has suggested that this has led to the marginalization of the interests and needs of 'problem populations', and has created a 'hostile environment' for immigrants ('health tourists') and the unemployed who are accused of abusing public finances. The mobilization of anti-immigrant sentiments in the Leave campaign is also discussed by Magdalena Nowicka in her analysis of focus groups of Polish migrants to the UK. Interestingly, nativist fantasy has been shared by at least some groups of migrants. Polish citizens believe in the idea of a neoliberal meritocracy and see themselves as productive components of the UK economy, close to white English culture. However, particularly in the aftermath of Brexit, they have become increasingly aware of the practices of exclusion and the social hierarchies that prevent them attaining upward social mobility.

Questions of political representation and agency relate not only to socio-economic, cultural and ethnic inequalities but also to geography and territorial integrity. Allan Cochrane has demonstrated how the concentrated power and wealth in London and the South East has dominated political thinking and decision-making: 'London is the UK's world city and in that role it has helped to maintain and reinforce patterns of inequality across that wider geography'. Tom Montgomery and Maria Grasso, who have analysed survey data on collective actions against austerity policies, confirm similar patterns of political participation related to social class and geography. Their respondents who work in sales and services and those who live in London have shown significantly higher levels of political activism. As Hugh Mackay has discussed in his chapter, across Wales the vote to leave the EU was not quite as strong as in England despite Wales being poorer in socio-economic terms. This is partly because Wales is less divided as a society with an elite less detached from the people, and because Welsh national identity had little impact on the voting behaviour in the referendum. Welsh-speaking and cosmopolitan communities were more likely to support Remain.

The third phase of Brexit, after Article 50 was invoked, has challenged the unitary nature of a UK that is dominated by England. Citizens of Scotland and Northern Ireland, where the majority voted against leaving, as well as Wales, have had little means to have their voices heard in the negotiations about the future relationship with the EU, although the border between Ireland and Northern Ireland was a crucial stumbling block on the road to Theresa May and Boris Johnson's Brexit deals. Klaus Stolz has suggested that, although political disenfranchisement is also prevalent in Scotland, Scottish voters did not believe that leaving the EU would enhance their agency. Rather, it was the opposite: the EU was seen as an enabler of 'Scottish agency' (self-government) against a 'broken promise of democracy' by the UK government, which since Thatcher had disempowered collective institutions, pursued a neoliberal agenda and, more recently, implemented austerity policies, all of which were seen as against Scottish interests.

Though not part of the UK, the Republic of Ireland has held a decisive position in the Brexit negotiations, challenging the territorial integrity of the UK. Similar to the case of Scotland, Kevin Bean has argued that Irish political actors have endorsed EU membership as a means of restraining British influence and promoting their sovereignty and political agency. As a member of the EU, Ireland's key priority in upholding the Good Friday Agreement and preventing a hard border with Northern Ireland has been central to the EU's position and has overruled the will of a state soon-to-become a non-member. As Derek Birrell and Paul Carmichael have written, however, in Northern Ireland, the Democratic Unionist Party (DUP) was able to enhance its power and influence during the Brexit negotiations due to its confidence and supply agreement with the Conservative government. The DUP's opposition to a 'backstop' agreement that would treat Northern Ireland differently to the rest of the UK, however, has contributed to problematizing a deal with the EU. At the same time, the suspension of the Northern Ireland Assembly and Executive, along with Sinn Féin's refusal to take their seats at Westminster, means that the interests and concerns of people in Northern Ireland are only partially represented.

Restoring agency under the legacy of austerity and Brexit?

Across this volume, the notion of agency has been accented in different ways. Some chapters have used the notion of agency in the context of collective action and political participation, for instance through membership of activist groups (Montgomery and Grasso), protest or strike (Truxal, von Rosenberg), or the ability to influence decisions (Bean, Birrell and Carmichael, Guderjan and Wilding, Morelli, and Stolz). Other chapters (Clarke, Forkert, Griffiths, Mackay, Nowicka, and von Rosenberg) have discussed the role of public services, education, welfare and entitlement of citizen rights as facilitators of agency. Here, notions of representation and acknowledgement have been particularly important for understanding a sense of agency, whether in relation to social class (Clarke, Montgomery and Grasso, Mckenzie, and Morelli), ethnicity (Forkert, and Nowicka), geography (Birrell and Carmichael, Cochrane, Montgomery and Grasso, Mackay, and Stolz) or even gender (Montgomery and Grasso, and Mckenzie). The multifaceted context of political alienation, social exclusion, geographical disparities and a conflict of values explains why many bought into the idea of restoring a sense of agency and the power of the people. Some authors (Montgomery and Grasso, Mckenzie, and Morelli) have interpreted support for Leave as a form of resistance. Other contributors to this volume (Clarke, Cochrane, and Guderjan and Wilding) have highlighted how nationalist or right-wing populism appealed to people who believe in a nostalgic past in which they held a privileged position in society.

Recent public demands for more direct democracy stem from a dissatisfaction with politicians, who are perceived as manipulative and out of touch with their voters. However, 'poorly chosen or badly implemented reforms may further alienate a restless citizenry' (Whitehead, Welp and Ruth, 2017, p. 218). In their chapter Guderjan and Wilding have expressed serious doubts that an exclusionary, illiberal populism, such as adopted by the more radical elements of the Leave campaign, will restore people's agency. They have argued that, instead, it will be damaging not only economically, but also politically and culturally, as it favours the majoritarian interests of a dominant hegemonic group over deliberation. A fundamental change in the distribution of wealth and power would be necessary to enhance people's agency. It goes without saying that this is highly unlikely in a climate of economic turmoil and with the government's overriding interest in remaining in power.

In the Introduction to this book, it was suggested that voting Leave was an extreme example of acting otherwise because the expected benefits outweighed the anticipated disadvantages. However, the opportunity costs of leaving the EU may not have been perceived as very significant for those who have already suffered severe socio-economic decline. Voting Leave was an expression of frustration by agents who have been deprived of the means, solidarity and self-confidence to take collective action to improve their situation. While the relative costs, or at least the fear of the damage of Brexit, may be higher for more mobile and better-off agents who have backed Remain, voting against the will of an elite seemed like a rare opportunity to be heard and acknowledged.

Mckenzie has argued that middle-class cosmopolitans have not understood the needs of the working classes but instead have continued to work with pejorative narratives. Voting Leave was not necessarily guided by a belief in achieving real change – in some sense it was actually intended to stop and even reverse changes brought about by European integration, globalization and immigration. This is one of the main reasons why many British voters have turned away from the liberal ideas that have for a long time shaped British identities, values and politics, and have instead embraced a nativist, xenophobic and exclusionary politics. Liberalism has increasingly promoted economically focused notions of individualism, emancipation, self-expression, and choice; it has deviated from the socially liberal ideas of state intervention and solidarity of the late 19th and early 20th century (Leach, 2015; Pabst, 2018, p. 502). Crouch has suggested:

> Liberalism, conservatisms original nemesis in European history, was for the rights of the individual, particularly in the context of rejection of the constraints imposed by conservatism and its elites. As such, liberalism is not necessarily opposed to collective action or public goods, and certainly is not synonymous with the market […]. (2017, p. 222)

While social liberalism has in the past promoted social solidarity and collective action, a meritocratic reading of liberalism is restricted to advocating equal rights for all. In view of a highly unequal distribution of economic, political and cultural resources, however, not every citizen can effectively exercise or attain their rights. As Edmiston (2018, p. 8) put it: 'If social citizenship has macrostructural, rather than democratically determined, origins, citizens are regarded with little, if any, political agency to endorse, deliberate or contest ideals surrounding the common good.'

With regard to social class, 'organised labour has been effectively disciplined: British workers have less capacity to challenge capital collectively, and have become more vulnerable to its fluctuations and demands' (Umney, 2018, pp 47–8). Although not only a British phenomenon, self-employment has grown considerably in the UK. Rather than providing workers with freedom, the self-employed are more vulnerable, exposed to financial risks and lack the structure for collective actions, which has resulted in a precarious work force (Umney, 2018, p. 88). Forkert and Clarke have suggested in their chapters that to restore the agency of those 'left out', horizontal solidarity needs to be rebuilt and class struggle needs to re-emerge to enable collective actions and challenge the views and ignorance of the political elite. Interestingly, Montgomery and Grasso have found the potential to re-engage in class struggle not among those from the traditional, manual, working class but among those working in sales and services. The latter are subject to the precarious labour markets of the 'gig economy', and it would be interesting to investigate further why they are more politically active than other classes, and how age and education have an impact on political activism. As von Rosenberg and Truxal have pointed out, access to fundamentals such as education, the arts and the judicial system are prerequisites for the strengthening of political activism.

Pabst has suggested finding a 'postliberal centre ground' which would strengthen collective actors:

> In an age of economic and cultural insecurity, the liberal-progressive consensus is breaking down. [...] There are also signs that British politics is moving in a postliberal direction, rejecting the economic and social liberalism that has been dominant for the past four decades. In the economy, postliberalism signals a shift from rampant market capitalism to economic justice and reciprocity. In society, it signals a shift from individualism and egalitarianism to

> social solidarity and fraternal relations. And politically, it signals a shift from the minority politics of vested interests and balkanised group identity to a majority politics based on a balance of interests and shared identity. Linking strands of postliberalism together is an emphasis on the embedding of state and market in the intermediary institutions of civil society, which give people agency-professional associations, profit-sharing businesses, trade unions, universities, ecological groups and devolved government. (2017, pp 500–1)

It would be the wrong conclusion here to suggest turning away from acknowledging and encouraging social and cultural diversity in favour of an exclusionary class politics. Instead, overcoming social inequality, injustice and dominant power structures requires enabling solidarity and empathy across agents, even though they have different experiences. Illiberal and xenophobic views should not be tolerated but, at the same time, discourses that stigmatize the 'undeserving poor' are also discriminating and cause a divided society.

Shortly after the referendum, in her 'one nation' speech, the then new Prime Minister Theresa May seems to have understood parts of the underlying problem that led to Brexit:

> That means fighting against the burning injustice that if you're born poor you will die, on average, nine years earlier than others. If you're black, you're treated more harshly by the criminal justice system than if you're white. If you're a white, working class boy, you're less likely than anybody else in Britain to go to university [...] If you're a woman, you will earn less than a man. If you suffer from mental health problems, there's not enough help to hand [...] The government I lead will be driven, not by the interests of the privileged few, but by yours. We will do everything we can to give you more control over your lives. [...]. (Doherty, 2016)

However, despite this rhetorical commitment to tackle social injustice, her government made no meaningful social reforms to counter precariousness and poverty. Perhaps this is unsurprising given the decades-old commitment of successive governments to greater liberalization, rather than state-led intervention. Ultimately, the conditions which generated Brexit, although in some senses deeply historical, have (intentionally or otherwise) been created through public policies, most recently in the form of austerity.

Conclusion

This book has demonstrated the value of multi-disciplinary perspectives on Brexit, and the utility of studying the implications of Brexit in a breadth of spheres, or policy areas. Crucially, it has argued that Brexit is strongly connected to austerity policies and questions of agency.

Brexit has revealed the problematic state of Britain, and there are valuable lessons to be learnt from it. This book has given some answers on who voted Leave and for what reasons. It may be argued that the outcome of the referendum has been the work of many actors and agents, which renders it difficult to assign responsibility for outcomes to one actor. Yet, as Choat has argued, an analysis of agency has to account for the properties and capacities of agents and actors and the context in which they operate, as the 'rigid structures of power and the reproduction of relations of domination and exploitation' are enduring:

> To seek causes and establish accountability is not necessarily to blame or condemn an individual agent; rather, it means trying to establish a hierarchy of causation that can identify which actants are more important than others and that can grasp the structures within which they act. The ability to ascribe responsibility in this way is arguably a defining feature of any politically useful concept of agency. (2018, p. 1036)

The questions of inequality in agency, representation and recognition emphasized in this book demonstrate the need to rebalance relations of power across social classes and across territories and geographies – including decentring the power of London and South East England.

At the time of writing this book, the increasingly desolate state of the UK government under the leaderships of Theresa May and Boris Johnson, and the massive task of Britain's withdrawal from the EU provide little hope that such inequalities will be addressed. Instead, the traditional centralist reflexes of Westminster hinder constructive debate among stakeholders who are severely affected by Brexit, including citizens of all strata, opposition parties, the devolved nations, and of course, the EU and its member states.

As Brexit and associated politics develop, further research is required to extend the spectrum of related fields or spheres that this book has addressed, including gender and diversity politics, forms of action, and actors, such as trade unions, NGOs and others. There is great potential and empirical need to deploy core concepts from multiple disciplines to tease out how these dimensions of British society can best be understood, as well as to apply systematically an agency perspective to other phenomena and other nations. In this respect, this book has made a first step with the hope that others will follow.

References

Choat, S. (2018) 'Science, Agency and Ontology: A Historical-Materialist Response to New Materialism', *Political Studies*, 66(4): 1027–42.

Crouch, C. (2017) 'Neoliberalism, Nationalism and the Decline of Political Traditions', *The Political Quarterly*, 88(2): 221–9.

Doherty, C. (2016) 'Theresa May's first speech to the nation as prime minister – in full', *The Independent UK Politics*, 13 July.

Edmiston, D. (ed.) (2018) *Welfare, inequality and social citizenship: Deprivation and affluence in Austerity Britain*, Bristol: Policy Press.

Leach, R. (ed.) (2015) *Political Ideology in Britain*, London: Palgrave Macmillan.

Pabst, A. (2018) 'Postliberalism: The New Centre Ground for British Politics', *The Political Quarterly*, 88(3): 500–9.

Umney, C. (ed.) (2018) *Class Matters: Inequality and Exploitation in Twenty-first Century Britain*, London: Pluto Press.

Whitehead, L., Y. Welp and S. P. Ruth (2017) 'Let the People Rule?', in S. P. Ruth, Y. Welp and L. Whitehead (eds) *Let the People Rule? Direct Democracy in the Twenty-First Century*, Colchester: ECPR Press, pp 207–19.

Williams, R. (1977) *Marxism and Literature*, Oxford: Oxford University Press.

Index

Note: Page numbers in *italics* contain relevant tables.

A

activist groups
  and agency 51–6
  and attitudes to EU 54–5
  and gender 52, 55
  and geographical location 52–3, 55–6
  and social class 53–4
agency
  and activist groups 51–6
  and the Conservative Party 62–4
  and the cultural sector 62–7, 237
  definitions and theories of 5–7, 62, 77, 78–9, 81–2, 104, 131, 244
  and disenfranchisement 104–8
  and the economy 93, 96–7
  in education 24, 25
  and EU referendum 83, 104–5, 196; *see also* 'take back control'
  and immigration 131
  and legal aid 77–83, 237
  in Northern Ireland 203–4, 211, 214–15, 239–40
  overview 235–45
  and populism 104, 108–14, 240–1
  and praxis 90–1, 96–9
  and public services 20, 30, 139, 236–7
  and Republic of Ireland 221, 224, 227–8, 230, 239
  in Scotland 190–1, 199, 200, 239
  in Wales 185–6
  and welfare benefits 30
  and the working class 42, 43, 47, 97–9, 100
agriculture 92, 93–4, 96, 198, 205, 209
Ahearn, Laura M. 62
Ahern, Bertie 222
Alston, Philip 30
alternative dispute resolution (ADR) 76
Amin, Ash 167
Anderson, Bridget 137
anti-austerity groups 52–5

anti-capitalist groups 52–5
Archer, Margaret S. 62
Article 50, 126–7
Arts Council England (ACE) 60, 70, 71
Arts Council of Northern Ireland 60, 61
Arts Council of Wales 60–1
Atos Healthcare 28–9
austerity
  during and after Second World War 4
  as 'dangerous idea' 46
  definitions 46, 146
  United Nations report on 30
austerity policies (under Coalition government/Conservative governments)
  and the contracting state 20–2, 24, 27, 29–31
  and the cultural sector 59–61, 66–71
  economic and social impact 4–5, 7–8, 41, 98, 100, 106, 146, 235
  and education 23–5, 69–70
  effect on public funds 39
  and international aid 46
  justification for 3–4, 19–20, 46, 61, 73, 146
  and legal aid 73–4, 75–7, 79–81, 83–4
  and local government 22, 46
  and the NHS 25–7, 46
  overview 3–5
  viewed by Polish migrants 151, 154
  and welfare benefits 27–9, 46, 46–50

B

banking crisis (2008) *see* global economic crisis
'Bedroom Tax' 27, 50
Behr, Rafael 117
Bethnal Green, East London 36–7, 41, 42
Big Society 62, 63, 67, 237
Blaenau Gwent 177, 184
Blair, Tony 42, 64, 222

Blake, David 95
Blyth, Mark 46
Bourdieu, Pierre 6, 33, 36, 39, 99
Brexit
  as ambivalent phenomenon 103–4
  and fantasy 117–19, 123–4
  three phases of 233–5
Brexit campaign *see* Leave campaign; Remain campaign
Brexit negotiations
  and devolution 198–200, 201, 205–8
  Irish border issues 212–14, 219–20
  stages of progress with 234–5
Brexit Party 146
Brexit populism *see* populism
Brexit referendum *see* EU referendum (2016)
Brexit voters/Brexiteers *see* Leave voters
British economy *see* economy
Britishness 122, 140, 176, 182–5
Brown, Wendy 119, 121
Browne Review (on higher education) 23–4

C

Cameron, David
  and austerity politics 3–4, 19–22, 30–1, 73
  and Big Society 62, 63, 67, 237
  and the contracting state 19–22, 30–1
  and EU referendum 2, 92, 122, 234
  and 'welfare tourism' 140–1
capitalism
  Fordist capitalism 121–2
  and relative economic decline 91–2, 100
  and the welfare state 119–20
  and the working class 35, 37, 42–3
  see also anti-capitalist groups
car industry 92, 95, 96, 123
Carnegie libraries 68
Child Benefit 27
Choat, Simon 244
Citizens Advice Bureaux 79–80
Clarke, Harold D., et al 164
Clarke, John 62, 73, 80, 83, 131; *see also chapter pp117–28*
Coalition government (1940-1945) 75
Coalition government (2010-2015)
  focus on deficit reduction 46
  and higher education 23–4
  and immigration 134
  and the NHS 25–7
  Open Public Services white paper 21–2
  and rescue of banks 61
  and schools 23, 24–5
  and Scotland 195

  and the welfare system 27–9, 46–50
  see also austerity policies
Common Travel Area (CTA) 208–9, 222
Conservative governments (1979-1997) 35, 65, 70, 191–2
Conservative governments (from 2015)
  and Brexit 112–13, 120–1, 126, 198, 212–14
  'confidence and supply' arrangement with DUP 198, 203–4, 209–10, 211, 214
  and the creative industries 64–5
  and the cultural sector 63–4
  and immigration 134
  see also austerity policies
Conservative Party
  2015 general election 41–2
  2017 general election 1, 207
  and agency 62–4
  and Big Society 62, 63, 67, 237
  'Broken Britain' narrative 35, 48–9
  internal divisions 10–11, 92
  in Scotland 207
  in Wales 179–80
contracting state 20–2, 24, 27, 29–31
Corbyn, Jeremy 5, 65–6, 90–1, 99, 181, 182, 210
Cox, Jo 110
Creative Europe 71
creative industries 3, 64–5; *see also* culture
Creative Scotland 60, 61
Crouch, Colin 241
culture
  creative industries 3, 64–5
  government funding 59–61, 66–71
  other sources of finance 60–1, 71
  and Scottish nationalism 192
  use of term 59
cuts to public services *see* austerity policies

D

Dallmayr, Fred 192
Darling, Alistair 38
Davies, Andrew R. T. 179–80
Davis, William 123
deindustrialization 37, 47, 48, 54, 121, 191
Delors, Jacques 193
Democratic Unionist Party (DUP)
  2017 general election 209
  'confidence and supply' arrangement with Conservatives 198, 203–4, 209–10, 211, 214
  influence on Brexit process 10, 203–4, 213, 214–15

INDEX

political differences with Sinn
  Féin 209, 210–11
position on Brexit 210, 214–15
Department for Culture, Media and Sport
  (DCMS) 60
devolution
  and austerity politics 22, 23
  and Brexit negotiations 198–200,
    201, 205–8
  and cultural sector 60
  and education policy 23
  and EU matters 205–8
  and health policy 25
  and London 165–6
  repatriation of powers 198–9, 207, 211
  and welfare policy 27
  see also National Assembly for
    Wales; Northern Ireland; Scottish
    government; Welsh government
disability allowances 28
'discount justice' 74
disenfranchisement 104–8
'Don't Stop the Music' campaign 66
Duncan Smith, Iain 27, 29
Dundee 99
Dwyer, Peter 137

E

economy
  agriculture 92, 93–4, 96, 198,
    205, 209
  car industry 92, 95, 96, 123
  financial services 92, 94–5, 96, 123, 168
  impact of Brexit 11, 92–7
  Keynesian and neoliberal
    approaches 91–2
  manufacturing sector 89, 92, 95–7, 123
  Marxist interpretations 91–2
Edmiston, Daniel 105, 242
education 21, 23–5, 34, 69–70, 134,
  181, 206
elites
  business elites 96, 98, 189
  in London 168, 169–71
  and populism 109, 113
  in Republic of Ireland 224
  in Wales 175–6, 179, 181–2
  and the working class 41
Elizabeth II, Queen 171
employment *see* labour market
England
  constitutional position within UK 171
  national identification 122, 140, 176,
    182, 183–4
  poverty rates 178
  regional inequalities 166–8
  regional institutions 67–8

voting patterns in EU referendum *162–3*, 168–71, 172, *176–7*, *205*
English Baccalaureate (EBacc) 70
English National Opera (ENO) 67
EU referendum (2016)
  impact on immigrants in UK 110
  as opportunity for agency 83,
    104–5, 196
  as political misjudgement 89
  question 83
  results and voting patterns 8, 83, *162–3*,
    168–71, *176–9*, *183–5*, 186, *205*
  turnout 107
  see also Leave campaign; Leave voters;
    Remain campaign; Remain voters
European Communities Membership
  referendum (1975) 189
European Economic Community, UK
  joining of 2, 183
European Union
  approach to Irish border issue 212–14
  and disaffected electorates 229
  effect of Brexit on internal debate 11
  and neoliberal globalization 43
Euroscepticism 2–3, 183, 196
Extinction Rebellion 115

F

Farage, Nigel
  and Brexit Party 146
  comments following EU referendum
    result 112, 124
  and immigration 9, 50
  and the National Health Service
    (NHS) 139–40
  populist approach 8, 196
  and 'take back control' 123
feminist groups 52–5
financial services 92, 94–5, 96, 123, 168
Fordism 47, 121–2
Frank, Thomas 35
Freedland, Jonathan 40
Fridays for Future 115

G

gender
  and activism 52
  inequalities 49–50
general election (2015) 36, 41, 42,
  107, 197
general election (2017) 5, 90–1, 99, 115,
  207, 209, 214
general election (2019) 99, 214
Gerbaudo, Paolo 127–8
Geuntner, Simon, et al 138–9
Giddens, Anthony 5–6, 62, 104, 113
'gig economy' 47, 56, 242

249

Gilroy, Paul 118, 141
Gini Coefficient 106
global economic crisis (2008)
  and austerity politics 19, 45, 46, 73
  causes 3–4, 38, 92
globalization 43
Good Friday (Belfast) Agreement 10, 209, 211, 212, 215, 222, 225–7
Gordon, Ian 166, 167
Gordon, Michael 121
Gove, Michael 23, 24
Greater London Council (GLC) 65
Guardian, The 40, 70

H

Hall, Peter 166
Hall, Stuart 63, 110, 124
Harvie, Christopher 192, 193
Hawes, Mike 96
Hay, Colin 6
Haylett, Chris 40
Heal, Sharon 66
health *see* National Health Service (NHS)
'health tourism' 132–3, 135–6, 137, 140
Helmshore Mills Textile Museum, Rossendale 68
higher education 23–4, 34, 206
Higher Education Council 23, 24
Highmore, Ben 135
Hills, John 39
Housing Benefit 27, 29, 38, 39; *see also* 'Bedroom Tax'
housing policy 34
Humphrys, John 219
Hunt, Jeremy 66, 132, 139–40

I

immigration
  in Brexit debate 8–9, 50, 90, 110, 196
  creation of hostile environment 50, 133–5
  'health tourism' 132–3, 135–6, 137, 140
  and legal aid 76–7
  and the National Health Service (NHS) 131–6, 137, 140, 141–2
  and Republic of Ireland 222, 224
  and Scotland 142, 198
  'welfare tourism' 140–1
  see also migrants; Polish migrants
Independent Group for Change 10
Institute for Fiscal Studies (IFS) 20–1
Irish border 121, 125–6, 204, 208, 210, 212–14, 219–20
Irish government
  and Good Friday (Belfast) Agreement 211
  and Sinn Féin 204
  and special status for Northern Ireland 212–14

J

Jacques, Martin 110
Jefferson, Tony 124
Jennings, Will 164
Jessop, Bob 127
Johnson, Boris
  becoming Prime Minister 1, 10, 113
  and Brexit 10–11, 113, 196, 235
  as London mayor 166
  and populism 115
justice *see* legal aid

K

Keynesian economics 91
Khan, Sadiq 166
Koch, Insa 122
Kynaston, David 4

L

Labour governments (1945-1951) 75
Labour governments (1997-2010)
  Conservative blaming of 3, 46, 61, 73
  and the creative industries 64
  response to global economic crisis 38
  and Scottish devolution 194
  see also New Labour
labour market
  and austerity politics 106
  and Brexit 54–5
  and deindustrialization 47, 54, 56, 121–2
  'gig economy' 47, 56, 242
  and women 49–50
Labour Party
  2015 general election 42
  2017 general election 90–1, 99
  2019 general election 99
  under Corbyn 99, 209–10
  cultural policy 65–6, 70
  divisions on Brexit 10
  in Scotland (Scottish Labour) 190, 193, 195
  in Wales (Welsh Labour) 61, 177, 179, 180, 181, 182
Lammy, David 164–5, 170
Lancet, The 26
Lansley, Andrew 25, 26
Law Society 77, 81
Leave campaign
  and immigration 8–9, 50, 110, 196
  and the National Health Service (NHS) 139–41
  representation of migrants 146–7

INDEX

in Scotland 196, 197
slogans and rhetoric 111–12, 118, 238; *see also* 'take back control'
and sovereignty 119–21
Leave voters
  characteristics of 108, 177–9
  disenfranchisement and lack of agency 105–8, 113, 241
  the 'left behind' 40–1, 164, 169, 179, 183–4
  in Scotland 99, 196
  as viewed by Polish migrants 148
  voting patterns 8, *162–3*, 168–9, *176–9*, *183–5*, 186, *205*
  in Wales 175–9, 180, *183–5*, 186
Lee, Phillip 11
legal aid
  and advice organizations 79–80
  and agency 77–83
  alternative dispute resolution (ADR) 76
  and austerity policies 73–4, 75–6, 79–81, 83–4
  and Brexit 83, 84
  and civil disputes 76
  creation and development of system 74–6
  and criminal cases 77
  and immigration cases 76–7
Liberal Democrats 11, 27, 179, 193, 197
liberalism 241–2
libraries 68–9, 70
life expectancy 98
Light Infantry Museum, Durham 68
Live Theatre, Newcastle 68
Livingstone, Ken 166
local government
  2013 elections 8
  cuts to public services 22, 48
  funding for cultural sector 60, 61, 67–8, 69
London
  2011 riots 82, 170
  and activist groups 52–3, 55–6
  as city state 165–6, 170
  and financial services 94–5
  inequalities within 166, 169–71
  infrastructure projects 167
  Olympic Games bid 167
  relationship with English regions 165, 166–9
  support for cultural organizations 65
  voting in EU referendum *163*, 171
  and the working class 36–7, 41, 42
  as world city 167, 168, 170–1, 238–9
Lukács, Georg 90, 98–9

M

Maastricht Treaty 2
Magna Carta Libertatum 74
Major, John 2, 222
manufacturing sector 89, 92, 95–7, 123
Massey, Doreen 167, 168
May, Theresa
  and 2017 general election 5, 64
  and austerity policies 19, 154
  and Brexit 2, 10, 40, 117, 126, 235
  and immigration 50, 132, 133, 135
  and new Scottish independence referendum 199
  'one nation' speech 243
  and populism 112, 238
  post-Brexit vision 120–1
  resignation 1
McCann, Phil 167
McEntee, Helen 219
Merkel, Angela 148
middle class
  and activism 53–4, 56
  and income 98
  interpretation of working class vote 41
  Leave voters 8, 106, 108
migrants
  impact of austerity policies 146
  migration from EU to UK 145, 235
  relations with British majority 148, 149
  representations of in Brexit campaign 146–7
  and respect for sovereignty 149, 154
  see also Polish migrants
Milanovic, Branko 97–8
Miller, Gina 126
Modi, Narendra 120
Morris, William 65
museums 66, 67–8, 70
Museums Association 66
music education 69

N

Nairn, Tom 171
National Assembly for Wales
  2016 election 177
  Assembly Members (AMs) 179–80, 180–1
  political parties 61, 177, 179–80, 181, 182
  reputation in Wales 181
  see also Welsh government
National Farmers Union (NFU) 94
National Gallery 60, 67
National Health Service (NHS)
  under Coalition government 21, 25–7
  'health tourism' 132–3, 135–6, 137, 140

and immigration 131–6, 137, 140, 141–2
and Leave campaign 139–41
neoliberalization and conditionality 98, 132, 136–9
spending on 21, 137–8
in Wales 181
National Theatre 67
Neill, Alex 196
neoliberalism
effects 33–4, 136
ideology 63
neoliberal rationality 139
New European, The 40
New Labour
and cultural sector policy 60, 65, 67
and education 23, 69
idea of the creative industries 64
and immigration 133–4
'reform-and-invest' approach 19–20
social exclusion agenda 35
'Third Way' 39
and Welsh Labour 181
see also Labour governments (1997-2010)
New Local Government Network (think tank) 22
NHS *see* National Health Service
Nissan 92, 96
Northern Ireland
and activism 52–3
and agency 203–4, 211, 214–15, 239–40
and Brexit negotiations 205–7, 211
and Common Travel Area 208–9
cultural sector funding 60–1
education system 23
and EU funding 205–6, 208, 226
Good Friday (Belfast) Agreement 10, 209, 211, 212, 215, 222, 225–7
health policy 25
and Irish unity 50
party-political differences 209–11, 212–14
poverty rates 178
rights to Irish passports and identity 208, 226, 227
and special status/special arrangements 212–14
suspension of Assembly and Executive 203, 211
the 'Troubles' 208, 222
voting in EU referendum 163, 176–7, 205
see also Irish border
Nottingham, East Midlands 37–8, 41
Nottingham City council 39

O

Offe, Claus 119
Olson, Mancur 91
Osborne, George 20–1, 22, 27, 29, 30
O'Toole, Fintan 228

P

Pabst, Adrian 242–3
Parker, Simon 22
Paterson, Lindsay 192–3
Peace and Reconciliation Funding programme (PEACE) 205–6, 208, 226
pensions 21, 27
Philipps, Rhodri 126
Pickles, Eric 30–1
Piketty, Thomas 97
Plaid Cymru 177, 180
Polish migrants
and assimilation 147, 238
attitudes to immigration 147, 148, 150
migration to UK 145
responses to EU referendum result 148–9, 153–4
scope and methodology of studies 147
views on Poland 153
views on public services and welfare 150–3, 154
populism
and agency 104, 108–14, 240–1
'authoritarian populism' 110
challenges to 115
and disenfranchisement 104–8, 114
and immigration 110, 132–3, 140–1
as 'inclusive' and 'exclusive' 109, 238
as 'thick' and 'thin' ideologies 109–13
and vulnerability of society 103, 114
postcolonial and post-imperial legacies 3, 118, 122, 141–2, 169, 171
poverty
'deserving' and 'undeserving' poor 34, 235
and the Leave vote 106
rates of 178
and welfare benefits 27, 47
and women 49
public services
austerity and the contracting state 20–2, 29–31, 41–2, 132
and government agency 139
see also education; legal aid; National Health Service (NHS); welfare benefits; welfare state

R

Rees-Mogg, Jacob 95
Reid, John 133–4

Remain campaign 118, 146, 179–80, 182, 197
Remain voters
  in the creative industries 3
  in London 171
  in Scotland 196–7
  voting patterns *162–3*, 171, *176–7*, 178, *183–5*, 186, *205*
  in Wales 176, 177, 178, 179–80, 182, *184–5*, 186
Republic of Ireland (ROI)
  and agency 221, 224, 227–8, 230, 239
  attitudes toward and relationship with EU 220, 223–5, 228–9, 229–30
  and Brexit 212, 219–20, 225–7, 228–30
  and Common Travel Area 208–9, 222
  economy 222, 224, 225, 229
  emigration and immigration 222, 224
  and Good Friday (Belfast) Agreement 222, 225–7
  as Irish Free State 221–2
  and national project of independence 221, 227–9
  relationship with Britain 221–3, 225, 228–9, 229–30
  rights of Irish citizens in UK 208, 222
  rights of Northern Ireland citizens 208–9
  see also Irish border
Reynolds, Albert 222
Rhodes, James 66
Royal Opera House 60, 67
Royal Shakespeare Company 60, 67
Rushcliffe Committee 75

S

Savage, Mike 35
Save the Arts (campaign group) 66
Sayer, Andrew 35
schools 21, 23, 24–5, 69–70, 181
Scotland
  and activism 52–3
  and agency 190–1, 199, 200, 239
  arts and culture 192
  attitudes to Europe 114, 189, 192–4, 195–6, 197, 200
  and austerity politics 23, 197
  and Brexit negotiations 198–200, 201
  debates post EU referendum 114
  and devolution 27, 193–4, 198–9
  and EU funding 205–6
  EU referendum campaigns 196–8
  EU referendum results 106, *163*, *176–7*, 197, *205*
  and immigration 142, 198
  and independence 1, 50–1, 114, 142, 194–6, 196, 198, 199–201

national identity and identification 176, 182–3, 192
poverty rates 178
and Thatcherism 191–2
Scottish government
  campaign for new independence referendum 198, 199, 206, 207
  cultural sector funding 61, 66, 67
  establishment of 190, 194
  and European single market 142, 198, 206
  funding for culture 60–1
  and health policy 25, 140
  participation in Brexit negotiations 205–8
  response to austerity policies 61
Scottish independence referendum (2014) 1, 90–1, 99, 140, 191, 194–6, 197, 199, 233–4
Scottish National Party (SNP)
  and 2015 general election 197
  and 2017 general election 207
  and Europe 194–6, 197, 198
  social-democratic agenda 61
Serota, Nicholas 70
Shapiro, Susan P. 78
Sillars, Jim 196
Sinn Féin
  and 2017 general election 209
  campaign for united Ireland 50
  and Irish government 204
  political differences with DUP 209, 210–11
  position and strategy on Brexit 204, 210
Skeggs, Bev 35–6
social class *see* elites; middle class; working class
social housing 41–2
Solomon, Nicola 66
sovereignty
  and collective power 127–8
  and empire 3, 118
  and Republic of Ireland 221, 227
  role in Brexit campaign 119–21, 196; *see also* 'take back control'
  and Scotland 197
  as viewed by Polish migrants 149, 154
St Ann's estate, Nottingham 37–8
Stoker, Gerry 21, 164
Stolcke, Verena 150
strike action 80, 84
Sturgeon, Nicola 197

T

Taguieff, Pierre-André 119, 124
'take back control' 43, 103–4, 113, 114, 118, 121–4, 141, 235

Taylor-Gooby, Peter 21
Thatcher, Margaret 2, 4, 30–1, 39, 110, 191–2
Theatre Royal, Newcastle 68
theatres 67, 68
Thrift, Nigel 167
Toyota 96
trade unions 8, 34, 47
TransSOL project 52–5
Trump, Donald 120
Tzouvala, Ntina 122

U

UK Independence Party (UKIP)
  and immigration 9, 110
  and nationalism 140, 172, 183
  and populist approach 8, 238
  in Wales 177, 180, 182
  and working class voters 107, 146
unemployment 132, 137, 178
  allowances 27, 28
Univeral Credit 27, 29
universities 23–4, 34, 134

V

Varadkar, Leo 229
Vote Leave campaign *see* Leave campaign

W

Wales
  and activism 52–3
  cultural and egalitarian traditions 176, 180–1
  education system 23
  and EU funding 205–6
  national identification 176, 182–3, 184–5, 186
  public institutions 181
  social-democratic tradition 175, 181, 185–6
  voting in EU referendum 163, *175–80*, 181–2, *183–5*, 205
  Welsh elite 175–6, 179, 180–2
  Welsh language 176, 177, 185, 186
  Westminster politicians 180
  see also Welsh government
Walker, Andrew 77
Warwick Commission 69
wealth inequality 5, 33, 39, 97–8, 106, 139, 166–7, 168
Webb, Steve 27

welfare benefits
  and austerity policies 27–9, 37, 41, 46–50
  and conditionality 137
  'welfare tourism' 140–1
  see also Work Capability Tests
welfare state
  and capitalism 119–20
  the four pillars of 75
  neoliberalization and conditionality 132, 136–9
  'welfare tourism' 140–1
Welsh government
  and culture 60–1, 66, 67, 179–80
  and EU referendum campaign 179–80, 182
  health policy 25
  participation in Brexit negotiations 205–8
  response to austerity policies 50
  and Welsh Labour 177
  see also National Assembly for Wales
Welshman, John 34
Whitehead, Margaret 26
Williams, Raymond 3, 59, 235
Windrush scandal 9, 50, 90, 235
withdrawal legislation 10–11, 198–9, 206–7, 209, 213, 219–20
women
  and austerity policies 49–50
  feminist groups 52–5
Women's Budget Group 49
Work Capability Tests 27, 28–9
working class
  and activism 53–4, 56
  and agency 42, 43, 47, 97–9
  and Brexit 91, 98–9
  and income 98
  labelling and rhetoric 34, 35–6, 40–1, 48–9
  Leave voters 8, 40, 41–2, 42–3, 106, 237
  and London 36–7, 41, 42
  voter estrangement 36, 41, 42
  and wealth inequality 33–5
Wright, Tony 104–5, 107
Wyn Jones, Richard 184

Y

Younge, Gary 118
youth clubs 69
Yuval-Davis, Nira 134

www.ingramcontent.com/pod-product-compliance
Lightning Source LLC
Chambersburg PA
CBHW070916030426
42336CB00014BA/2443